DISCOVERING EDEN

Adventure In The Crown of The Continent
Glacier National Park and North Fork of the Flathead Valley
A True Story

By

Donald Sullivan

To John + Megan
— Great Friends
+ North Fork lovers!

Donald Sullivan

"Away, away from men and towns,
To the wild woods and downs,
To the silent wilderness,
Where the soul need not repress
It's music."

Percy Byssche Shelley

****

This Book is Dedicated to

SARAH McMAHON

In her tender youth, she found
Montana's wild woods and downs
Soaring mountains, icy streams
Peaceful days, happy dreams,
And fell in love.

FOREWORD

Part of the year I live in the urban megalopolis that stretches from Richmond, Virginia through Washington, D.C. and New York City, all the way to Boston. My life there is different, very different, from the one I've lived in the remote northwest corner of Montana, the rugged mountain landscape known as the Crown of the Continent. I find it amazing that these two incredibly different worlds reside on the same planet.

Few of my friends in Annapolis, Maryland and Washington, D.C. have experienced the West. These friends of ours can't imagine what one might do with ones' self in a land of space and emptiness and silence, far from the constant stimulation of today's avatar world. That's a shame because everyone should have at least a taste of life away from the constant demands of their smart phone. Everyone should sample life's possibilities apart from the crowded, competitive, high-speed maze known as "modern civilization." I wrote this book, in part, for those fellow souls who have not had that taste, that they might catch at least a glimpse of what the world was like ten and twenty thousand years ago, a simpler time before i-pads and smart phones created today's new reality. That world was – and is– a world of the "here and now" where tomorrow doesn't matter much and today does; where there's time to study a flower and skip stones over a lake and listen, really listen, to a friend. I hope, through these words, that I might convey at least a hint of the "nourishment of the soul" that vast vistas across empty landscapes can provide. I hope readers who are strangers to unhurried days and silent nights might begin to suspect that peace, freedom, awe and joy such as they've never known are possible.

Of those who visit Glacier National Park, not everyone is motivated or physically able to hike the backcountry. Only a small fraction venture beyond the umbilical of their automobiles. Park officials say 98% of visitors just drive through. For them,

Glacier's backcountry remains beyond the reach of their cameras. I've had the good fortune to hike across Glacier Park, from south to north and from east to west, west to east and most of the high trails in between. This book, attempts to let those who have not been there glimpse what it's like in the backcountry and reveal the rainbow of experiences hikers may encountered there. Some of my experiences were good, some trying, some dangerous. Many more were simply awe-inspiring. Those hardy souls who are far more experienced in Glacier's backcountry than I – and there are many - may crack a smile and shake their head at the naïveté of a city boy just learning the ropes in the early years. I have endeavored to paint an unvarnished picture of my inexperience and occasional bad judgment in the hope that others may, like me, learn from my mistakes.

A word about history; the North Fork of the Flathead Valley has a lot of it but very little is written down. People who first settled this wilderness are gone, those who knew them nearly so. I worry that the stories of those incredibly tough, hardy, persistent, self-reliant souls will be lost. One of the early settlers was Tom Reynolds. Tom arrived in the North Fork in 1928 and lived there by himself until he died in 1992 at age 96. The incredible life Tom lived is a story that must not be lost and is included herein. I'm reasonably confident it is accurate. Sue and I knew him the last eleven years of his life. We heard his story first-hand. I have kept a book full of notes on tales he told to me. Joe and Joan Lang and Sue recorded interviews they arranged with Tom. I travelled to Great Britain and secured Tom's birth certificate in Bournemouth, England. I visited the London Records Office to get what few records remain of his 13 year service in the British Army. The adjutant of the King's Own Scottish Borderers in Berwick Upon Tweed, Scotland was immensely helpful in tracing the movements of the Regiment during Tom's enlistment. I've had the good fortune of interviewing some of the men who worked with Tom in the Forest Service during the 1940's, 50's and 60's and with neighbors, some who knew Tom for more than 40 years. Hours spent on the internet have provided research that filled in some blanks. I hope you'll agree, after reading Tom's story, that his life is a piece of history worth preserving.

Compared to some who have lived in the North Fork for forty, fifty even sixty years and more, Sue and I are relative newcomers. Our own personal history goes back only a third of a century. Even so, a lot has happened during that time that has not been recorded and needs to be. I've endeavored to do so. My thanks go to Cecily McNeil, Larry Wilson and other neighbors for their memories. Sometimes mine isn't what it should be.

An attempt is made to lay out the serious environmental and cultural issues facing the North Fork when Sue and I got there. I've tried to present in a factual, unbiased way the considerable efforts residents have made in determining the future direction of this unique place. My hope is that this narrative allows the reader to make up his own mind about divisive issues such as logging, Forest Service practices and – perhaps most challenging – the issue of paving the North Fork Road. We'll see.

In reading A.B. Guthrie, Jr. and Ivan Doig, two Pulitzer Prize winning writers who were born and raised within 12 miles of one another on Montana's Front Range, I am struck by how similar are the worries of people who lived one hundred years ago to those of us who live in the North Fork today. Drought is a frequent visitor to northwest Montana and, during July, August and September, fire is never far from people's minds, be it 1910 or 2010. No history of the North Fork in recent years would be adequate without addressing the wildfires that have swept through this country over the past thirty years. Wildfire has burned out some residents, threatened the lives of others and changed the landscapes of the North Fork and Glacier Park for longer than we will live. I confess that the notes I've kept over the years do not exist for 2003 when the Robert and Wedge Canyon Fires ravaged the lower and upper portions of the North Fork. Those were pretty busy days and worry dogged me day and night, not a situation conducive to note writing. Consequently, the Robert/Wedge Canyon Fire story relies on Forest Service records as well as Sue's and my recollections.

I've come close to losing my life three times – four if you count an encounter with a monster thunderstorm over Missoula when Sue and I were flying our plane to Kalispell. In telling these stories, I have done my best to avoid the temptation of employing exaggeration or hyperbole. I tell these stories as accurately and dispassionately as I can, exactly as I remember them, without embellishment.

I want to thank my wife Sue for her encouragement and support, – which has been invaluable – not just in writing this book but also in charting and shaping the experiences we've had in Montana. She has been at my side – or I at hers – for the 47 years we've trod the ground of the Crown of the Continent. Sue has been a constant source of inspiration, energy, enthusiasm and good sense. Through her interviews with Tom Reynolds, she has provided invaluable source material on his life. I have relied heavily upon her recollection of events we've shared over the years in crafting this book. Many's the time she's remembered an important event I'd forgotten or saved me from error. Our daughter, Heather McHugh, too, has been an important source of support and encouragement, for which I am grateful. Heather is very much a part of the North Fork, having visited Granite Park Chalet for the first time before she could walk. My thanks extend to the many friends and neighbors – in the North Fork and beyond – who have, over the years, shared their memories, knowledge and impressions, a vital repository that, I trust, has made a better narrative.

Don Sullivan

CHAPTER 1

THE HIGHLINE

I kept the accelerator pressed hard against the floor. For the past two hours, the speedometer on our borrowed 1964 Ford Fairlane wavered between 103 and 105 miles per hour. Thank God there was no speed limit. Had to make the most of the two week vacation I'd been given by the ad agency I worked for in Chicago. I'd scrutinized the map before we left and figured Highway US 2 was the fastest route across Montana on the way to Glacier Park. It ran more or less straight west, just south of the Canadian border. Montanans called it "the highline." Glasgow, Chinook, Havre, Shelby were all behind us. I squinted into the blazing sun that was lowering in the west. The two-lane ribbon of asphalt we were on stretched out flat ahead of us, the dry Montana landscape a shimmer of heat

The hot wind screaming into the open windows of my parents' sedan did little to cool us. In 1965 few Fords had air conditioning. At least ours didn't. I glanced down at my watch; seven PM. We'd all be glad to stop for the night in Cut Bank. I looked over at Sue, my wife of two years. God she was beautiful, even with the wind pulling strands of her hair every which way and the heat glistening on her face. "We should be there in fifteen minutes," I yelled over the sound of the wind. Sue smiled. "Good," she said with a weary smile. "The kids are really hot."

Our 10 month old toddler, Heather, was in a porta-crib on the floor behind us. Debbie, Sue's six-year-old daughter who we would soon adopt, was lying on the back seat, curled up presumably to escape the hurricane wind. Seat belts, like Interstates, were still in America's future so the kids were free to move about.

We were in love with the West, or at least our romanticized image of the West and two hundred miles back, excitement overcame discomfort. In the distance we'd spotted dark, low shapes; the mountains we'd been anticipating for more than a year! Or at least we thought they were mountains. When they turned out to be nothing more than hills – the Sweet Grass Hills, our map said – we went back to sweating. And now, a little more than two hours later, still no mountains, just brown flatland with few features, fewer dwellings. There weren't even fence posts. Montana, I learned, remains one of just two open range states where cattle have the right of way and ranches don't need fences. In this Western emptiness, anything of interest, even road signs were welcome, especially the one in front of us that read "Speed Zone Ahead." That could only mean Cut Bank.

A cluster of low buildings intermixed with a few trees came into sight and I let up on the accelerator, allowing our speed to coast down. We passed a small white sign with black lettering that announced "Cut Bank." As we coasted into town, we passed small, shabby houses followed by an oil distributing company, mechanics' garage and filling station. Toward the town center, Cut Bank's appearance picked up some with modest but neatly kept houses surrounded by green lawns and shade trees. The downtown was a couple of blocks of two-story buildings housing various retail outlets and a movie theater. "I wonder where the campground is," I said, as much to myself as to Sue. "The tour book didn't say," she replied. "It's just listed here in Cut Bank."

I pulled into what I figured was the only other gas station in town. A boy of 15 or 16 wearing a baseball cap came out of the darkened service bay, wiping his hands on an oily rag. "Regular or high test?" he asked, reaching for the handle on the side of the gas pump that he had to turn to clear the previous sale. The price on the pump for a gallon of regular showed 36 cents, a nickel above back home. "Regular," I replied. The young man nodded, clicked the metal numbers on the pump to "0" and racked the nozzle out of the pump. "Not from around here," he observed. I shook my head. "Chicago."

Sue opened the back door to the car and picked up the baby. "Come on," she said gently, taking Debbie by the hand. "Let's go to the bathroom. Some cool water on your face will make you feel better. We'll get a cool drink."

8

After sticking the nozzle into the filler of our yellow Ford, the attendant grabbed a wet sponge and hustled around the car to clear the windshield of bugs we'd met on the highline. "Do you know where the campground is?" I asked. He paused, a puzzled look on his face. Then he brightened. "Oh, I know what you mean," he said. "Old man Merton's place. It's on the left, just before you go down the hill there," he said pointing west. "Folks camp out there sometimes."

I counted out $5.15 to pay for the tank of gas, then inventoried the money in my wallet. We'd saved for the trip and left home with $250. After buying gas and two nights at campgrounds, we had just over $210 left. We'd get by.

While standing in the gas station, I'd noticed that, although the car wasn't moving, the wind hadn't stopped. It had slowed some but still had enough velocity to whip dirt up from somewhere to the south and blow it across the highway. I felt the hot, gritty, dry particles on my face and in my hair. Sue returned with the kids, put them in the back and climbed into the passenger's seat. She gave me an uncertain smile. "I hope we'll find some shade in the campground," she said.

We turned off the highway where the boy had indicated and in one block we were out of town again, facing an empty field enclosed by a barb wire fence, not a tree in sight. A small house stripped of most of its paint stood a half block to the east. A hand-lettered sign marked the entrance to the field. "Campground," it read. I pulled in. Sue and I got out and looked around. The wind blew, dirt swirled and the lowering sun continued to burn into hundred degree air. The baby began to cry. Sue opened the door and picked her up. Debbie followed them out and she, too, began to cry. As I went to pick up Debbie, my foot hit something hard. I looked down at a ten inch dried cow paddy. Cow paddies were everywhere. "This is a pasture, not a campground," I exclaimed. I looked at Sue and the kids. Debbie's tears left little brown trails through the dust that the wind had blown onto her face. "What should we do?" Sue asked. "I don't even see any water here." I looked about me, then at my watch. It was already near eight o'clock. I turned my gaze to the west. Still no mountains. I surveyed the pasture again. "Do you trust me?" I asked. Sue looked at me, brushed fallen hair from her eyes and nodded. "Yes," she replied. "I trust you."

"OK," I said, "get the kids back in the car. We're going to Glacier Park. I know it's late, but we're not staying here."

The eastern boundary of Glacier National Park is one of the most spectacular scenes in North America. On the run west to Browning, the Front Range of the Rocky Mountains rises up suddenly, unexpectedly, thrusting up out of the flatland like a jagged stone castle wall that some clumsy giant threw up before time began. Snow capped peaks carved into horns, arêtes and escarpments by unimaginable rivers of ice rise up into the air, seven and nine thousand feet above the monotonous plain. Dusky valleys and steep canyons cut by knives of glacial melt hide sparkling blue and green lakes and rivers

Unfortunately, we missed it. Before we reached Browning, it was dark. We followed our headlights to the town of East Glacier, then the signs to the Park. Montana Route 49 took us under a gigantic concrete viaduct over which the Great Northern Railway once transported wealthy Eastern dudes and their ladies to the Crown of the Continent, the moniker bestowed on Glacier's mountains by George Bird Grinnell in the 19th Century. Our route wound its way through a tunnel of darkness, giving us glimpses of cottonwoods covering the small foothills east of the Park through which we drove. In a few miles, a sign pointed left, taking us off 49 to the Park entrance.

Blackness engulfed us. There were no lights anywhere, no towns or gas stations, no ranch houses, nothing to give us a sense of what was around us. But while we didn't see the mountains, we felt their presence. The air coming in the windows suddenly cooled. It was fresh, sweet, clean, bracing. As it swirled around us, bathing our tired, sweaty bodies in the breath of unseen glaciers high above, I sucked it in and grabbed for Sue's hand. "My God, can you believe this air?" I exulted. "It's mountain air." "Yes," she replied, "it's wonderful! We must be getting close." She looked back at the children. Debbie was sitting up, fingers on the window sill, looking out into the blackness, no doubt wondering what had happened and where we were, while Heather slept.

By the time we passed the Two Medicine entry station to the Park– unmanned at night – we were rolling up the car windows. When the car began to climb, our spirits rose with it. I figured we must be near our destination – Two Medicine Lodge Lake Campground. "Thank God we left Cut Bank," Sue said. "I feel so much better." She looked back at the children. "The kids do too." I smiled. It was night, we were hungry and tired to near exhaustion, but we were at last safe from sweltering heat and endless plains. More important, we had reached the object of our quest, a quest born of dreams dreamed for more than a year in our small Evanston, Illinois apartment; the West, Montana, the Rocky Mountains, Glacier National Park!

A large brown and white sign appeared in our headlights announcing Two Medicine Campground. I slowed the car to a stop and saw the awful "FULL" placard. While the bubble of our enthusiasm didn't exactly burst, I felt deflated. What are we to do now? I asked myself, glancing back at the girls. Heather had begun crying again and Debbie looked as though she was about to. I pulled up to the ranger check-in station, hoping to find help, but it was empty. "What do we do?" Sue asked. I had no answer. We proceeded into the campground hoping against hope to find an empty spot. A man was standing to the left of the road, next to a silver Airstream trailer parked in the first campsite. I pulled up, and rolled down the window.

He was an older gentleman, gray haired and balding on top. He wore glasses and his full, rather handsome face bore a warm smile. "I'm wondering if there are any open campsites," I asked. The gentleman bowed down and looked into our car, surveying the occupants. "I'm afraid not," he replied. "Why don't you pull in here next to our trailer. It will be alright. I'll tell the rangers we're all together."

11

"You sure?" I asked. By this time, the gentleman had stepped into the grassy area next to his trailer and was motioning me forward. I pulled in and killed the engine and lights. The next thing we knew, a matronly lady about the gentleman's age was opening Sue's door. Later, Sue said she looked like Mrs. Santa Claus. She was white-haired, rather plump, wearing a dress and funny shoes. "Hello, Dear," she said to Sue. "Why don't you get the children out and bring them into the trailer. They look all tuckered out. I'll heat some water and we'll get them washed up. They'll feel so much better."

I got out, unsure yet of my bearings, not quite able to decide what to do next. "Are you tenting?" the gentleman said. I nodded. "I'll help you set it up. It's late and you must be tired." That brought me around. I opened the trunk and found the green canvas Sears Roebuck tent we'd borrowed from my boss. With the help of the kindly Airstream owner and his flashlight, he and I succeeded in getting the aluminum poles together and the tent hung on them. He and I pulled out the bedrolls we had with us along with our Coleman white gas lantern, ice chest, assorted stuffed animals and a couple baby bottles.

Inside, Mrs. Santa put a kettle of water on her stove, helped Sue get the girls out of their clothes and gave them warm, sudsy baths. While Sue was stuffing the freshly scrubbed girls into their PJ's she said, "Have you eaten yet?" Sue shook her head. "No, not yet." "Well," the lady said, "we'll have to do something about that. I'll heat milk for the baby," she said. "Do you have some bottles that need washing?" As she spoke, she began opening cabinet doors and pulling out the makings of a hot meal for the three of us.

Sue came out just as I was setting up our two-burner Coleman camp stove. "You won't need that," she said. "This nice lady has fixed dinner for us. Come in."

"You're kidding!" I exclaimed, dead tired and incredibly grateful. I followed Sue into the trailer. Two happy girls, wet-headed and rosy-pink in their pajamas, looked up contentedly at us from their places at the table. Debbie chattered away with Mrs. Santa while Heather drained a bottle of baby formula. Dishes steaming with boiled potatoes, hot soup, left-over roast beef and green beans were soon on the table. "Well sit down and help yourselves," the gentleman said. "We've eaten." I could not remember a better – or more welcome – dinner than the one we had that night.

When we'd finished our repast, it wouldn't do for Sue to help with dishes. "Get these dears to bed," the lady ordered. "And you go right with them. You look exhausted." I went outside and lit the lantern, then carried Heather – who'd fallen asleep – into the tent. Sue and Debbie followed and crawled into their sleeping bags while I went to thank our benefactors. The trailer door was closed, so I knocked. The gentleman opened it and peered out. A moment latter Mrs. Santa stuck her head out around him. "I can't thank you enough for all you've done," I said. "There are no words. I don't know how we can ever repay your kindness."

A knowing smile creased the gentleman's face. "We're glad to have the opportunity to lend a hand," he answered. "We're happy we happened to be here tonight."

"We are so glad to have met you and Sue," his wife added. "The children are such dears. Take good care of them, won't you? Now you just go and get some sleep."

The Coleman filled the tent with light and shadows until, once we were all tucked in, I turned the knob that shut off the flow of white gas. Then darkness as complete as any I could remember engulfed us. "It's dark as the inside of a cow," I quipped, but Sue gave no answer. She was sound asleep.

Sometime in the wee morning hours, I felt a tug on my arm. Heather was crying. "She's hungry," Sue whispered. "We need to heat a bottle." I propped myself up on one arm, found the matches and lit the lantern. I leaned the bottle against the glass of the lantern, using its heat to warm the milk. It would take a while and I drifted off, only to be wakened moments later by Sue.

"Something's burning!" she exclaimed. I turned quickly to the lantern. I'd allowed the nipple on the baby bottle to rest against the hot metal top of the lantern and, indeed, it was melting. I grabbed the bottle away from the lantern while the remaining rubber bubbled and smoked on the top. Sue searched her bag and found another nipple. "I'll be more careful this time," I promised.

Hours later, I was awakened by a bright green light. The sun was up and illuminating the canvas tent like a giant lantern. The 9X9 foot space in which we slept afforded little room when filled with a large wooden porta-crib and three sleeping bags, so when I sat up, bleary-eyed, Sue woke. "Morning," I yawned, shivering a bit in the coolness of the morning. "How are you feeling?"

"I'll tell you in a minute," she replied. "I can't ever remember sleeping so soundly."

I crawled out of my bag, pulled on the jeans I'd been wearing since we left Evanston, and unzipped the tent fly, anxious to see what lay outside. I stepped out and gasped. I was shocked, awed by what I saw. Rising up over me across the glassy outlet of Two Medicine Lake, not three hundred yards away, was a mountain so near, so massive, so high, so magnificent that I felt tiny, an ant, insignificant, unworthy. All I could do for a moment was gawk, speechless. Never had I been confronted by something so impossibly massive, so unexpectedly wonderful, so completely humbling.

I called to Sue to come out. She, too, gasped. "Oh my gosh!" is all she could say. We stared, unable to take it all in or look away. The mountain rose three-quarters of a mile straight up from the shore of Two Medicine Lodge Lake, so high that we could not see its summit. I pulled her to me and put my arm around her. We craned our necks at the spectacle looming above. The morning sun illuminated its fractured brown and gray stone face. Fissures and angles carved into the pinnacle eons ago cast shadows that revealed its tortured shape in bold relief, a shape no artist could conceive.

To our left, the blue-green waters of the lake stretched out for several miles. Ripples began to rise with the breeze. In the distance beyond the head of the lake, other stone monsters soared into the blue sky, blue as any sky I could remember. In time, we'd learn their names; Rising Wolf, directly above us is one of the most massive mountains in Glacier Park. Across the way, thrusting up and out toward the lake like the prow of some gigantic ship is Sinopah, named for the Blackfeet wife of Hugh Monroe, an early 19th Century trapper given the name Rising Wolf by the tribe of which he became a part. To the right of Sinopah lay Mt. Helen and to the left Painted Teepee, Never Laughs and Apistoki Mountains.

Save for the hump behind us formed by rubble left by an ancient glacier, we were encircled by peaks that scaled the sky. Deep green forests blanketed the flanks of these mountains while patches of snow still clung here and there to their cheeks. Nature's grandeur was on display everywhere; in deliciously clear blue-green waters of the lake, among the smooth pebbles lining its shore, in the bright red Indian paintbrush at our feet and green boughs of spruce and fir shading the campground. It was more beautiful, more grand, more wonderful than we had – or could have – imagined.

Though not a particularly religious person, I sensed that I was in the presence of the Creator, that we were standing on holy ground. As my eyes reached up again to the flanks of Rising Wolf, I felt that my eyes were somehow touching the face of God. Tears filled them. Sue and I looked at one another. Her eyes told me this was a seminal moment, one that would change our lives.

Inside the tent, Debbie began to stir and Heather made waking sounds. Sue turned away and went inside. It was then that I realized the silver Airstream trailer was gone, along with the pickup truck that pulled it. Our tent stood alone. I walked over to the campground road and looked up and down, toward the entrance, then behind me. Our benefactors were nowhere to be seen. "Sue," I called. I ran over to our tent and stuck my head inside. "They're gone!" I exclaimed.

"Who's gone?" she asked.

"The Airstream," I answered. "The folks who helped us last night. What were their names?"

Sue appeared startled, then puzzled. "I don't remember," she replied. "I'm sure they said their names, didn't they?" Neither of us could remember.

"In any event, they're gone," I said. "I wish I knew who they are. I'd like to find some way to thank them."

Sue thought for a moment. She picked up Heather and came out of the tent. "I think I know who they are," she said. "They are our guardian angels."

I looked back at the spot where the Airstream had been. Perhaps they were, I thought. Perhaps they were.

Though we were raised two hundred miles apart by families of very different backgrounds, growing up, Sue and I experienced similar family vacations. "See the USA in your Chevrolet," and "Discover America" were advertising slogans that resonated with newly mobile post-World War II families, ours included. So every couple of years, our parents would take us on two and three week driving vacations that spanned America, introducing us – and them – to the far-flung wonders of this great country. Both our fathers pushed their cars - and their families - to the limit, aiming to maximize the number of miles covered each day, calculating average speed, trying to beat the previous day's record and boasting about how many total miles they'd covered when they returned home. Stops for gas were like Indianapolis pit stops; everyone would jump out of the car, run to and from the bathroom and jump back in. When we reached the objective of one leg of our trip, we would grab the Kodak Brownie, jump out of the car, take a few pictures of whatever it was we were so anxious to see, then jump back in so we could race toward the next attraction.

Sue and I agreed early on that we did not want this kind of vacation in our life together. We wanted to go somewhere, spend time in one place, feel the ground under our feet, breathe the morning and evening air, explore and experience the place, not just take a mental snapshot, fill an album and check off one more place on an itinerary.

Our families had taken us, separately, to many of the same destinations; Plymouth, Mass., Washington, D.C., the Grand Canyon, Pacific Ocean, Pike's Peak and many others. But the one that held special memories for us both was Glacier National Park.

Having seen that first morning how truly spectacular the Park was, more spectacular even than we'd remembered, we decided that we would use every moment of this first vacation to explore as much of it as we could, while still feeling its ground beneath our feet. Two Medicine Lodge Lake, as it was called in 1965, was but one narrow valley in the million acre national park. We would spend two more nights there, we decided, then move on to other wonders in Glacier until the very last moment when time and distance dictated that we must race back to my job.

After breakfast, I put Heather in the child back-pack we'd bought in Chicago and the four of us headed off down the blacktop that leads to the boat dock we'd seen pictured in the brochure procured that morning from a ranger. The baby, facing backwards, kicked her feet contentedly and made happy noises, swaying in her seat on my back to the cadence of my pace.

We soon came to a large old log building on the shore of the lake. Its Swiss chalet architecture charmed us, with fancy log work around a covered porch, large stone chimney and peaked roof cut off in the front. A sign out front labeled it as the dining room of one of nine chalet complexes built in 1913 by the Great Northern Railway. Louis and James Hill, Great Northern Chairmen, saw the establishment of Glacier National Park in 1910 as an important potential revenue source for the railroad. Their idea was to bring wealthy people from the East and Midwest to the alpine wonders of the Park and back again on their ribbon of steel that runs across the country and along the Park's southern boundary. To accommodate their vision and their travelers, they constructed three grand hotels in the Park and nine chalet compounds throughout the backcountry. Park visitors would get off the train in East Glacier (then called Midvale), be transported a short distance to the gargantuan Glacier Park Lodge for a formal white-tablecloth dinner followed by a ball complete with full orchestra. The next morning guests would be introduced to their saddle horses and wranglers who would take them on a cross-country tour through the Park. Lodging facilities decked out in Swiss architecture and called chalets were situated in remote mountain locations chosen for their spectacular beauty, one day's ride apart. One month later, the adventurers would reach the other side of the Park, departing for their homes from the rail stop known as Belton.

Following World War II, the ubiquity of the automobile and decline of passenger rail travel led to the abandonment and destruction of all but two backcountry chalets, though the magnificent hotels remain. A half-dozen chalet buildings reachable by car remained as well, including the Two Medicine dining room which, we discovered, had been turned into a store selling hot dogs, T-shirts and trinkets.

We went to the west-facing shore of the lake to take in the spectacle afforded by this American fjord and enclosing peaks. Then off we went for our first adventure; a trip on The Sinopah, a classic wooden boat built in the late 1920's to take tourists to the head of the lake where trails into the wilderness begin. We listened with unbridled enthusiasm to Bill, the boat captain, as he named the mountains around us, gave us a brief lesson in Glacier Park geology and pegged the depth of the lake at 140 feet.

Twenty minutes later, Bill pulled the boat up to a small dock. We, along with fifty or so hikers and tourists, got off. A ranger was there to lead the group on a nature hike to Twin Falls, a popular attraction three quarters of a mile up the valley. We chose to go it alone. We were exuberant, impatient to see, experience everything. We didn't want to be slowed down by a group whose slowest member would determine its pace. So off we went by ourselves, ahead of the pack.

The first thing we encountered was a yellow sign warning "THIS IS BEAR COUNTRY." The warning served only to heighten our excitement further. It didn't occur to us to be afraid. But as the trail passed along a bog wetted by the clear waters of a creek feeding the lake and dense forest began to close in around the trail, we felt it advisable to take the precaution of making noise. We talked loudly and clapped our hands, not exactly afraid of meeting a bear, but just in case. Soon our pace slowed. Debbie, just six, could not long keep up with our rapid advance. Sue and Debbie fell behind. I looked back, anxious to get on and after a few moments of rest, we were all together again. After a half-dozen similar rest stops, the ranger and group of tourists appeared in the distance behind us. They soon caught up, passing us by. We overheard the ranger explaining about bear grass and cow parsnip and willows and the like. It was sounded interesting. Sue and I looked at one another. We fell in line at the tail end of the group. We had a lot to learn.

Five minutes later we came to two streams cascading side-by-side down 150 foot high cliffs strewn with immense boulders. We stood below the waterfalls, letting the rising mist swirl around us as we watched, savoring the sight of white water racing down, crashing, dividing, splashing, roaring as it dodged between the boulders in its path. Sue and Debbie made their way through a jumble of rocks to the edge of the retreating stream at the foot of the falls. Sue took off Debbie's shoes and socks so she could cool her small feet in the icy water. I scanned the cliffs for a route to the top but the ranger was already rounding up his group for the return hike and we didn't want to miss the boat. Besides, I had Heather on my back. "Some day," I promised myself. "Some day."

The next morning we decided we'd rent one of the fishing boats available at the dock and try our luck on the lake. When we left Evanston, I'd packed a couple of rods and assorted fishing gear I'd had as a kid. After all, part of my image of the West included pulling trout from pristine wilderness lakes and streams and cooking them over an open campfire. We took Debbie, Heather, fishing gear and packed lunch down to the lake and headed off across its bright blue waters, our wooden boat scooting along in front of a five horse outboard motor. We had no experience in fishing Western lakes but figured we'd try what worked back home, on lakes we'd fished in Wisconsin and Michigan. If we didn't catch anything, so what? The air was warm, the sun bright, sky clear and mountains huge. Feasting our eyes on the surrounding grandeur from the vantage point afforded by our boat would be a great way to spend our last day at Two Medicine.

But soon after dropping our lines in the water, lightning struck! Sue's rod bent sharply and she reeled in a fine, fat eight inch brown trout. I was so shocked I nearly forgot to net the fish to bring it in. A half hour later, I felt a tug on my line. I pulled back and hooked another. Soon I was putting it on our stringer. Two fish! We would have fish for the fire that night.

"Can I try?" Debbie asked. We baited her hook and helped her throw her line out. "Wouldn't it be great if Debbie could catch one?" Sue asked. Surprisingly, little Debbie had remarkable patience. After a half hour of no action, she kept at it, reeling in when her bobber got too close to the boat, waiting while I put another worm on, learning how to cast out. When the fish hit, it nearly pulled the rod out of her hands and into the water. Sue jumped forward to help her reel it in. When the fish got close enough for me to see it, I couldn't believe its size. "Don't pull too hard," I yelled. "Just reel it in slow and steady." I grabbed the net, dipped it into the water but the fish took off again, racing under the boat. With all the excitement, I had all I could do to keep the boat from capsizing. In time, the monster tired and I was able to help Debbie bring it in. It was huge! Had to be near two feet long and six inches thick. It flopped around on the bottom of the boat until I was able to get it on the stringer along with the other two fish and back into the water.

Sue took Debbie's pole and before we headed back to the dock, caught another nice sized trout. I untied the stringer from the oar lock to bring it up out of the water so I could put Sue's latest catch on it. In the process, I somehow dropped the end of the stringer into the lake! Debbie's monster fish gave two shakes of its head and was off, gone back into the deep, cold water. I was chagrined. Debbie had caught the biggest fish and I'd lost it. She cried and I nearly did too. "It's all right, Don," Sue said. "Debbie caught it and that's the important thing. She'll always remember that. Besides, it's been a wonderful day, fish or no fish." Sue has always had the marvelous ability to see the silver lining, an ability that has helped us get through tough times, an ability I've admired all our lives together.

The next morning we took down the tent, rolled up our sleeping bags and put everything back into the trunk of the Fairlane. Two Medicine had provided one of the most wonderful experiences of our lives, but it was time to discover other wonders in Glacier. We drove back out past the Two Medicine entry station, turning north on twisty, steep and somewhat scary Highway 49 toward the town of St. Mary. As the road climbed, the views it afforded opened up, revealing a vastly different landscape from heavily wooded Two Medicine valley. I stopped the car at an overlook. The Front Range, we saw, is virtually devoid of trees, its stark vertical landscape brown and dry and empty like the flatland plains further east. The naked ribs of mountains and brown, barren hills beneath held their own awesome beauty, but beauty of a very different kind; the beauty of enormity, of distance, of visual freedom. Down below, the only breaks in the barrenness were narrow bands of cottonwoods clinging to lowlands wetted by the north and south forks of Cut Bank Creek. Elsewhere the wind swept unhindered across the vast, lonely Montana steppes. Sue and I stood close, wind whipping our hair as our eyes savored a planet so different, so much more peaceful, so infinitely better than the one we walked on Michigan Avenue.

The most popular and, arguably, most spectacular feature of Glacier is the road across it, Going to the Sun Road. The 52 mile road, constructed between 1925 and 1933, is considered to be, along with Hoover Dam and the Golden Gate Bridge, one of America's greatest engineering feats. It climbs steadily from St.

Mary Lake in the east into the heart of the Park, taking motorists up among some of the most awesome peaks of the Livingston Range; Red Eagle, Citadel, Piegan, Reynolds, Clements, Oberlin. Passing through a tunnel bored into the stubborn stone of Going to the Sun Mountain, the Road reaches its summit at the Continental Divide, 6,664 foot Logan Pass.

West of the Pass, the Road begins its descent. Within a half mile, it becomes a narrow, winding niche carved into vertical sides of the Garden Wall, an 8,000 foot high, 35 mile-long mountain chain sharpened into a narrow arête eons ago by glaciers. In places, unrelieved vertical rock forced builders to carve the road into the cliffs in such a way that the rock above the road actually arches back out over the roadbed, forming a sort of roof just a few feet above vehicles passing beneath. Only an 18 inch thick, two foot high rock barrier separates motorists on the opposite side of the road from vertical precipices falling two- and three thousand feet to the valley floor. On its way down to Lake McDonald, 3,500 feet below, the Road descends over stone arches bridging roaring waterfalls, around precipitous promontories and through a second tunnel.

Sue and I both had vague recollections of the road from our childhood visits but, like our experience at Two Medicine, we were unprepared for the magnificence we encountered now. Driving up from St. Mary townsite, the landscape changed and changed again. Climbing past the sparkling, wind-whipped waters of nine mile long St. Mary Lake, we entered lush green forests of alpine fir, spruce and pine, leaving behind the parched Front Range. Climbing higher, the forests thinned: trees grew smaller, some gnarled by ferocious winds and frigid temperatures of the higher altitudes. Finally there were no more trees, only tundra and stone scraped naked by an arctic climate. As we drove up Going to the Sun Road, I felt almost as though I was an eagle soaring up, riding the winds to the heights of the earth. We were excited, thrilled, awed.

We stopped at Logan Pass, parked the car in the lot and got out, sucking in the cold, thinned air. We grabbed coats out of the trunk for the kids and ourselves even though the sun was shining brightly on this late July afternoon. I put Heather in the pack and the four of us headed up to the visitor center where we viewed wildlife displays featuring creatures of the high country, some we'd never even heard of; ptarmigan in white winter feathers, a tiny, adorable rodent called a pika and Columbia ground squirrels, see-through burrow and all. The last display featured a cast of a giant grizzly bear footprint along with a grizzly skull. It was hard to imagine a living animal that big running free in America, right here in the Park. The display gave us new awareness of this grand animal – and new respect. We would not again dismiss the possibility of danger when we ventured into the wild.

We were given a free trail map of the immediate area by a ranger, bought a book called Guide to Glacier authored by a famous Park naturalist, George Ruhle, and hastened outside. Sloping terraces of rock covered by light green tundra stretched south to the base of Reynolds Mountain, a towering horn carved on three sides in the great ice age. A rocky path leading up from the visitor center through the tundra disappeared over a ridge to the west. The trail map showed that the trail leads to Hidden Lake, described as one of the most beautiful in the Park. So up we went. How hard could it be? It was only a mile and a half and we could see the top from the visitor center, or so we thought.

A few hundred yards up the trail we began to feel the pull of the trail's surprisingly steep grade and thinness of 7,000 foot air. Debbie needed a rest, for which Sue and I were secretly grateful. After pausing a few moments to catch our breath, up we climbed again, not to be defeated by this trifling hill. Only later did we learn that the trail rises 550 vertical feet, the height of a 50 story building! After numerous rest stops and an hour of hiking, we reached the top of what we learned was a terminal moraine, a huge pile of ground-up rock left by a retreating glacier. But to our chagrin, it was not the top of the trail. Our destination, Hidden Lake Overlook lay somewhere above.

When we finally reached the overlook, it was immediately clear that our effort was worthwhile. Far below lay the spectacle of

Hidden Lake, a sparkling alpine gem embraced by towering peaks crowded close around. In the far distance, high above, lay the gray-green surface of Sperry Glacier. The flanks of surrounding mountains were cloaked in deep greens of alpine fir, winter snow still spotting the ground beneath. Blue waters gathered at the north end of the valley, squeezing into a quiet stream nestled between grassy banks. A few hundred yards beyond, the stream disappeared over an unseen precipice into a distant abyss. Beneath a massive headwall of gray shale, a peninsula dotted with alpine fir curved gracefully into the lake, making me wish I could go down and explore, draw near, experience more completely the enchanting cirque.

Debbie wasn't entirely sure about the worth of the hike until she spotted a mountain goat standing amongst the subalpine fir, just a few feet away. Then she saw a second. "Look," she exclaimed, pointing. "A baby!"

"Yes," Sue replied, "a mama and baby mountain goat. Aren't they wonderful?" We snapped pictures of the goats - who paid absolutely no attention, the lake, the mountains and each other, in awe of where we were and everything that surrounded us. Our enthusiasm, that had been subdued somewhat by the strenuous climb, blazed anew. This was heaven!

We returned to our car and started down Sun Road toward Sprague Creek Campground on the west side of the Park. Almost immediately, Sue spotted a hiking trail snaking from the Pass across the tundra saddle below. "Oh, my gosh!" Sue exclaimed, pointing with her finger. "Look! That trail goes out onto a ledge. Look how narrow it is!"

I slowed the car to a stop near a hairpin curve a quarter mile below the Pass and looked. She was right. The trail left the tundra and curved around onto a narrow ledge carved into vertical stone. To the right of the ledge, the stone wall rose straight up a thousand feet or more; on the left, it fell straight down to the roadbed below. Perhaps three or four feet wide, the frighteningly narrow ledge continued level while the road beneath dropped rapidly, increasing the vertical distance between them. "Wow," I replied, "that must be five hundred feet, straight down!" Sue pointed. "There are people on the trail, several of them."

My eyes followed the foreboding dark gray ledge and in a quarter mile or so, it emerged once more as a trail, traversing a steep mountain slope dotted with fir and spruce. "I wonder where that goes?" I said. My eyes returned to the road and I started our car rolling downhill again.

Sue studied the trail map we'd been given. "I think that's what they call the Garden Wall trail," she said.

"It's supposed to be the best hike in the Park," I replied.

Sue looked up at the trail we were passing beneath. Her expression suggested real doubt. "Maybe," she said, "but I can't imagine walking out onto that ledge." Sue, I knew, had always had a bad case of acrophobia.

As we passed beneath the trail, we felt as though our car was on that narrow ledge, for the road west of the Pass becomes a twisty notch hewn into vertical rock just barely wide enough for two cars to pass. Waterfalls cascade down from above, disappearing into culverts beneath the road before shooting out into space on their race to the valley floor. Sue, too nervous to look down, admonished me more than once to keep my eyes on the road and my foot off the gas. In places, the stone walls arching above us crowded so near that I feared the outside mirror on our car might be knocked off.

Beyond a broad sweeping bend that opened the sky wide to our view, we approached a black wall of porous rock thirty feet high and several hundred yards long. Showers of water streamed from the rock. Wild cascades of giant droplets smacked down onto our car, making loud, pounding sounds. We felt as though we were going through a celestial carwash. I turned on the windshield wipers. Sue and Debbie giggled. What a ride! On one side, nothing below us for thousands of feet; on the other, water splashing down onto us from a wall crowding us toward the precipice. We were glad we'd come up from St. Mary first. The Road west of the Pass was even more spectacular – and scary.

We would always consider Sprague Creek the most beautiful roadside campground in Glacier, situated as it is, on the shores of magnificent Lake McDonald, the largest lake in the Park. Shaded by red cedars in one of the world's few temperate-zone rain forests, Sprague Creek is unique. We pitched our tent on a forest floor cushioned by a blanket of needles. Through the trees, the waters of the lake, only steps away, shimmered blue and white, ripples on its surface pushed east by a gentle breeze. Golden light of early evening filtered down through the trees as we lit our Coleman stove and put the makings of dinner on a nearby picnic table. A large gray Canadian jay swooped silently overhead, landing in a tree nearby. He looked at the picnic table, cocking his head, appearing to assess his prospects of stealing a morsel before fluttering away. After dinner, the sun sank behind brooding Howe Ridge to the north. Sue got Heather into her sleeper and put her to bed. The temperature dropped and silence, broken only occasionally by muffled sounds of nearby campers, descended. We snuggled down into our sleeping bags, heads filled with delicious visions from our day, tired and as happy as we'd ever been.

The sun rose early the next morning but didn't reach Sprague Creek immediately, shaded as it is by the towering shapes of Edwards Mountain and Mt. Brown. Still, Sue and I were up early, leaving the kids asleep. Diffused morning light illuminating tenuous fog tendrils lent an ethereal feel to our campground; majestic, silent, reverential, reflective of eternity. Coffee perked on the Coleman. While we waited for it, I opened Ruhle's Guide to Glacier. Together we perused its contents, searching out information on hikes we could take and wonders we could discover. "I think we should pick some easy hikes to start with," Sue advised. "Hidden Lake was tough going for Debbie."

I nodded. "Yes, I admit I was puffing too. Heather's getting heavier by the day! Let's take a day off from hiking and see what's around here," I suggested.

Lake McDonald Lodge, near the head of the lake, was our first stop. More enchantment! Perhaps the most beautiful of the three magnificent hotels in the Park, it sits on the site of a hotel built in 1893 by George Snyder. In those days, tourists were transported by horse-drawn carriage to the hotel from Belton 15 miles distant over a rough rut cut through dense forest. In 1895, Snyder bought a 40 foot steamboat to ferry them up the lake. Nine years later, John Lewis purchased Snyder's hotel and, in 1913, moved it to a nearby location to make room for the existing structure, calling it the Lewis Hotel.

Lake McDonald Lodge, as it has come to be known, is perhaps the best example of the Swiss architecture employed throughout the Park by the Great Northern builders. Stone and stucco foundations support the massive log structure. Intricate log work railings enclose second and third story balconies that overlook the lake. Dozens of baskets filled with bright blue lobelia, showy red geraniums and white Queen Anne's lace hang from decks and dot walkways around the hotel. Heaven again, man-made this time!

Inside, we found the lobby equally impressive; open three stories to a vaulted ceiling, it is surrounded by log work-enclosed walkways two and three stories above. A stone fireplace five feet high and ten feet across faces windows looking out onto the lake. Eight foot long chandeliers of parchment decorated with vivid Indian motifs shine down on well-worn leather armchairs below. We gawked, especially at the many animal trophies that looked down on us from above; mounted heads of moose, elk, deer, antelope, mountain goats, big horn sheep, grizzly bears, eagles and some animals we could not identify. These, we learned, were trophies shot decades before by Snyder for the purpose of decorating his hotel.

We walked down to the water's edge just fifty feet from the Lodge. Sue took Debbie's shoes off and she immediately waded in.

"Don't get your shorts wet," I ordered. I took Heather out of the pack and Sue fed a bottle to her. I walked the short distance to where Snyder Creek flows into the lake, loving the wonderful sight presented by the mingling of the waters. Meanwhile, Debbie delighted in the cold, clear water, testing its depth until her shorts were thoroughly soaked. Sue only giggled.

The sign on the dock said the beautiful old tour boat, the DeSmet, would depart for a lake cruise in a little over an hour. I studied the sign displaying the price of a ticket; three dollars for adults. Debbie and Heather would be free. "What do you think?" I asked Sue. "It's a lot of money."

"I'd like to," she replied, "if we can." I checked the contents of my wallet, looked at my three girls and handed six dollars to the man at the ticket booth. After the hour ride on the glassy waters, I was glad we'd gone.

Easy hikes accessible by Going to the Sun Road, we discovered, lay mainly east of Logan Pass. The next morning we decided to drive back up over the Pass and down the way we'd come. Our aim was to see popular Sunrift Gorge, then hike the half mile down to Baring Falls.

It was a short but fairly steep walk up from the side of the road where we parked our car to the overlook. We immediately discovered why Sunrift Gorge is so popular. It's amazing! Over uncounted millennia, Baring Creek has sliced down through solid rock, leaving an arrow-straight sliver of chasm a thousand feet long, a hundred feet high and a dozen feet wide. Looking through the dim light that cloaked its narrow walls, we could see bright green patches of sunlight beyond. Magnificent! On its way through the Gorge, Baring Creek throws up a fine spray that perpetually nourishes thick green moss blanketing its upper ledges. Dappled light filtering through overhanging branches of fir bring forth in surprising brilliance the blue and red and white blooms of delicate wildflowers growing up through the moss.

That afternoon we explored Baring Falls and took the short spur trail to the shore of St. Mary Lake. The following day we packed a lunch for the three mile hike in to Florence Falls, passing lower but no less magnificent St. Mary Falls on the way. We were in awe of all we saw; mountain majesty everywhere. This was better, much better even, than the expectations produced by brochures we'd savored in Evanston. Glacier Park was heaven right here on earth.

Since arriving at Sprague Creek Campground, Sue and I had read and re-read George Ruhle's description of the Garden Wall trail in his guide book and each time my enthusiasm grew. The trail, almost completely above tree line, traverses high alpine country, affording unparalleled views all the way to Granite Park Chalet. A picture of the Chalet, one of only two original back-country chalets left, showed the beautiful old stone structure situated on a promontory overlooking a valley thousands of feet beneath. A profusion of wildflowers blanketing the steep, grassy alpine slopes gave the geological feature along which the trail ran its name. This was, the book said, not only one of the most spectacular hikes in the Park, but also one of the easiest. The urge to take it became almost overpowering. I felt it represented an experience that we simply couldn't afford to pass up.

But a number of factors needed to be considered. First, there was that ledge. Could Sue, with her acrophobia, get safely across it? And did I want to subject her to that? Second, the length of the hike was a concern. While the guide book described the trail as more or less level with little climbing, it was nearly eight miles to Granite Park Chalet and another four miles down from there to Going to the Sun Road. Shortly after we were married, Sue had a terrible skiing accident. Both legs and both ankles were shattered and on first examination, doctors thought she might never walk again. After five operations and a year's convalescence, she proved them wrong. But could she walk twelve miles? Could Debbie? And third, apart from goats at Logan Pass, we hadn't seen any large animals yet, but the book said we might. I could not discount the possibility of bears again.

At our campsite that evening, we discussed the warm-up hikes we'd taken. We'd made the six mile round trip to Florence Falls without incident and Debbie had put up with our prodding without too much travail. Heather seemed to enjoy riding in the pack on my back and expressed no discontent as long as her diapers were dry and she wasn't hungry. "What do you think?" I asked. "Can we make it OK? The Chalet is only two miles farther than we went today." My enthusiasm was obvious.

Sue did well to hide her apprehension. "I think we can if we take it slow," she replied. "Debbie can't go very fast."

"Yes," I replied, "but there won't be much climbing." I took her hand and looked into her eyes. "I know you're not wild about going over that ledge, but it's only a short distance and people do it all the time. Besides, I can put a rope around your waist on the way across if that will make you feel better. What do you think?"

Sue smiled. "I think we should go," she replied. "It will be wonderful. The Chalet looks so pretty in the pictures. We can probably get Debbie a candy bar or something there." She gave my hand a squeeze and smiled brightly. "Let's do it. I'll pack a lunch and take extra diapers and several bottles for Heather. We'll be fine."

Driven by my desire to take this hike, I stuffed down deep in my consciousness the real truth; Sue was frightened of the ledge, concerned about her and Debbie's ability to hike 12 miles, and worried about dangers we might encounter. I chose not to acknowledge in my own mind the fact that her acquiescence was most likely a product of her love for me and desire never to disappoint.

The next morning dawned bright and clear, perfect weather for a day in the high country. Our plan was to hike the eight miles along the Garden Wall, stop at Granite Park Chalet for a snack, then hike four miles down to Sun Road. We'd seen motorists pick up hikers and figured we could get a ride back up to our car at Logan Pass without much trouble. We'd be back at our campsite by nightfall.

Sue made our lunch and put it, along with three full baby bottles, a supply of diapers and a spare jumper for Heather, in the day pack she would carry. We got the girls up and after breakfast headed for Logan Pass.

We pulled into the parking lot around ten thirty. I opened the trunk and got out the carrier Heather would ride in, Sue's day pack, our camera and a length of rope. I put the rope in Sue's pack before we headed for the bathrooms at the visitor center. After everyone had done their duty, Sue tied knots in Debbie's sneakers. I put Heather in her carrier, we shouldered our packs and made for the trailhead on the opposite side of Sun Road. The sky was bright blue, the breeze gentle and air cool enough to require jackets. I checked my watch. It was nearing eleven, still plenty of time, I thought.

Our trail descended gradually through a lovely green alpine meadow dotted with yellow glacier lilies. We were the only hikers in sight. Cars and pickups shouldered past one another on the road descending beneath us. A mountain to the south, hard by the road, towered above while to the west, the landscape dropped away to nothingness. Logan Creek, three thousand feet below, appeared as a silver thread. This awesome valley proceeded many miles west, flanked on one side by snow-clad Heaven's Peak and on the other by long, sheer stone flanks of the Garden Wall. My eyes followed the trail to a high, flat-topped beehive-shaped hump that protruded south from the Garden Wall some distance ahead. Our map labeled it as Haystack Butte and indicated that our trail went behind it, between it and the Garden Wall. As I surveyed our route, I thought to myself, "We're actually going to that remote, wild, beautiful, distant place; we're hiking into the backcountry!"

A feeling unlike any I'd ever experienced swept over me: freedom, an overpowering sense of freedom. We were alone at the top of the world, leaving civilization behind, entering remoteness, immersing ourselves in the wild, dependent on no one but ourselves, constrained only by our own imagination, courage and ability. Free.

"Look!" Debbie cried, pointing. "More mountain goats!" Not far off our path, in the middle of the meadow we were crossing, were four white mountain goats, two mamas and two babies. "Take a picture, Daddy," she squealed. I turned on the single-lens reflex camera we'd bought on time, focused its long telephoto lens and snapped off a half-dozen shots. Then I aimed the camera at the mountain spectacle that surrounded us, attempting to capture not only the beauty in which we were immersed, but also the emotions I felt. It was good we'd brought a lot of film.

Continuing on through the meadow, it wasn't long until we faced the dreaded ledge. I stopped and looked back at Sue. I sensed her fear, though she smiled cheerfully. "Come up by me," I said. "Turn around so I can get the rope out of your pack."

"I know we won't need it," she said, "but it will make me feel better."

I retrieved the rope and tied it around her waist, keeping a secure hold on the other end. I held out my other hand. "Here," I said, "take my hand."

"No," she replied. "Take Debbie's hand. I'll follow behind her."

I took Debbie's hand in mine and knelt down to her level. "There's nothing to be afraid of," I said. "I'll hold onto you. You won't fall. You'll be perfectly safe. Are you scared?"

Debbie shook her head. "No, I'm not scared", she said, "but I think Mommy is."

"No," Sue said, kneeling down. "I'm not a bit scared." She gave Debbie a hug. "We'll be just fine." She looked at me. "How far is it to the other side?"

"Not more than a hundred yards or so," I replied, my estimate perhaps optimistic. "Keep your eyes on the path and don't look down. Stay close to the wall and you'll be OK. It's plenty wide enough. Nobody will fall."

I led us out onto the dark grey ledge and, though I had never been afraid of heights, when I looked down onto the roofs of the vehicles below, I felt butterflies swarming in my stomach. The drop was breathtaking, truly straight down. I kept to the center of the ledge thinking this would demonstrate to Sue – who edged along the wall, feeling its surface with her hands – that its width provided an ample margin of safety. We proceeded slowly, the distance between us and the road below growing with every step. I saw that we needed to watch the path, for the ledge was strewn with rocks of various sizes and shapes, presumably having fallen from somewhere above.

I paused to look back at Sue. "You OK?" I asked.

"Don't stop!" she cried. "Just keep going!"

As I turned and started forward again, my heart leapt into my throat. A sizeable animal had started out onto the ledge from the other side. It was heading our way. I stopped short. "What's that?" Sue cried, pressing her body closer to the wall, both palms flattened against it. Debbie's hand tightened in mine and she clung to my leg.

The animal came toward us. It was light colored with streaks of white and brown and grey in the long fur that covered it. I judged its stocky body to be not quite two feet high when walking on all fours and maybe three feet long. It certainly wasn't a chipmunk! It marched resolutely forward. I could feel my heart speed up. As the animal drew near, the shape of its head reminded me of a beaver. But beavers don't climb mountains, I told myself. I wondered if it was dangerous. Had I not been frightened of this animal and our tenuous position on the ledge, I would have admired it. Indeed, it did look something like a beaver, with two large upper teeth protruding beneath a black button nose. I held my breath as the creature closed the distance between us to a few yards, wondering what it would do and what I would do. Would it attack or would it attempt to go around us? Closer and closer it came. Suddenly it stopped, not more than five feet in front of me, and sat up on its hind legs!

"What is it?" Sue cried. "Is it dangerous? What does it want?" Debbie looked at it, wide eyed.

"I don't know what it is," I replied. As the animal continued sitting up on its haunches, I began to relax. "It looks like it's begging," I said. "Do you think it's looking for a handout?"

"It does look like it's begging," Sue replied.

I backed away from the animal to get closer to Sue, being careful not to let Debbie or myself step too close to the edge. The animal dropped back onto four legs and waddled after me, keeping the same distance. Then it sat up again.

I turned Sue's back toward me so I could reach into her pack. "Be careful!" she cried. "Don't push us off!"

"This will just take a second," I said. "Stay quiet." I reached into the pack and found one of the peanut butter and jelly sandwiches she'd made. I turned back to the animal. It continued to sit up, watching me. I broke off a piece of sandwich and dropped it on the ground. The creature instantly went down on all fours, reached out a paw, snatched up the morsel and ate it. Then it sat up again'

"He is begging!" Debbie cried, suddenly delighted by this strange creature.

I broke off another piece of sandwich. This time I threw it a few feet beyond the little fellow, in the direction we were headed. It quickly retreated to this second morsel, snatched it up and ate it. The hairy creature turned back toward us and sat up again. I looked at Sue and let out a sigh of relief. "That's what he wants," I said, "a handout. He likes peanut butter and jelly."

"Keep giving him the sandwich," Sue said. "Let's get off this ledge."

I'd throw a piece of sandwich beyond the animal, it would retreat to where it had fallen, eat it, then look back for another. Piece by piece, the peanut butter and jelly sandwich led the creature – and us – off the ledge.

When we finally emerged safely from the ledge onto the trail, I breathed a sigh of relief. Sensing that its gravy train had come to a stop, the animal scurried down a steep slope below the trail and disappeared beneath a large rock.

I went to Sue and embraced her. "You did great," I told her. "We're OK now. I can take the rope off."

Still somewhat shaken by our experience, she returned my embrace and attempted a weak smile. "Boy," she said, "for a minute I thought we'd either be eaten by that animal or pushed off the cliff. I'd really like to know what it is."

"The guidebook will probably tell us," I said. I opened Sue's pack again and drew out the little yellow book. I thumbed through until I found the section on Park wildlife. Sure enough, one of the black and white photos showed an animal that looked exactly like the one on the ledge. "It's called a hoary marmot," I said. "It lives among the rocks in the high country and eats roots. It gets its name because of the color of its fur – like hoarfrost."

Sue grinned. "I wish we'd seen that picture before we left."

I put the book and rope back into Sue's pack, checked Debbie's shoelaces and off we marched toward unknown wonders. The trail dropped gently through subalpine fir dwarfed by winter cold and vicious winds, then broke out into fields of showy wildflowers. "Oh my," Sue said, "look at these flowers! They're incredible." She stopped to examine some bright blue flowers shaped like bells. Anxious to move forward, I said, "Come on. It's a long hike. We need to keep moving."

The trail reversed its descent and we began to climb. The sun became hot and Debbie grew tired. We stopped for a rest and took off our jackets. Looking back, I saw we'd come only a short distance. A mile? I couldn't judge. I encouraged Debbie and Sue to begin again.

Soon the trail made a wide turn to the left. Rectangular grey boulders were strewn here and there on the mountainside amid bright green grasses and spectacular fields of wildflowers. "My feet hurt, Mommy," Debbie said. We stopped again and stepped out of the way of several hikers who had overtaken us. I itched to move faster. "Can we stop here for lunch?" Sue asked.

When I looked at my watch, I was surprised at the time. It was already past noon. I surveyed the trail ahead. In what I guessed was about a half mile, it began to climb in earnest. "Let's wait 'till we get up there," I said, pointing above us to where the trail disappeared behind Haystack Butte. "The view will be better and we need to keep moving."

Time and again, marmots and ground squirrels pulled our attention away from our path. It was difficult to keep our eyes on the rocks in the trail. Vast views surrounded us. Despite my desire to get on more quickly, my heart was near bursting with exhilaration. I hoped Sue and Debbie shared my joy.

We stopped to rest and gather our strength where the trail began its steep climb. "Do we have to go up there?" Debbie asked, the tone in her voice a sorrowful protest. "It will be alright," Sue said, putting her arm around her. "We can stop and rest whenever you like."

I knew that was both the right and wrong thing to say. It was right because it was all that could be said; it was wrong because saying so would cause more delay. Our progress to this point had been frustratingly slow and the climb ahead was sure to slow it even more. I was becoming worried about the time and how far we had yet to go. I consulted the guidebook. Were we halfway? It was difficult to estimate, but from the description, I concluded we weren't. Perhaps I'd underestimated the time it would take our little family to cover the 7.8 miles to the Chalet. Perhaps I'd overestimated a six-year-old's stamina – and patience. A new realization dawned. We were new to this.

Up we climbed, the magnificent views becoming more so with each step. But the sun beat down and the steep grade took its toll. Heather didn't seem heavy on my back when we began our trek at Logan Pass, but now I was struggling, sweat running down my face, lungs sucking thin air, legs tiring. The baby, on the other hand, didn't seem to mind a bit. She slept. I worried about Sue's legs. The Doctors at Northwestern University, our alma mater, had pieced the bones together, but how strong were they? I didn't know.

Sue marched on behind, uncomplaining, but Debbie was crying more or less continuously now. Even frequent rest stops didn't help much. I was tempted to prod her along by saying that we had a long way to go to reach the Chalet, but held my tongue. I mustn't say anything that might discourage Debbie – or Sue, for that matter.

After what seemed an eternity, we reached a place where the trail bent back upon itself, reversing direction. A switchback. We stopped. I rested my legs and filled my lungs. Everyone got a drink from one of the water bottles Sue carried. I wondered how she felt. I looked up the trail and thought I could see where it leveled out. There was hope. I pointed. "Look," I said, "you can see the top. We'll stop there and have lunch."

When we reached the saddle behind Haystack Butte, the optimism I'd felt when we first started out began to return. It was a tough, hot climb and we'd all suffered to one degree or another, but we'd made it. We'd reached the top. As I marched forward across the saddle, the weight I'd felt on my back seemed to lift, my legs regained their spring, sweat dried and I breathed easy. Heaven again.

The area around us was strewn with rectangular blocks of stone bigger than our Ford Fairlane. To Debbie's – and our – delight, patches of snow remained here and there between the boulders, feeding rivulets of icy water onto the trail and down the mountainsides. We went for the nearest snow and scooped up handfuls, feeling its delicious iciness. I made a snowball and threw it at Sue. I missed. She fired back, her aim better. Refreshed and happy, we found a large flat rock to have our picnic on.

Sue drew Debbie close to her. "Let's take off your shoes," she said. "Put your toes in the water. It will cool your feet off and make them feel better. You'll see." Shoes and socks off, Debbie jumped down and made for the melting snow. When she felt the icy water run over her feet, she turned back quickly to look at us. A grin lit up her face and she squealed with delight. She jumped up and down in the snowmelt, splashing water in every direction.

My watch said two o'clock, but now that we were at the high point on the trail, the time didn't seem to matter as much. We were halfway, I judged, and the difficult part was behind us. Sue changed Heather's diaper and gave her a bottle while I took the remaining sandwiches out of her pack. With the oranges and trail mix she'd packed, there was still plenty to go around.

As we ate, my eyes searched the talus slopes above, hoping to see more mountain goats or perhaps a bear. I spotted something in the distance. "Is that a rock?" I asked, pointing. Sue squinted in the sunlight. "I think that's an animal," she replied. "Yes," she said, "it's moving. Look!" she cried. "There are several of them! They aren't mountain goats and they certainly aren't bears." I focused our telephoto lens on the distant objects. "I think they're big horn sheep," I said, handing the camera to Sue. "Here, take a look. They're hard to see because their color blends into the rocks." To our delight, the herd moved down lower, giving us a close-up view of their magnificent curved horns and noble faces. "This is great!" Sue exclaimed. I was glad to see her enthusiasm. I snapped picture after picture while they grazed unperturbed. Wouldn't it be fun, I thought, to bring these pictures back home to show our families?

Looking east, my eyes followed our trail back to Logan Pass in the distance, several hundred feet below our picnic spot. But this, I saw, would be our last view of the Pass and set of mountains surrounding it. Once our trail descended around Haystack Butte, our view of Oberlin Mountain and the ethereal 294 foot ribbon of spray called Birdwoman Falls would be blocked. Looking west, I saw a new and different landscape, a solid phalanx of peaks sheathed in snow, equally magnificent but different; distant, cold and somehow a little sinister.

My watch read two thirty; time to head out. Granite Park Chalet was still nearly four miles distant, I judged, if Haystack Butte was the halfway point. Sue put Debbie's shoes and socks back on, I returned Heather to her carrier and we set off west, spirits high once again.

Within a hundred yards, my heart sank. I had been wrong about the trail. It didn't descend from the saddle behind Haystack at all. It resumed its climb and the grade looked at least as steep as the climb we'd just made. "Oh no," Sue said, when she realized the truth. "I thought you said it was all downhill."

I was chagrined. "I know," I replied. "I thought that's what the guide book said." Both Sue and Debbie looked as unhappy as I felt. My eyes scanned the trail ahead, hoping to see it level out, but it continued up, up and still up more as far as I could see. We could expect no relief from hard labor anytime soon. We climbed slowly, silently, eyes no longer admiring the sheer western slopes of Haystack Butte. Everyone, even Debbie, seemed to understand that we must husband our strength. As the sun beat down on the steep, rocky trail, even I didn't mind frequent stops. We were in survival mode. I became angry; angry at the guidebook, angry at the trail, angry at myself for having gotten it wrong. No longer worried about the time and our slow pace, I just wanted us to reach the top. Eventually we got there. The trail leveled and began a gradual descent. We stopped to catch our breath and congratulate ourselves.

We found the mountain slopes above and below the trail to be much steeper west of Haystack. After an hour of hiking, we reached a point where the slope that our trail traversed was nearly vertical. We came to a place where it curved south before disappearing around a corner, only thin air beyond. The trail took a sharp turn to the north, the apex exposing hikers to nothingness on all sides. Before we reached the promontory, Sue called a halt. "I don't like this," she said. "I'd like the rope." I got it out of the pack and tied it around her waist again.

While this portion of the trail was not to Sue's liking, I loved it. I found it exhilarating to stand at the sharp point where the trail turned back upon itself, surrounded by depth and distance on every side. As I looked south across the wide valley three thousand feet in depth, I imagined that this must be how birds feel when they soar above the earth; limitless vistas, limitless possibilities, limitless freedom. Awesome! I wished Sue could appreciate it as I did.

Once past the promontory, the grind of hiking what was seemingly an endless trail distracted us considerably from the awesome scenery through which we were traveling. Debbie cried, not only from the exertion and tedium a child experiences during a long hike, but also because her feet hurt. Sue had noticed a developing blister at our lunch stop but there was nothing to be done. We didn't have any band aids. We both felt sorry for her and I, a little guilty.

Our slow, jerky stop-and-go pace continued hour after hour. We'd husbanded our water but finally it gave out. Few streams presented themselves on this side of Haystack and I was unsure if the water was safe to drink. My back ached from the weight I was carrying and my feet hurt from the pounding I was giving them. But I couldn't complain. Sue, with her damaged legs, probably suffered more. Heather grew tired of riding in the pack on my back and cried, so I carried her in my arms for a time. We were down to the business of simply getting there, though I could not judge where "there" was. The map I had lacked detail and the guidebook, while descriptive, gave me no clear indication how far we'd come or how far we had yet to go. But two things were clear; Haystack Butte was well short of halfway and I had screwed up. Both Sue and I knew that, though it remained unsaid.

As the sun marched implacably northwest, shadows cast by mountain walls predicted sundown within the next few hours. We came to a place where the trail left the flowers and grasses we'd been hiking through and entered stands of stunted alpine fir. We were no longer above treeline. Perhaps this meant we were getting close, I thought. I was eager for any clue, any indication that the Chalet might be just around the next corner.

Suddenly Sue stopped. "Look!" she said, pointing through the trees into the distance. "Is that a lake? Could it be Lake McDonald?" Beyond the valley facing us, far in the distance, I could just make out a tongue of light blue water, difficult to notice in the blue mountain haze. "My gosh!" I exclaimed. "It could be!" I tried to judge the distance. "It must be a good ten miles away." Sue was more observant than I, always able to see things that I would miss. She's still in the game, I told myself, relieved that she had not given in to exhaustion or lost her appreciation of where we were.

The trees thinned and our trail took a sharp right turn, heading north past beautiful stone ramparts darkened by water trickling from somewhere above. Tired as we were, we couldn't help appreciating this wonderful grotto. It was Sue, again, who called my attention to something in the distance. "Look!" she exclaimed excitedly. She pointed west across a shallow valley around which our trail traversed. "Is that the Chalet?" We all looked. At first I didn't see it. The Chalet, built of stone quarried from nearby cliffs, blended into the landscape. "Yes," I replied, "that's the Chalet!"

At last the object of our obsession these past hours was within sight. The quaint stone buildings we'd seen pictured in the guidebook sat majestically on a plateau beneath Swiftcurrent

Mountain and above McDonald Valley. We were all relieved and excited. I bent down and put my arm around Debbie. "See," I said, pointing, "that's where we're going. We can rest there and maybe get a candy bar before we go down to the road and get a ride to our car." She nodded and wiped a tear from one eye. "OK, Daddy," she replied.

The balloon of excitement created when the Chalet came into sight was deflated considerably when we calculated the distance that still separated us from it. Even looking directly across the valley, the Chalet buildings appeared tiny. And our trail circled the valley, perhaps doubling the distance we must hike. "How far do you think it is?" Sue asked. The day had proven I was no judge but I said, "Probably a mile." It looked like more but I was afraid to say so.

Three quarters of an hour later, we arrived at the base of the plateau on which the Chalet sits. To reach it, only fifty yards distant, required a climb up a modest grade. At that moment, it looked to me like the route to Mount Everest. I heaved a sigh, hitched up my britches and headed up.

When we reached the courtyard between the Chalet and smaller stone building behind it, we were too exhausted to feel anything; not joy or pride or even relief. We paused for just a moment to admire the old stone structures and their magnificent setting before making for the porch and front door on the opposite side of the Chalet. We needed to get off our feet.

I pulled the heavy wooden door open and followed Sue and Debbie inside. Gas lights illuminating the large room cast a friendly glow. Our entrance was greeted with nods and smiles by people eating dinner at a half dozen wooden tables. A girl in her late teens or early twenties chattered cheerily with the hikers while she bustled about, filling glasses on the tables. "Look," someone said pointing to me, "he's carrying a baby!"

I swung Heather's carrier off my back and set it and her on the floor. Debbie immediately made for a bench at an empty table and flopped down. I helped Sue with her day pack and we eased our tired, aching bodies down next to Debbie.

A young man with a friendly face came out from what I guessed was the kitchen and, when he saw us, appeared surprised. "We didn't expect any more hikers today," he said. "Hey, you've got a baby!" he exclaimed, seeing Heather who was fussing and squirming in her seat. "We don't get too many hikers this age. I guess you carried her all the way, huh? How old is she?"

"She's a little over ten months," Sue replied. "Could we get something to drink?

"Oh sure, you bet," the young man replied. "I'm Brian. I'll be right back." A few moments after he hurried away, a tall, handsome, matronly woman with graying hair swept out of the kitchen. She was wiping her hands on the apron she wore. "I'm Kay Luding," she said. She bent down to the baby and stroked her head. "Who's this?"

"That's Heather," Sue replied. "She's a little fussy right now."

The woman picked the baby up out of her carrier. Heather looked startled and began to cry. "Now, now," the woman cooed, rocking her in her arms. "I think you'll be just fine now that you're out of that awful seat you've been stuck in." The baby stopped crying, looked up into Kay Luding's face and settled down into her arms. The young man who had met us returned with glasses of lemonade which we immediately sucked down.

"I'm Don Sullivan and this is my wife Sue," I said. "And this is Debbie."

The woman turned her back and went behind a glass-fronted counter near the entrance to the kitchen, taking Heather with her. She put a large book that looked like a ledger on the counter top and her eyes scanned it for a moment. Then she returned to our table. "I didn't think so," she said. "You don't have a reservation."

43

"No," I said, "we don't. We didn't intend to spend the night. I didn't realize how long it would take us to get here."

Kay frowned. "I can see that," she said. "You aren't thinking of trying to hike down to the road tonight, are you?" she asked. "It's a long way and it will be dark in a couple of hours. Besides, we've been watching three grizzlies in the meadow down below. I can't let you take these babies down the trail tonight."

I looked at Sue again. This woman no doubt knew what she was talking about. Our exhausted bodies – and minds – craved rest. We weren't ready to get back on the trail. Hiking in the dark could be dangerous, especially with bears around. We were all hungry. But we hadn't planned for anything like this. The money I had in my wallet was just enough to get us back to Chicago. I didn't know what to do

Kay's nose crinkled and she looked down at the baby in her arms. "Sue, Heather needs a change."

Sue looked into her pack and pulled out a cloth diaper. "It's the last one I have," she said. "I don't have another bottle for her either. We have to go down tonight."

Kay handed the baby to Sue. "Go in the back and change the baby," she said. "I'll get dinner for you and there will be no more talk about going down tonight."

"How much does it cost to stay here?" I asked. "We only have enough money to get us home."

"Where's home?" Kay asked.

"Chicago," I replied. "Near Chicago. Evanston, Illinois."

Kay frowned again. "Well," she said, "that is a long way. But so is the trail down to the road. You'll spend the night here. Don't worry about paying me. Now get ready for dinner."

The girl who had been serving the other hikers came to our table with plates and silverware and napkins. "Your baby is so cute!" she said. "I don't think we've ever had a baby up here. At least not this summer. It's really exciting!"

"What's your name?" I asked.

"Sarah," she replied. "This is my first summer up here. I'm from back East. Ohio. I just love it here. I hope to be back next summer."

Sue returned with Heather who looked fresh-scrubbed and happy. She'd changed her diapers and put on a clean jumper she'd included in the pack. "Kay gave me some hot water to wash up with," she said. "You can take Debbie back and wash up too. They're mixing up some powdered milk for Heather. I think that will be OK."

Warm water in a white porcelain basin, a bar of soap and a towel were waiting for us near the sink in the kitchen. When I'd finished washing, I was surprise at the miraculous result soap and water could produce. My fatigue and pain had been washed away along with the trail dust and dried sweat that had coated my face. I felt like a new man.

Brian came out of the kitchen holding one of Heather's baby bottles, filled with milk. "We mixed in more powdered milk than the instructions on the box called for," he said. "Kay said baby formula is richer." He turned the bottle upside down and shook a few sprinkles of milk from the nipple onto his wrist to test its temperature. "I heated it up. I don't think it's too hot," he said, handing the bottle to Sue.

Sue smiled at the young man's eagerness to do the right thing for our baby. She tested it herself. "It feels just right," she said. "Thanks." As soon as the nipple came near Heather's lips, she grabbed the bottle and attacked the milk. "She likes it," Brian said with a grin. "There's more powdered milk in the kitchen. Just let me know."

"What are you going to do for diapers?" I asked.

"Kay said she'd give me a large napkin and that will work for tonight," Sue replied. "They're washing the dirty diapers along with the jumper Heather had on today. They'll dry overnight on the clothesline out back.

Shortly thereafter, Sarah and Brian brought roast beef dinners out to us. "It's canned," he said, indicating the beef. "Everything has to be packed in on Mules so we don't have fresh meat or vegetables. The beans are canned too, but the potatoes are fresh. I peeled them myself." Fresh or not, Sue and Debbie and I agreed this was the best meal we could remember.

When we'd finished, Kay came out and said, "Come with me. I'll show you where you'll spend the night. The guest rooms here in the Chalet are all filled, so you'll have to take the one empty room I have in the building out back. That's where the kids who work here stay. It's not fancy but I think you'll be comfortable enough."

The room in the single story stone building was small but clean. It was just large enough for a bunk bed, a table with a pitcher and basin on it and a chair. "Debbie and I will take the upper bunk," I said. "Heather can sleep with you. OK?"

"You know I don't like heights," Sue said with a grin. "This is wonderful."

Indeed it was; our little room provided a snug sanctuary in the wilderness, a sanctuary from fatigue and pain and danger. It would allow us to sleep soundly, secure in the knowledge that nothing would harm us this night. In the morning, the sun would rise again. We'd be rested and fresh and all would be wonderful.

"Why don't you come back and sit on the front porch?" Kay said. "Sarah will bring out some hot chocolate while we watch the sunset."

We gladly accepted Kay's invitation and joined guests clustered around a spotting scope set up near the porch. Everyone was looking down into an open meadow below the Chalet, pointing and talking. As we drew near, a hiker who had been looking through the scope motioned me over. "Take a look," he said. "There are three grizzlies down there. It looks like two adults and a cub." Looking into the eyepiece, I saw my first bear! Its distinguishing hump and thick, broad head said "grizzly," even in the fading light. The heavy animal's movements were slow and deliberate, projecting grace and power and magnificence. I called Sue over. "Take a look," I said. "A grizzly."

She studied the animal. "Boy," she said, "I'm glad we aren't taking the trail down tonight. I'd hate to meet up with him. But this is really thrilling, watching it from up here." While we watched the three bears move about the meadow, Kay came out and joined the group. "What are they doing?" I asked.

"Oh, they've probably dug up some garbage from the dump," she replied. "We bury our garbage over there." She pointed west. "It's why we get so many bears up here."

Brian and Sarah brought out cups of hot chocolate while Kay and a Park ranger entertained the group with exciting bear stories and wilderness tales. The roseate glow of the sun behind the mountains eventually faded into darkness and we lost sight of the bears. Conversation ebbed and it was time to turn in. Heather had fallen asleep in Sue's arms. I helped Sue to her feet, took Debbie's hand and we headed back to our room. This, we agreed, was an evening we'd never forget.

The mattress on the bunk bed was, I discovered, decidedly thin but it didn't matter one bit. Laying down on it was heaven. Only then did I realize how truly tired my body was. Debbie and I snuggled deep beneath the thick comforter Kay provided. Debbie was asleep instantly but I lay awake for a time. Startlingly bright moonlight streamed through the window. Tired as I was, I wished to savor the experience of being in the old stone structure high in the Rocky Mountains, miles from anything, surrounded by beauty and silence and grizzly bears. It was the fulfillment of indistinct boyhood dreams I'd had of what wilderness must be like, only immeasurably better.

Sue stirred in the bottom bunk. "What's that?" she whispered.

"What's what?" I asked.

"That noise," she replied. "Don't your hear it?" I had heard it but hadn't paid attention.

"What is that?" she asked again.

I listened to scratching, scrambling sounds on the rough stone floor below, racing from one side of our room to the other and back again. In the silence of the wilderness, it sounded like dogs and cats chasing one another. "Mice, I think," I replied.

"Oh great!" was all she said. I smiled. Most other women would have freaked, I thought. Not Sue. I heard her snuggle Heather and herself down deeper in their covers without another word.

Brilliant cold woke me in the morning. Sun streamed through the window onto the stone floor, illuminating steam produced by my breathing. My God, it was cold, I thought. I dreaded the prospect of leaving the warm cocoon Debbie and I had created beneath our comforter. I stuck my hand out just long enough to look at my watch. Seven thirty. I listened to sounds in the courtyard outside. Some of the guests staying in the Chalet were up moving about. Breakfast, Kay had said, was served between seven and nine. I heard Sue wake in the bunk below when Heather stirred and began fussing. "It's really cold this morning," I said. "Everybody OK down there?"

48

"Heather's hungry and needs changing," Sue replied, rousing herself from her bunk. "I'll need to take her into the Chalet to get a diaper and wash her up. There's a layer of ice in the wash basin."

After Sue and Heather departed for the warmth of the Chalet, Debbie and I gathered up the things we'd scattered about and put them back into Sue's day pack. We straightened up our little room, then headed for breakfast. Hot coffee and warm pancakes were entirely as wonderful to Sue and me as the roast beef dinner we'd eaten the previous evening. When we'd finished, Brian brought out three baby bottles filled with warm milk for Heather and sandwiches for the three of us to eat on our hike down to the road. Sarah retrieved the diapers they'd washed from the clothesline out back and held Heather while Sue arranged things in her pack.

It was time to go. I went into the kitchen to find Kay Luding. She was barking orders to the cook while snatching pancakes off a griddle on the wood stove. I waited for a pause in the activity. "We were in trouble last night," I said. "I know that now. There's no way I can thank you enough for all you've done for us."

Kay wiped her hands on her apron, her face betraying no emotion. "Where are those babies of yours?" she asked. She turned and made for the dining room. When she reached our table, she picked Heather up and put her in one arm. Then she knelt down and wrapped the other around Debbie. "Getting these babies down safely is all the thanks I need," she replied.

Tears glistened in my eyes. I'd never met anyone so kind, so loving, so generous. What do you say to someone like that?

Sue, too, was choked up. "Thank you so very much," she said. "I don't know what we would have done without you."

Kay stood up and handed Heather back to Sue. Then she gave Sue and me a hug. "Every once in a while I get the chance to help someone out. I'm glad it was you. Now scoot. You still have four miles ahead of you and the trail is steep. Don't let it get too late."

Back at our campsite at Sprague Creek, Sue and I decided we all needed a day to rest and decompress. The following day we drove to the village of Apgar at the foot of Lake McDonald to pick up some groceries and wash clothes and diapers. No such luck. We needed to go out of the Park to nearby West Glacier to find what we needed.

When Sue sorted our laundry, she realized that the jumper Heather had worn the day we hiked to the Chalet was missing. "We must have left it on the clothesline," she said. While our clothes were washing, we replayed our adventures on the Garden Wall a dozen times. Tired legs, sore feet and dangers posed by wild animals were forgotten. Our enthusiasm for Glacier Park and yet-to-be discovered wonders had only grown.

We dreaded the thought of leaving but I had to be back at work in a few days. I figured we could leave as late as Saturday morning and still be back home Sunday night. With no speed limit, we could make 800 miles a day. We studied the guidebook and map of the Park, trying to decide how to squeeze the most into our remaining vacation time without subjecting the kids and ourselves to anything overly ambitious.

One section of the Park caught my attention and I kept coming back to it. Fjord-like Kintla Lake lay in the far northwest corner of the Park, thrusting into the belly of the Livingston Range like a knife. The guidebook described it as the most remote Park destination reachable by car. We'd seen gorgeous pictures of Kintla and of Bowman Lake, which lay just to the south. They were in remote wilderness; "out among 'em," as my grandfather would say, miles from anywhere.

Our map showed a Glacier Route Seven going up the west side of the Park all the way to Kintla, a few miles south of the border with Canada. Why not? I asked myself. The trip didn't look to be more than forty miles or so, maybe an hour's drive. Focused entirely on the Park, we had no interest in anything beyond its boundary. Consequently, when I studied our map, I didn't notice a parallel road going north outside the Park. That was an oversight I'd learn to regret.

Sue and I agreed that we'd drive to Bowman Lake Campground and spend one night, then proceed some fifteen miles farther north to Kintla. After spending a night there, we'd return to a campground on Going to the Sun road and depart for home the following day.

The next morning we packed our tent into the car and headed for Bowman Lake. We retraced our route to Apgar and continued west over a bridge spanning McDonald Creek just below where it flows from the Lake. Soon we came to a sign that pointed to the right. "Logging Lake," it read. I checked our map to be sure this was the road we wanted and found that indeed, our route would take us near Logging Lake. We turned onto a narrow gravel road that led east to Fish Creek Campground. Just beyond, it swung north.

Within a hundred yards, gravel gave out and we found ourselves on a bumpy dirt road strewn with rocks of every size and shape. The roughness of the road slowed our progress to twenty miles an hour, then fifteen. This was nothing like the smooth paved roads we'd encountered at Two Medicine or Going to the Sun Road. I shifted uncomfortably in my seat. So much for thinking we could reach Bowman Lake in an hour. I did not look at Sue for fear my expression would betray my misgivings.

Soon the road climbed steeply, then descended just as steeply. It became rougher and narrower by the minute, deteriorating in places to a series of muddy tire ruts. I kept my eyes glued to the ruts to avoid rocks as big as beavers. We came to a lush meadow dotted with small ponds which might have been home to beavers, but if so, I would never see them. Dense forest crowded in against the road as we crept north, the Fairlane's suspension bottoming from time to time . "Should we turn around?" Sue asked.

I shook my head. "We'll be OK. In any case, there's no place to turn around."

We ground and bumped north for an hour and came to another steep grade, this one worse than the first. Our pace slowed to a crawl. I shifted down to low gear and the wheels spun in soft earth for a moment, then caught traction. The Ford's hood pointed skyward and I held my breath until we crested the grade. On the way down, a steep embankment within inches of our slippery rut fell a hundred feet or more to a rocky stream bed. Sue gripped the door handle and fear showed in her eyes. "I don't like this, Don," she gasped.

There was nothing I could do but proceed down the steep hill, keeping our speed to a minimum and our tires as far from the precipice as possible. When we reached the bottom, we both breathed a sigh of relief. The road leveled out and became smoother. "I think we're past the worst of it," I said.

However, fifteen minutes later we came to a place where the road seemed to have washed out. The roadbed sloped sharply to the left, tipping our car at a precarious angle. Dense forest crowded in on both sides, branches nearly touching our car. We could only go forward. I looked up at Sue on the upside of the car. She was alarmed. "We won't tip over, will we?" she cried. Suddenly we heard a loud metal scraping sound coming from the car. I jammed my foot on the brake, my heart thumping in my chest. "What's happening?" Sue screamed. I had no idea. When I unglued my eyes from the road and looked around, I saw the problem. The metal radio antenna on my side of the car had hit a low-hanging wire that paralleled the road. Neither of us had noticed it before.

"What is that?" Sue said, pointing to the wire. "Is it a light line? My God, we might be electrocuted!" I tried to remain calm and think about what I should do. I remembered reading that if your car touched a live wire, you'd be safe so long as you didn't get out. "We need to stay in the car," I said. "We'll be OK." I inched the car forward, hoping to disengage the hanging wire from the metal antenna. The wire scraped along for a few seconds, then separated from the antenna as the road dropped beneath it. The roadbed leveled out and everybody breathed again.

We continued north. Two hours in, we came to a beautiful meadow shaded by massive pines. I pulled off the road and Sue got the kids out of the car. "Would you get the lunch?" she asked. "Look, Mommy!" Debbie cried, pointing to deer grazing in the meadow. Sue put her arm around her and they watched three lovely does in the peaceful glen. "They're wonderful!" she said.

I studied the map again while we ate our lunch. "I think this is Sullivan Meadow," I said. "Kind'a neat. I wonder where it got its name? I'm guessing these trees are Ponderosa Pine. I remember seeing pictures of trees like these in the guidebook."

"How much farther do you think Bowman Lake is?" Sue wondered.

"I think we're better than half way," I replied. She groaned. "Only halfway? We've been going for two hours. The girls are tired and frankly, so am I"

"If this is Sullivan meadow, there should be a ranger station a little way ahead," I said. "We can talk to the ranger."

In about a mile we came to an old log cabin. A sign read, "Logging Creek Ranger Station." We stopped and got out. There were no vehicles in the parking area. I went up to the cabin door and tried the knob. The door was locked. I peered in a window. The place was deserted.

My heart sank and a twinge of fear sneaked into my gut. I'd hoped to find a ranger who could tell us where we were, what the road ahead was like and how far we had to go. The empty ranger cabin brought home the reality of our isolation, heightening my awareness that we were on our own, perhaps out of our element. What if we had a flat tire, I asked myself? What if the engine quit? What if we slid off the road? Would anyone look for us, anyone come to our rescue? I suddenly itched to be out of this wild place, back to paved roads and gas stations and normalcy. The remoteness I had sought now felt more threatening than exciting. It seemed I had again underestimated the risks and challenges posed by wilderness and our ability to deal with them.

We got back into the car and continued our journey. Within a hundred yards, we came to another obstacle. A newly constructed concrete bridge spanned a broad creek that ran near the ranger station. I slowed to a stop as we approached it, for I saw that the road did not rise to meet the end of the bridge. The concrete bridge roadbed stood a good eight or ten inches higher than the road we were on. Could the Fairlane climb up onto it, I wondered? What would that do to our tires? Sue and I got out to look the situation over. It seemed that, prior to the construction of the bridge, the road had gone down an embankment and forded the creek. There was no way our car would make it through the rocky streambed. We had only two choices; turn around and return the way we'd come or try to get our car up on the bridge.

"What do you think?" I asked.

"It's more than two hours back the way we came," Sue replied. "What do you think"?

I walked up onto the bridge again and looked carefully at the difference in height, then returned to the car. I bent down and examined the distance between the bumper and the road. "I think it will make it," I said, "if the tires hold up. I'll give it a shot and if it seems like it's going to hurt the car, I'll stop. You and the kids stay here until I get the car across the bridge."

I edged the front tires up to the bridge and steadily applied pressure to the accelerator. The back wheels spun and rocks flew for a few seconds before the front of the car raised up and bounced onto the concrete. It made it! At least the front wheels had. I eased forward again until I felt the rear of the car raise up onto the bridge. It was smooth sailing for a hundred feet or so until I came to the drop at the other end. I eased the car back down off the bridge and got out to check for damage. I motioned for Sue and the kids to come ahead. "It's OK," I said, "we made it."

Forty five minutes later we came to the Polebridge Ranger Station, a collection of old log buildings of considerable charm. We were all relieved to see signs of civilization. Several cars and pickup trucks were parked nearby, suggesting that this time we were not alone. We found a building with a sign by the door that read "Ranger Station" and went inside. The ranger on duty seemed surprised when he saw our little family. He rose from his desk and approached the counter that separated us. "Camping at Bowman?" he asked.

I nodded. "How far is it?"

"Six miles," he replied. "You'll find the Bowman road about a quarter mile north. You won't have any trouble finding an open campsite. How many nights do you plan to stay?"

"Just tonight," I replied.

"Plan to do a little fishing?" the ranger asked.

"That was the plan but it's gotten late. We didn't realize how long it would take us to get here. The road is awful. We almost didn't make it. Do you know that the bridge by Logging Creek Ranger Station is way too high for the road?" I asked, allowing my annoyance to show.

"You didn't come up the inside road, did you?" the Ranger asked.

"What other way is there?" I replied.

"Don't you know about the outside road that goes through Polebridge?" he said. "That road is much better and a whole lot quicker. Not many people try to come up the inside road."

I wondered why I hadn't talked to the rangers at the visitor center in Apgar. Another mistake. I felt foolish and embarrassed.

It took a half hour for the Fairlane to navigate six miles up the rough, tortuous road to Bowman Lake and when we arrived, it was already late afternoon. "It's taken us the whole day to get here," I complained. "It's my fault."

Sue got out of the car and looked at the lake. "Don't worry," she said, "it's worth it."

I got out and joined her. Bowman Lake was even more beautiful than its pictures. Rainbow Peak to the south and Numa Ridge to the north framed this narrow alpine lake that stretched many miles into the interior of the mountains. I smiled and put my arm around her. Now that the harrowing trip up the inside road was over, I could relax. She was right. It was worth it, every mile.

Sue helped me pitch our tent beneath a thick canopy of Douglas fir. While she put our sleeping bags and assorted gear inside, I went to work building a campfire using wood stacked nearby. It was nice, I thought, for the Park Service to provide firewood. I pulled hotdogs from the ice chest and a can of beans from the trunk. We were all hungry. The aroma of wood smoke drifting through the trees mixed wonderfully with the smell of evergreens. While we heated the beans and roasted our hotdogs, two does stood quietly among the trees a few yards away, watching. We savored the sizzling franks. Filet Mignon could not have satisfied us any better than those hotdogs and beans. Sitting around a campfire by the edge of a mountain lake roasting hotdogs was the essence of everything we'd dreamed of, everything we'd sought on our race across the country.

When dinner was finished and the dishes done, we walked a hundred feet down to a pebbly beach by the water's edge. The sun had begun to set. Sue and I found a log to sit on and watched the sheer mountain ramparts towering above the lake turn crimson in the setting sun. We sat silently by the water, watching shadows creep up the mountain flanks until even the peaks had lost their light.

Sue and I put our arms around one another while Debbie threw rocks in the lake and little Heather slept in her carrier at our feet. Sue looked into my eyes and smiled. "Purple Mountain Majesty," she said, laying her head on my shoulder.

CHAPTER 2

GROWING UP

It is often difficult to pinpoint events that change and shape our lives. Often times, lives change gradually with the accumulation of experiences and factors over which we have little control. In some ways, that is true of Sue's and my life. But an indelible mark was left on our soul in 1965, a mark that would forever change the course of our lives and shape of our character. In this case, we can pinpoint exactly where and when that event took place; it happened when I unzipped our tent that first morning at Two Medicine and the two of us stepped outside. From that moment, we were no longer captives of our upbringing, no longer strangers in empty lands, no longer city people.

The images of Rising Wolf towering above us and reflective calm of Two Medicine waters would remain with us, never far beneath our consciousness. They influenced where we would live, the values we would teach our children and how we would spend much of our time and money. They would lead us to wonderful and sometimes terrifying experiences that very few people ever have. They would introduce us to life-long friendships and to challenging work that needed to be done to preserve places we love. Life for us would never be the same. We saw that then, but only, like St. Paul writes, "as through a glass darkly." We did not know how fundamentally our lives would be changed, nor could we guess that I would nearly lose mine several times along the way.

The following year, my fledgling career in the advertising business showed signs of promise. I was promoted from assistant account executive to account executive and my income rose modestly from the $4,800 annual salary at which I'd started. Consequently, with scrupulous frugality and creative budgeting, we were able to buy a car that would take us, our new tent and assorted camping gear back to the mountains; a brand new bottom-of-the line 1966 Ford station wagon.

Our first trip to Glacier Park had revealed that I was really a city boy. It taught me how ignorant I was about the business of camping and hiking in the wilderness. I had not been able to accurately gauge how long one mile is or the time it would take our family to hike it. I did not understand the importance of water or the potential for dehydration. I underestimated the effort it takes to climb one hundred vertical feet, much less one thousand. I didn't appreciate the real dangers to which a hiker can be exposed in venturing away from campgrounds and parking lots. That first trip taught me a lot. We'd be better prepared next time.

During the winter following our introduction to Glacier National Park, we read Ruhle's Guide to Glacier cover to cover, front to back. We selected sights we wanted to see and hikes we wanted to take, then laid out a schedule that would squeeze everything in. Hunkered down in our small Evanston apartment during that long Chicago winter, we counted the days until summer and our two weeks of freedom arrived. When they finally rolled around, we got ready to head for Glacier National Park for the second time.

With a budget not much greater than the previous year, we planned to camp out and avoid restaurants. Sue had the idea that we could save time and effort when we made camp in the evening if we pre-packaged the food we would need each day. She calculated what we would need and bought all the non-perishables in Evanston. Then she and Debbie and I sat on our living room floor dividing the food up into individual meals, labeling them "breakfast", "lunch" and "dinner". All Sue had to do at our campsite was select a bag that contained everything needed for the meal she was about to prepare. It proved to be a time and money saver. And it was fun. We could all, in our own way, imagine where we would be and what we would be doing with each plastic bag we filled. Sue's bright idea became a tradition that lasted many years.

Joe Hoskins, Sue's dad, was raised on a farm in western Illinois in the early years of the Twentieth Century. Living with hard work and few luxuries as a boy, it was difficult for him to understand why Sue and I would want to spend our vacations sleeping on the ground and cooking our meals in the open on a portable stove.

Growing up in a horse-and-wagon era, he just couldn't appreciate why anyone would want to walk when you could drive, no matter how good the scenery. He worried about bears and other unknown dangers Sue and I and his grandchildren might encounter "out in the woods," far from civilization. When we tried to explain our love for Glacier Park and hiking and camping, he didn't say much, but he didn't have to. To Joe, this was more than a bad idea, it was folly. Before we left, he asked us to check for general delivery mail at the post office in the towns of East Glacier and West Glacier and made us promise to write him. The prospect of being tethered to post offices and taking time from our precious vacation days in the Park to check for mail was irksome, but I readily agreed. It was something Sue wanted to do for him.

The images of Rising Wolf Mountain and Two Medicine Lodge Lake that we carried in our heads drew us back to where we'd encountered them. We needed to validate our memories by repeating the experience. Were Two Medicine and Glacier Park really as fantastic as we remembered? We needed to know. I was nervous. Attempts to repeat wonderful life-changing experiences often lead to disappointment. But not this time. Two Medicine, we found, was every bit as grand as we remembered; just as magnificent, just as awe inspiring, just as wonderful. How devastated we would have been had it been otherwise.

We pitched our tent beneath the ramparts of Rising Wolf and breathed in the mountain air, absorbing the essence of country we had come to love. After two days of reacquainting ourselves with Two Medicine and savoring the experience, our schedule called for us to head to Many Glacier in the northeast quadrant of the Park, an area rich in scenery that we had yet to see.

The morning Sue and I took down our tent and stowed our stuff in the station wagon, the weather had turned cloudy and blustery. Sue pulled the collar of her jacket up tight around her neck and looked skyward. The tops of Sinopah and Rising Wolf were gone, dissolved halfway up in dirty gray cotton. "I'm glad we're moving," she said with a shiver. "It's cold and it looks like rain."

We drove Highway 49 north to St. Mary as we'd done the previous year. When we reached the highpoint of the road, clouds scudded low over our car on their flight to the east. The landscape looked remarkably different this time; darker, lower, smaller. This was a surprise and somehow a little unsettling. We'd seen only blue skies and sunshine the previous year.

We continued north beyond St. Mary to Babb, Montana, a scruffy dab of habitation on the Blackfeet Indian Reservation. The paved road to Many Glacier turned off the highway at the Babb Bar, the biggest building in town, and proceeded west to the Park entrance. The road snaked along a river wild with surging whitewater racing down out of the mountains. We came to a sign that read "Rough Break" where the pavement ended and gravel began. Wind racing to keep up with the raging waters swept up great clouds of dust from the gravel, driving it hard against our windshield. Cottonwood trees by the sides of the road shook ferociously, bending in the direction the wind was headed. We passed a large lake whipped into a white froth by the gale, not guessing that the gray clouds overhead obscured one of the great vertical escarpments of the Park just to our right. I felt as though we were entering some wild netherworld, a landscape tortured by wind and water desperate to escape the mountain ramparts that lay ahead, eager to gain their rest on flat plains below.

We pulled into Swiftcurrent Campground and took our pick from a half-dozen open campsites. Just then rain began, large droplets but few, spaced widely enough that we could nearly dodge them. Heather, almost two and Debbie now seven, stayed in the car while Sue and I struggled to stake down the corners of our flapping tent before putting the metal poles together and raising it. The raindrops became smaller but closer together. The wind pulled at my hair and jacket as I went around the tent, checking its moorings. Sue put our sleeping bags, Coleman lantern and assorted gear inside before I brought the girls in. The rain had, by this time, increased to a wind-driven downpour. We decided to lie back on our sleeping bags, listen to the rain drumming on our tent, and watch its walls snap in and out in the howling wind. We were eager to see the peaks surrounding Swiftcurrent Valley and the

Many Glacier Hotel, but for the time being, we were prisoners in our tent.

As the afternoon wore on, Sue and I began to think about where and how we could cook dinner. The wind and rain would prevent me from lighting the stove outside even if I succeeded in lighting a match. We'd learned the previous year that food inside the tent was not advisable because of bears, so no cooking inside the tent. "Perhaps the storm will let up," Sue suggested. But the roar of the wind continued unabated through the afternoon. All that was left for us to do was take a nap.

When we woke, we decided that our only option was to cook dinner in the back of our station wagon. I unzipped the tent and ventured out into the blowing rain. I opened the tailgate of the car and, after a half dozen attempts, got both burners of the stove lit. Somehow Sue managed to fix a hot meal in that cramped space and we ate in the car.

The dull, gray afternoon light faded without a let-up in the storm. I lit the Coleman lantern as we huddled inside our tent. Sounds of wind and rain beating against canvas and rattling metal poles seemed louder and more worrisome in the descending darkness. Debbie was frightened and began to cry while Sue snuggled Heather down inside her bag to shield her from the awful noise. I attempted to comfort Debbie, but at the same time, wondered about the effect the storm might have on unseen mountains towering above us. Could the storm unleash torrents of water, drowning us in a flash flood? Could the howling wind tear chunks of rock off unseen cliffs? I didn't know. We'd never experienced weather like this, certainly not in a tent far from civilization.

Sounds of the raging storm combined with the snapping and rattling of the tent drained our energy. Sue and the kids became quiet. I turned off the Coleman lantern, immersing us in total darkness. I closed my eyes and, in time, was able to drift off to a troubled sleep.

Sometime in the middle of the night, a terrible shaking and shuddering jolted me awake. It was pitch black. My heart leapt into my throat. "What's happening?" Sue cried. Before I could answer, I felt the tent give way to the howling wind. Wet canvas tangled with collapsed aluminum tent poles crashed down upon us. Sue and the girls screamed. I searched frantically for the flashlight I kept next to my sleeping bag. The black chaos in which we were ensnared was disorienting. I could not remember where I'd put it. I thrashed around in the darkness, trying to extricate myself from my sleeping bag. The weight of flapping wet canvas pressing down upon us created the terrifying feeling that we were being buried alive. A light came on somewhere. "I found my flashlight," Sue cried. "Get us out of here!"

I was becoming panicky. We had to get out. I had to find my flashlight. Sue's light was trapped on the other side of the tangled mass that held us down and showed as just a dull green glow through the canvas. Without my flashlight, I would never be able to locate the door of the tent and find the zipper needed to free us. As my hands scrambled frantically in the darkness for my flashlight, I became furious with myself for being so frightened, so helpless.

Finally my fingers touched the round barrel they sought. I switched the flashlight on and crawled toward what I believed was the front of the tent. I played the light over the wet canvas covering my head and located the zipper. "I found the door!" I cried. "I'll get us out!" I ripped the zipper open and crawled through the flattened door of the tent out into shrieking wind and drenching rain. I bent down low and fought the wind to bring the tent opening in the direction of where Sue and the kids lay. Sue's head popped out, face and hair streaming water. "Thank God" she cried. "Get the kids into the car."

By the time everyone was inside the sanctuary of our station wagon, we were soaked to the skin. Sue handed Heather to me to hold. "It's OK," I said, attempting to calm our two terrified children, my own heart continuing to pound. "We're safe. Everything's OK."

Sue crawled over the seats into the back of the wagon to get dry clothes for the kids. "We'll be just fine here in the car," I said. "We'll stay here tonight. Nothing can hurt us." Torrents of rain blasted down on the car and periodic gusts shook it back and forth, but we would be OK. I had no idea in what condition our tent and all our gear might be, but it didn't matter. We were safe.

Sue and I slept little that night and when dull gray-green light hinted the arrival of morning, we were wide awake, anxious to see what had happened to our things. The wind had dropped but a light rain continued. From the car, we could see the forlorn site where the tent had stood. Its green canvas lay twisted like bedclothes after a restless night, collapsed tent poles on top. The scene reminded me of a giant green spider that someone had stepped on.

"Stay here," I said. "I'll get our stuff out of the tent." When I lifted the canvas and probed inside the door, my fears were confirmed. Our sleeping bags were wet. How in the world could we dry them, I wondered? The Coleman lantern and other gear was wet, too, but seemed OK. I lifted my soggy sleeping bag up to show Sue who watched from the car. We could only hope the rain would end soon so we could dry the bags in the sun. Otherwise we'd spend another night in the Ford. Our vacation budget could not accommodate a night in a motel.

To my immense relief, within a half hour, the rain stopped and patches of blue sky appeared overhead. Sue got the kids out of the car and sat them at a picnic table to get them fed.

I fished the bags and the rest of our gear out of the tent, then looked to the tent poles. Luckily they hadn't been damaged and went back together as before. With Sue's help, I put the heavy wet canvas back on the poles and opened the windows to encourage the tent to dry. The sleeping bags were a problem. All we could do, I figured, was open them and lay them out to the sun and hope they'd dry by nightfall.

We wondered what the storm might have done to other campsites and took a walk around the campground. We quickly discovered that ours was not a unique experience. Most other tents in the area had been blown down too. Like us, other campers were drying sleeping bags and raising collapsed tents. We chatted with our part-time neighbors about the incredible night we'd all experienced. Almost everyone was, like us, shocked at the storm's power. But one man, a local from a town west of the Park, was not. "The winds here on the east side are like that," he said. "It can blow like hell any time. Tents are blown down most every year. That's the risk you take when you camp in Many Glacier – or Two Medicine, for that matter."

Here was another lesson. I had not previously considered the impact weather could have on us. The past night showed how unpredictable mountain weather could be, how quickly it might change and what incredible power it could pack. This was hard for someone raised in flatland Midwestern towns and cities to fully grasp. It was difficult to believe that what we'd just experienced could happen any time. As a result, the lesson was acknowledged but not fully learned, the consequences of which – one day in the future – would nearly cost me my life.

The sun showed itself most of the day, enough to dry the tent and nearly dry our sleeping bags. We put them back inside before nightfall and reconciled ourselves to sleeping in bags that felt a little clammy.

During the next several days, the weather remained decidedly uncertain, sun and rain changing places frequently. We visited the thousand-room Many Glacier Hotel and were thrilled by its soaring lobby and amazing location only a few feet from the shore of beautiful Swiftcurrent Lake. Towering Grinnell Point on the other side reminded us of Sinopah Mountain at Two Medicine. Poised above the lake, it thrust up toward the hotel like a three thousand foot high arrow.

After poking around Swiftcurrent Lake and dodging rain showers, we decided that, with the weather being what it was, we would spend a few of our precious vacation dollars on the price of a boat ride. Actually, it was two boat rides. Chief Two Guns, an old wooden tour boat, took us from the hotel to the head of Swiftcurent Lake, at which point we got off and hiked 400 yards to a second lake. There we boarded a second boat, Morning Eagle, which motored smoothly to the head of Josephine Lake. Despite a light drizzle, we got off and hiked one mile to the foot of spectacular Grinnell Lake. Grinnell and Salamander Glaciers high above fed their melt waters into a thousand-foot-high waterfall at the far end of the lake. Surrounded on three sides by towering peaks, Grinnell Lake was, like much of Swiftcurrent Valley, awe inspiring.

Continuing rain kept us from our main goals of hiking to Iceberg Lake and Red Rock Canyon. Our short vacation was vanishing with the passage of each wet day. Much as we loved Many Glacier and longed to explore its wonders, we decided to head back west, across Logan Pass, to camp again at Sprague Creek. The weather on the west side of the Park might be better.

Dark clouds hung low as our Ford began its climb toward Logan Pass. Half way up we entered fog that dropped visibility to a few yards. Not a good sign. Sue, who was nervous about going over the Pass in the best of circumstances, was frightened. Indeed, I too, was nervous. I stared unblinking into the milky mist, keeping my eyes glued to the edges of the pavement lest we drive off into nothingness. We crept over the Pass and down the other side, emerging from the fog only when the road leveled out near the valley floor.

To our disappointment, it was raining hard when we arrived at Sprague Creek Campground and we decided to try waiting it out in the car. "I wonder how much it costs to rent one of those cabins we passed near Lake MacDonald Lodge," Sue said. "As long as it's raining, why don't we go back and find out?"

I knew we didn't have money to rent a cabin but, to make Sue happy, I figured it would do no harm to find out. We located the sign advertising cabins on the lake a quarter mile east of the Lodge and turned into a narrow lane leading down from the road through dense forest to a string of small brown wooden cabins facing the lake. Sue and I ducked our heads in the rain and dashed inside a cabin with an "Office" sign on the door. An older man with a friendly face looked up at us from a rocking chair. "How much to rent a cabin?" I asked.

"Ten dollars a night," he replied. "We have a couple cabins available. Looks like it's going to be nasty out there. Camping? He asked. "

I looked to Sue and hesitated, then turned back to the owner. "Yes," I said. "Thanks, we'll think about it."

The rain continued and, as nightfall approached, we wound up putting our tent up in the rain. The night was cold and everything inside the tent was damp. We bundled up the kids and ourselves in extra clothes before crawling into our sleeping bags. Nobody slept well that night as the cold rain continued to drum down.

When we awoke the next morning, our breath condensed in wisps of frigid steam. Debbie and Heather were miserable. We lay for a time in our sleeping bags, cold, damp and dispirited. "How long can this rain go on?" Sue groaned. I wished I knew. How long could we hold out in a wet tent, damp sleeping bags and clammy clothes, I wondered?

After an unhappy breakfast of cold cereal eaten in the car, Sue said, "Why don't we go into West Glacier and check to see if there's a letter from Dad?" I'd detoured to the post office in East Glacier the day before to let Sue check for mail, but general delivery had nothing for us. It annoyed me. But this day we had no plans. For sure there would be no hiking. Driving the eight miles along Lake MacDonald to West Glacier would be a good diversion. "Sure," I replied, "we have nothing better to do."

Despite the soaking rain, Sue was grinning when she emerged from the post office. She held up an envelope and waved it. "A letter from Dad," she announced when she got back into the car. She opened the envelope and removed a folded sheet of paper.

When she unfolded the letter, something fell out. I could see it was money. Sue gasped. "My gosh!" she exclaimed. "It's ten dollars! Dad sent us ten dollars!" She handed the ten-spot to me as though to prove that the unlikely event was really true. I was as surprised as she was. A child of the great depression, Joe was not one to throw money around. Given his frugality combined with doubts about the wisdom of our escapades in the woods, neither of us ever imagined that he would send money.

"That's why he wanted us to check for mail," Sue said.

I felt like a jerk for resenting our detours to the post office. She read the letter, then handed it to me. Joe ended his chatty epistle by saying, "I'm enclosing ten dollars. I figured you could use it." He could never know what an understatement that was!

"We can rent one of those cabins!" Sue exclaimed. "We can get out of the rain!"

I grinned. "Yeah, thanks to your Dad. Let's splurge. Let's get some groceries. You can make a special dinner."

"Could we?" Sue asked.

"Sure," I replied, "we'll celebrate!"

We went to the West Glacier Market nearby and Sue selected a canned ham, small bag of potatoes, carrots and some fresh fruit. We would have a feast! Our spirits were dampened no more. Even little Heather giggled. She knew something good had just happened.

We hoped that we would be able to dry our sleeping bags in the cabin and returned to Sprague Creek to retrieve them. When we arrived, the campsite looked truly forlorn. Cloud-filtered light painted a monochrome scene; cold, dim, cheerless. Pine branches gathered the rain into a dispiriting drip, drip, drip; puddles dotted the saturated ground, our tent sagged. Neither of us said anything while we gathered our wet things and put them in the car but I knew Sue was as grateful as I that we would not have to put our kids back in that tent and spend another night in the rain.

The grandest hotel on earth could not have felt more wonderful to us than the plain, old one-room cabin we rented that night. The door to the cabin opened into a kitchen just large enough to accommodate a sink, propane cooktop, refrigerator, wooden table and four chairs. A tiny bathroom with a metal shower stall and flush toilet – the first indoor bathroom we'd had since leaving home -was in the rear. Standing grandly in the center of the room was a propane heater the size of a mailbox, its black chimney pipe angling up into the open ceiling. Double beds flanked the heater with just enough room to get by. And lights – electric lights! All we had to do to light up the place was flip a switch by the door. What luxury!

I immediately went to the heater to get it going and warm the place up. The owner of the cabins had given me instructions on which knob to turn and where to put the match to get it going. Once lit, I turned the heat up all the way. We were all still wet and shivering. We put the kids on the bed and returned to the car for our groceries, sleeping bags and the things we'd need for the night.

In minutes the old heater was kicking out blessed warmth. Nothing ever felt so good as that hot, dry heater air! Had anyone else come into the cabin that night, I'm sure they would have thought it way too hot, but not us. Our bones were soaking up the heat, our clothes and bodies drying out.

Sue stirred around getting dinner. Within a few minutes she came to the bed where I was getting Heather out of her damp clothes. She had a frown on her face. "There's no oven," she said. "There's no way to heat the ham."

I thought for a moment. "Put it on the heater," I said. "It's hot enough to fry an egg." While I got the girls and myself showered and into dry pajamas, Sue heated our canned ham on the heater stove, boiled potatoes and carrots on the cooktop and presented us with a feast we would never forget.

I washed the dishes while Sue showered and changed. We rigged clotheslines across the cabin from one wall to the other and hung our wet sleeping bags on them. Thanks to that powerful heater, we knew they'd dry by morning. We crawled into bed and snuggled down under warm, dry covers, listening to the rain on the roof until we fell asleep. Never had we been more snugly happy than we were that night in our little old wooden cabin on the shore of Lake McDonald. It was a place and night we would always treasure in our hearts.

When we woke the next morning, we could scarcely believe what we saw. Sunshine! Bright, warm, clean sunshine streamed through the cabin windows in a vivid burst of energy. I jumped out of bed and went to a window. Blue sky above still, reflective waters of Lake McDonald signaled a dramatic change in the weather. Sue and Debbie quickly joined me at the window. "Wow!" Sue exclaimed, "I can't believe this. It was raining cats and dogs in the night."

"Yeah", I replied, "it's hard to believe that the weather can change so quickly. I think this just might have saved our vacation." Still in our night clothes, we went outside and walked to the shore of the lake, just a stone's throw from the cabin. I filled my lungs with the clean morning air. The smell of still-damp pines was delicious. We stood by the lake, gawking at the mountains like we'd never seen them before. The sight of Stanton Mountain soaring into the sparkling blue sky thrilled me and I felt like jumping up and down. Instead, I put my arm around Sue and we stood for a long while, soaking up the majesty of the place. The feeling of awe and excitement I'd experienced when I first stepped out of the tent in the shadow of Rising Wolf the previous year had returned. I realized now that clouds and rain would come and go, but they could never diminish my love for this magnificent country. The unchanging mountains of Glacier Park would always call me back.

****

Every visit to Glacier National Park brought new adventures, new learning and, occasionally, unexpected danger. Each winter we would read our guidebooks, discuss the trails, weigh the plusses and minuses and decide which one's we'd hike on our way- too-short vacations. Though we hiked the lowland trails through forests and along scenic whitewater creeks and waterfalls – like the trail to Avalanche Lake, for example – we preferred the high country, trails that climb above tree line where the views open up and you can see forever. Though the lowland trails are easier, the high-country is more exciting and rewarding.

Piegan Pass, accessible from Going to the Sun Road a few miles east of Logan Pass is one of those trails. On our second trip, we'd stopped at Siyeh Bend below the pass and stretched our necks, gawking at the clearly visible thin brown line that delineates the trail to Piegan Pass. The visible part of the trail climbs from tree line, traversing a steep, layered stone flank of Siyeh Mountain, to the saddle high above the road. Just looking at it gave us a thrill and before heading back to Glacier in 1968, it was on our "to do" list.

Heather, just 3, was too young to hike very far and nearly too heavy to carry. But it was either suck it up and carry her in the backpack carrier or forego hiking. I sucked it up.

As we'd learned, it was important to begin a long, strenuous hike into the high country early in the morning, for by mid-morning the sun could get hot. We got up at first light and arrived at Siyeh Bend by eight.

The trail ascends steeply from Siyeh Creek at the road, switchbacking up through a dense sub-alpine fir forest. As we climbed higher, the trees grew shorter and farther apart until finally we broke out onto the steep sedimentary stone layers of Siyeh Mountain. The slope across which the trail traverses appears nearly vertical, though in reality it's probably not more than 50 degrees. Still, it's plenty steep enough to send the unwary hiker all the way to the bottom should he set a foot wrong. From the point where the trail breaks out of the trees, the view is spectacular. The road lay nearly a thousand feet below and beyond that, the mountain falls away another two thousand feet to the valley through which Reynolds Creek flows. Sue was nervous. She felt exposed and vulnerable at this tremendous height, much like she did on the Garden Wall ledge. Still, trooper that she is, she hiked behind Debbie and me without a word of complaint.

About halfway across the massive face we were traversing the trail disappeared beneath a snowfield. The snowfield was about a hundred yards wide and fell five hundred feet or so to a large boulder field. Faint echoes of footprints made by hikers on previous days sketched the route across the snowfield to the re-emerging trail on the other side.

I stopped to consider the situation. Crossing it clearly posed a risk. The snowfield sloped as steeply as the rocky face across which the trail traversed. The snow was obviously slippery and I would have to carve foot-holds for each step. One slip would, in all likelihood, send the hiker on a fatal slide to the rocks below. I looked up the trail, beyond the snowfield. I reckoned it was less than a mile to the pass. Go ahead, or turn back? That was the question. "What do you think?" Sue asked.

I swung the carrier with Heather in it off my back and pulled her out. Then I turned back to the snowfield. I put a foot on the snow and kicked in a foot-hold, then another and another, working my way a few feet out onto the slippery snowfield. There was no doubt I needed to be very careful as I put one foot ahead of the other, but once the foot-holds were kicked in, it seemed manageable. If Sue and Debbie put their feet squarely in the foot-holds, I thought, they'll be OK. I looked back at Sue. "I think we can make it," I replied. "Just make sure you put your feet squarely into the footsteps I'll carve in."

Sue was frightened. "It's too dangerous," she said. "I think we should go back."

I turned back toward Sue and the girls, careful to keep my balance and my feet in the foot-holds, and retreated to the hard surface of the trail. With the footholds already kicked in, I found that navigating the snowfield didn't feel all that dangerous. "You won't have a problem if you just watch where you step," I said. "Plant your feet firmly in the footholds and everybody will be OK."

"I'm afraid," Sue said.

"I can tie a rope on you like I did at the Garden Wall," I replied. "I don't think you'll have a problem but if you slip, I can catch you."

"What about Debbie?" Sue asked.

"I can do it, Mommy," Debbie replied. "Don't worry. It will be fun."

Sue looked up at me. "OK," She said, "if you're sure we'll be safe, but I would like the rope."

I retrieved our rope from the pack Sue was carrying, put Heather back in the carrier and we started out across the snowfield. The sun on the white snow caused me to squint. The going was slow. I'd kick a foot-hold into the snow, step in it, kick the next one and so on, everyone following in my footsteps a few yards behind. "Don't look down," I advised, though I knew that advice was unnecessary.

About half way across, I heard Sue scream and felt the rope go taut. I was startled and it took all my strength and concentration to avoid being pulled off my feet and down the snowfield. I dug the heels of my boots in toward the up-slope as Sue hung on the rope a dozen feet below me. Terrified, I leaned back to brace myself, pressing Heather in the carrier on my back against the snow. She screamed. Debbie, behind me, was nearly hysterical.

"I've got you!" I exclaimed, holding onto the rope for dear life.

Sue's eyes were wide with fear as she looked up. "Don't let me fall!" she cried.

"Stay calm," I shouted, attempting to do the same. "You'll be OK. Try to dig your toes into the snow and I'll pull." Sue did the best she could in the ice encrusted snow that had been thawed and frozen many times. "Take it slow," I said. "We'll be OK."

She and I worked together to stabilize her position. I looked back at Debbie. "Stay still, don't move," I said. "Mommy will be OK. I've got her."

I pulled on the rope and Sue made little toe-holds below me, working her way back up foot by foot. It was slow going. When she reached us, she was shaking like a leaf, but so was I. We wrapped our arms around one another, wordlessly thankful for her safety. "I'll be OK now," she said, her voice shaky. She wiped tears from her eyes and a wisp of hair from her brow. She looked ahead, then back. "Let's go on. It's farther to go back than it is to go ahead and I don't want to try to turn around on this snow."

My legs were still a little rubbery when we reached dry ground on the far side of the snowfield. "Do you think you can make it back OK?" I asked.

"I'm not going back over that snowfield without getting to the top of the pass," Sue said. "That's what we came for. Lets go."

When we reached the saddle of Piegan Pass, the view was breathtaking. The naked, rocky summits of Piegan, Siyeh, Going-to-the-Sun and Reynolds Mountains stood close above us, seemingly so near that we could reach out and touch them. We experienced the feeling we'd sought, the feeling of freedom, exhilaration, of being at the top of a spectacularly grand world. We agreed that, since everyone was safe, our moment of terror was worth it.

Despite our close call, Piegan Pass would always hold a special place in Sue's heart. If she could hike just one trail in the Park, it would be to Piegan Pass.

****

I was given the marvelous opportunity by the Chicago ad agency that employed me to work on their largest account, the Procter & Gamble Company of Cincinnati, Ohio. P&G was respected as the best practitioner of packaged goods marketing in the world. It employed few agencies for its many brands of consumer products and demanded the best from their best people. Procter was smart, professional, demanding and fair. What a great learning environment for a young man not long out of journalism and business schools.

I liked Procter and they seemed to like me. After having been promoted on Mr. Clean, I was given additional P&G assignments including a new product which we ultimately named Pringle's. Marketers spend a lot of advertising money on new products, so this was a plum assignment. Two years of market testing convinced P&G to go national with Pringle's and my ad agency to promote me to account supervisor.

As new assignments and promotions came along, my income grew. Two years after we were married, Sue and I bought a modest house in a nice Chicago suburb with a down-payment loan of $2,500 from Sue's dad. Two years later, Sue bore us our third child, a son we named Patrick, after my grandfather.

Sue and I had always enjoyed looking at real estate and one day we discovered, quite by accident, the house of our dreams. It was a brick Tudor with mullioned windows set on several acres in a woodsy, upscale suburb. From time to time we would drive past the house just to admire it. "One day," we dreamed, "wouldn't it be great to have a place like that?"

When Patrick was two, we were shocked to see an ad for that very house in the real estate section of the Chicago Tribune. We immediately contacted the agent and went to look at it. The old, somewhat down-in-the-heels English Tudor sat on 3 acres of lawn, surrounded on three sides by a forest preserve. It wasn't Glacier

Park, but it was woods and deer and space and peace, and the house simply oozed charm. Though we knew we really couldn't afford it, we simply couldn't let that house go without at least trying to buy it. We figured and re-figured our expenses, made an offer and somehow managed to swing the deal. We were poor once more, but living in the house of our dreams, surrounded by woods and critters and echoes of that which we cherished in Montana. I didn't mind carrying a brown bag of peanut butter and jelly sandwiches to my office in the Loop each day, not one bit.

We returned to Glacier Park often over the next fifteen years, spending many – but not all – of our summer vacations exploring it. For certain, we wished to use our vacation time to immerse ourselves as much as possible in nature's wonders, wide-open spaces, outdoor adventure. But our "feet on the ground" experience was limited to Glacier National Park. What about other national parks, we wondered? Might not some others be even more grand?

There was only one way to find out. We decided that we would use our precious few summer vacation weeks in coming years to explore other places. But the prospect of giving up Glacier completely was too painful for either of us to contemplate. We agreed that we would spend every second summer vacation in Glacier Park, using in-between years to visit other national parks. And that is what we did; during the next 15 years, we took ourselves and our growing family to Rocky Mountain, North Cascades, Olympic, Grand Teton and Yosemite National Parks as well as to Yellowstone and the Grand Canyon. We pitched our tent, saw the sights and hiked the trails in each one. We were glad we did, for each, in its own way, is magnificent. But we kept coming back to Glacier. Nothing else quite matched up.

Heather was six years old when we took Patrick – a year-and-a-half – to Glacier for the first time. If we wanted to do any hiking, Heather would have to walk as Debbie had done that first year. Patrick would be on my back this time. We figured if Debbie could make it to Granite Park at age 6, so could Heather.

This time we were better prepared. We started early in the day, put proper hiking boots on us all, carried plenty of water and arranged to spend the night as guests at the Chalet. Heather skipped along the Garden Wall as fast as a veteran hiker and, when we arrived, she seemed less fatigued than I, who had shouldered our chubby son the 7.8 miles. When we entered the Chalet dining room, we found much to our amazement, Heather's blue jumpers displayed in the glass case by the kitchen. We'd left them on the clothesline that first trip. A small neatly lettered sign read, "Worn by the youngest person ever to reach Granite Park Chalet." We were pleased and honored and hoped to thank Kay Luding but she was not there. She'd moved over to supervise Sperry Chalet, the other remaining back-country facility built by the Great Northern.

Kay's move caused Sue and me to focus on Sperry, a potential hiking destination we had talked about back home. We'd read about it in our guidebooks and admired photos of the gorgeous old stone structure more than once. Seeing it and, at the same time, reacquainting ourselves with Kay proved a powerful temptation. But getting there, we knew, would not be easy, maybe even not possible. Back at our campground, we poured over the description of the trail up Snyder Creek to the Chalet and discussed whether or not we could make it. It was one hell of a climb. The guidebook showed the trail to the Chalet was nearly six miles long and climbed 3,650 vertical feet from Lake McDonald. We'd now had enough experience hiking Glacier's easier trails to know how much effort was involved in climbing one thousand feet. This would be a grueling experience. Could Sue, with her weakened legs and growing arthritis, make it? What about 12 year old Debbie and 6 year old Heather? And I had myself to consider. Could I climb that long, steep trail with 30 pounds of Patrick on my back?

We reasoned that we were now experienced hikers with numerous day-hikes in all parts of the Park under our belt. We knew what we needed to carry with us and, we reasoned, if we took all day to get there, that was OK. If we reached a point where the climb was just too tough, we could always turn around and come down. The temptation was just too strong to resist.

We made arrangements to stay the night at Sperry and on a bright early morning, the five of us headed for the trailhead across the road from Lake McDonald Lodge. A broad, smooth trail immediately entered a dense stand of red cedars, part of the temperate rain forest that runs along the south side of Lake McDonald. Within a few hundred yards, the trail turned left, narrowed and we began to climb. Although the morning air was cool, within five minutes we stopped to remove a layer of clothing.

Climbing steeply, the trail continued straight until it switchbacked to the right, sending us back on a long traverse the direction we'd come. As we climbed higher, red cedar gave way to lodgepole pine, their naked trunks supporting a thick green canopy fifty feet above our heads. Another half hour of strenuous effort brought us to a steep cutbank that overlooked Snyder Creek several hundred feet below. There the trail switchbacked left again. Up, up we toiled, one hour, then two. The grade was unrelenting. Everyone was suffering, especially Debbie who tended to be a reluctant hiker anyway. Unlike Heather, Patrick did not enjoy being in the carrier on my back. He became fussy and irritable. We stopped often to rest and rehydrate. As we climbed higher, the forest canopy overhead thinned and the sun began to reach us. Already sweating from the exertion of our climb, the merciless sun began to sap our energy and our appreciation of the shady forest took on a whole new dimension. We came to another switchback near a stream and stopped in a spot of shade to rest and have lunch. It was past noon. I swung the carrier off my back and removed Patrick while Sue took sandwiches out of her pack. "How much farther?" she asked. "I'm not sure how much longer the kids can go."

I wiped sweat from my eyes and consulted our topographical map. It looked to me like we'd come little more than halfway. "We still have a ways to go," I said, trying to balance my desire to continue with the hard truth of the matter. "Let's rest here for a while and see how we all feel after lunch. I'd hate to have come all this way for nothing."

Sue shot me a look that suggested displeasure, but said nothing. Instead, she dipped a handkerchief in the rushing stream and wiped the kids' faces with cool water. "That's a good idea," she said, more to the kids than to me. "We'll rest here and have lunch. I'm sure everyone will feel better."

Forty five minutes later, Sue put on her pack and I swung Patrick onto my back. He was not a happy camper and bawled his displeasure at being trapped again in the carrier. We headed up. The steep grade continued as before. A half hour later, the trees disappeared entirely and our trail entered tall, ugly weeds. Patrick bawled, Debbie cried and the sun beat down. The climb seemed endless. But Heather never complained, she just kept putting one foot ahead of the other. "You're doing great," Sue said. "Don't your legs get tired, Sweetheart?"

"Sometimes," Heather replied, "but when my legs get tired, I just crank up my tired legs and crank down new legs." I stopped and looked back at Heather in amazement.

"What a great idea!" Sue exclaimed. "How did you ever think of that?" Heather just grinned.

"I don't know how she thought of it," I said, "but I wish I had." I was about ready to call a halt and admit defeat when we rounded a bend in the trail and the view opened up. Ahead, sheer walls of naked stone rose several thousand feet above us. A patchwork of stone ledges cris-crossed a ridge at the foot of the walls, stairstepping down to a massive stone bench at the edge of a cliff 500 or more feet high. "Look!" Sue cried. She shaded her eyes with one hand and pointed up to the ledge with the other. "Could that be the Chalet?" I looked, searching the escarpment ahead with my eyes, but could spot nothing that resembled a building. "I don't think so," I replied. "I don't see anything."

Sue came up next to me and pointed with her finger to the dark ledge. My eyes followed her finger. Suddenly I saw it! It was difficult to separate the dark stones of the Chalet from the ledge it sat upon. "I see it!" I exclaimed. "You're right, that's got to be the Chalet! "Does that mean we're almost there?" Debbie asked, trying to see what we saw. Sue bent down and helped her identify our destination. "That's where we're going, Sweetheart," she said. "We'll get something good to drink and spend the night. It'll be fun, you'll see." Debbie didn't reply. She could see how high the Chalet was above us and how far we would have to go to get there.

Still, being able to see our destination provided the encouragement we all needed to continue toiling up the steep, hot grade. At least we had proof that the trail was not endless

Three quarters of an hour later, the trail led us, unexpectedly, to an oasis of sorts. A broad grassy meadow lay at the feet of the towering stone ramparts we'd been working toward. A stream fed by a waterfall cascading down the mountain wall flowed through the center of the meadow. Pines scattered here and there provided wonderful shade and at least the illusion of coolness. Gratefully, we took off our packs in a shady spot and eased our tired bodies down onto the grass. The relief we felt after our toilsome climb was nothing short of sublime. Not far off, a half-dozen saddle horses tied to a lodgepole hitch rail watched us suspiciously through round white eyes. These, obviously, were the critters that had dropped the smelly strings of 'road apples' we'd stepped over on the way up.

The Chalet, we sensed, could not be far off and we were anxious to get there. After a short rest, we crossed a little bridge over the stream and resumed our trek. We immediately came to a trail junction marked "Sperry Glacier." That trail led through the meadow toward a sheer mountain wall. Our trail swung right and, to our dismay, began to climb even more steeply than before. Thankfully, this climb was in the shade and better, didn't last long. Within a hundred yards, we crested a ridge and there, fifty feet in front of us, stood an old stone building. I suspect Sue and the girls felt something similar to the emotions I experienced; a mixture of blessed relief from our exertion, excitement at what we were about to experience, pride at having gotten there and awe at the incredible setting in which we found ourselves. But most immediately, my thoughts turned to getting weight off my back and a cool drink in my hand.

We crossed a broad, flat area that lead to a small door in the low stone building. Frankly, it didn't look at all like the pictures we'd seen. I didn't care. We had arrived and we all needed a rest. When I opened the door and we went inside, Kay Luding was waiting for us behind a glass display case similar to the one at Granite Park that held Heather's jumper.

"You people keep popping up in the least likely places," she said. She immediately came out from around the counter and gave Sue a hug. "When I saw reservations come in for the Sullivans, I knew it had to be you."

Patrick was the only one of us who was not happy to be there and to see Kay. He'd been fussy and crying off and on all day. Now, as I swung his carrier off my back, he set up a regular howl.

Kay immediately reached down and took him out of the carrier. "What's this," she asked, a pucker on her lips? She lifted Patrick up and cradled him in her arms. "It looks like you've got the grumpies," she said, a twinkle in her eye. "What's your name?" Patrick's reply was a continued howl.

"This is Patrick," Sue said. "He's got the terrible two's, I'm afraid."

"No, he doesn't have the terrible twos," Kay countered. She smiled at Patrick. "Patrick just has the grumpies. Do you know what we do with people who have the grumpies? We shake the grumpies out!" Kay began to carry him around the large room we were in and jiggle Patrick up and down in her arms. To our surprise, he stopped crying. He looked up into Kay's face with a startled expression. Then he began to giggle. Kay continued carrying him around the room, jiggling him up and down in her arms. "See?" she said, "we just have to shake the grumpies out and everybody will be just fine."

Kay carried Patrick around and bounced him up and down while the four of us collapsed into chairs. One of the girls we'd seen going to and from the back room brought out lemonade and sandwiches.

When we'd finished our scrumptious lunch, Kay said, "I'll show you your room. I bet someone would like to lay down and take a rest. It's in the Chalet next door."

"I thought this was the Chalet," I replied.

Kay smiled down at Patrick and jiggled him. "This is the kitchen and dining room. We'll be serving dinner between six and seven, so don't be late. The Chalet you see in all the pictures is next door. That's where the guest rooms are.

We followed Kay and Patrick out a door at the south end of the dining room and up a stone path to the magnificent two storied stone Chalet. The old Great Northern structure looked as though it came right out of a Swiss tourist ad. Its roof was steeply pitched to shed the loads of snow winter dumped on the high country. Two large gables with log-work balconies looked out from the second floor. A long, narrow porch with log-work railings led across the front of the building, from end to end, the entrance squarely in the center. It was just as beautiful as the pictures we'd seen. Like the dining room, it faced out over the high cliff we'd spotted from the trail. Far below lay the valley up which we'd hiked and in the distance, our starting point; the azure waters of Lake McDonald. To the south and east, the uppermost reaches of Lincoln Peak, and Gunsight and Edwards Mountains crowded close behind the Chalet. Stands of sub-alpine fir loosely blanketed the ledge on which it sits, lending a fairy-tale atmosphere to the scene.

"What's that?" Heather cried, pointing to a scrub fir enshrouded in a white, woolly substance. The white stuff was stuck to bushes all around the Chalet. From a distance, it resembled snow.

"Oh, that," Kay chuckled. She took Heather's hand and went to the tree. She reached out and pulled off a handful of the white stuff. "That's goat hair," she replied. She handed it to Heather. "The mountain goats are getting rid of their winter coats by rubbing up against the trees. Go ahead," Kay said, "pull some off." Thoroughly delighted, Heather and Debbie ran from bush to bush collecting mountain goat hair. They remembered the fun they pulling goat hair off the trees for many years

The rooms inside the Chalet were sparse; rough wooden floor, thin walls, iron beds, and a stand with a porcelain wash basin right out of the 19th Century. That was it. We all chose a bed and flopped down onto squeaky-springed beds with very firm – if not downright hard - mattresses. Though the sun was hot, the thick stone walls of the Chalet kept it cool inside. Heaven! "Why don't you all take a rest," I said, getting back onto my feet.

"What are you doing?" Sue asked. "Aren't you going to take a rest with us?"

"I thought I'd climb up to Sperry Glacier," I replied, attempting to sound casual. I knew Sue wouldn't approve. "I really want to see it."

"You've got to be kidding!" she exclaimed. "After climbing all the way up here? How far is it? It's still quite a climb, isn't it?"

"Yeah," I replied, "the guidebook says it's 1,600 vertical feet and about four miles."

"That's another eight miles round trip! I don't think you should try it. You just carried Patrick all the way up here. That's too much for one day. Besides, you'd need to be back by six for dinner. I wish you'd stay with us and rest."

On the strenuous climb up to the Chalet from Lake McDonald, my back and legs had gotten used to the 30 pound burden on my back. Without the load of Patrick, I felt wonderfully rejuvenated and alive, almost like I had wings on my feet. I was virtually bursting with enthusiasm and energy and couldn't possibly have slept. I itched to be on the trail to the glacier. "Don't worry," I replied,

"I'll be back for dinner. Kay said they serve until seven." I kissed Sue and rushed out.

I retraced the path down the short, steep grade that led to the meadow. There I picked up the Sperry Glacier spur trail that led toward towering cliffs nearby. It began to climb almost immediately. Soon I was atop a long, broad stone ledge that, to my surprise and delight, held a beautiful pool. I stopped to admire the place, as charmingly wonderful as any I'd seen. The flat stone surrounding the pool led to the opposite end of the ledge where the trail headed up again to another ledge. It, too, held a pool of crystal clear, mirror-still water. Tiny white and blue and green alpine wildflowers sprouted among green moss that edged the pool. I climbed from ledge to ledge, traversing each one, each one containing a pool seemingly more beautiful than the last. Up, up I climbed, enchanted by the amazing stone ledges. With each higher ledge, the view down the valley grew more magnificent. Exultation!

Looking up ahead, I could see a massive vertical wall towering above the ledges. As I climbed toward it, I wondered where the trail led and how I might be able to reach the glacier above. After a time, I came to the foot of the wall. There, the trail led to a steep stone staircase carved directly into the face of the massive escarpment. It was amazing! Narrow steps separated vertical walls of stone on each side of the staircase, giving the impression that they led straight into the heart of the mountain. I looked up, awed by the soaring walls crowding my shoulders, sky and clouds visible through the opening far above. I grasped a metal cable hand-hold affixed to the wall and started up.

Cold wind greeted me at the top. When I left Sperry Chalet and began my climb, the jeans and T-shirt I'd worn up from Lake McDonald were perfect for the warm breeze. But now I shivered. As I looked about, I was surprised. Dark clouds that I hadn't noticed while traversing the ledges, gave the landscape that stretched out before me a dark, monochromatic, almost foreboding appearance. Sperry Glacier was nowhere in sight.

I realized I was now standing atop Comeau Pass, about which I'd read in the guidebook. A plateau composed of a jumble of garbage can-sized rocks of every shape stretched into the distance as far as the eye could see. There was no discernable path to the glacier through the rock jumble and an instant of fear flickered within me. I wouldn't want to get lost in a place like this. It took me a moment to realize that the way ahead was marked by a series of stone cairns spaced a hundred yards or so apart that stretched out beyond my sight. Obviously these six-foot high pyramid-shaped piles of stone were put there to lead hikers to the glacier. I wondered how far it was. I looked at my watch. The climb to the Pass had taken longer than expected and I thought about turning back. Instead, I hurried toward the first cairn.

Clouds raced above me, so low I felt as though I could reach out and touch them. Cold wind tore at my hair. But nothing moved. There wasn't a sign of a tree or blade of grass or any living thing in this dull, gray, barren landscape. Sea of stone blocks stretched out in every direction. To the south, the lifeless jumble led to naked flanks of the upper-most reaches of Gunsight Mountain. To the north, the crazy-quilt plateau disappeared into nothingness, an abyss, I sensed, that fell to some unseen destination far below. Crossing that rock-strewn landscape without another human being in sight, I felt more alone than anytime in my life. I felt like walking on the surface of the moon.

After half an hour of picking my way from rock to rock, I came to a rise which provided my first glimpse of the dull, dirty gray-green sheet of ice I'd sought; Sperry Glacier. I'd never seen a glacier up close and was surprised that this one didn't look at all like postcard pictures of Alaskan glaciers. From this distance, Sperry appeared flat and smooth, almost as though it was pressed into the crags and crevices of Gunsight Mountain against which it lay. I moved closer, to the very edge of the ice. There I could see striations or crevices in the glacier. Beneath the dirty surface, the ice took on an ethereal bluish tint. It was a kind of beauty I'd never imagined.

I checked my watch. It told me that I needed to hurry back. Sue would worry if I didn't arrive at the Chalet by dinner time.

Conscious that this was an unforgettable memory, one that would remain with me always, I was reluctant to turn away. Sperry, I concluded, was magnificent, but not in the way of picture book glaciers; its magnificence seemed to me to be its isolation, its inaccessibility, its loneliness, its silence. I thought back to the hardy explorers who first discovered it in the late 19th Century and wondered how they had found it and what motivated them to reach it. As I made my way back to Comeau Pass and the ledges below, I felt a kind of distant kinship with these hardy adventurers.

My watch read a quarter past seven when I burst into the dining room, breathless from my race down the ledges. "Well, it's about time you got back!" Kay exclaimed. She was walking back and forth with Patrick in her arms, jiggling more "grumpies" out of him. "I was about to send a search party out for you," she said with mock seriousness. "Do you realize that you've climbed one vertical mile today? It's five thousand two hundred and eighty vertical feet from the lake to the glacier. And you had this bundle of joy on your back for better than half the climb! I'd say that's a full day's work. Sit down and I'll have the girls bring out your dinner before it's gone completely cold."

I went to the table where Sue sat with the girls and bent down to give her a kiss. "I'm sorry if I worried you." I said.

Sue smiled. "I'm glad you're back," she said. "I was worried."

"It took longer than I thought but I just couldn't turn back," I said. "The trail up to the glacier is incredible! I wish you could have seen it."

****

One evening in February of 1974, I came home from my office on Michigan Avenue carrying news that caused me both excitement and consternation. I was, at once, anxious to tell Sue and reluctant, for I knew my excitement would cause her worry and even pain. I began hesitantly. "I got a call from the president of an agency in San Francisco," I said, attempting to appear nonchalant.

Sue looked surprised. "Oh? What did he want?" she asked, her tone guarded.

I felt like someone who was walking out onto an ice-covered pond, waiting for the ice to crack. "He wants me to come out to talk about a job," I replied.

Sue's eyes searched my face. "You aren't interested, are you?"

I hesitated. "They just won the Hunt-Wesson account and they're looking for a management supervisor to run it. It's a big job."

Sue's expression changed to one of alarm. "Would we have to move?"

"Look, Sue," I replied, "I don't know much about the agency. They haven't offered me the job and I'm not even sure I should go out and talk to them."

"But you want to," she replied.

I hesitated. I didn't want to hurt Sue. Her whole life had been spent in the Chicago suburbs. Her aging mom and dad with whom we had a close relationship, lived a half hour away. Our local church was an important part of her life – and mine too, for that matter. She was involved in rewarding volunteer work with the church and local schools. Our many friends – some of hers life-long – lived on the North Shore. We'd only been in our dream house four years and hadn't yet done all the renovation we planned. We had great neighbors with whom we'd become fast friends. And neither of us had ever been to San Francisco. We had no idea what it was like. "I'd kind'a like to go out and talk to them," I replied. "I doubt anything would come of it."

"I really don't want to think about moving to San Francisco," Sue said. "What would I do there?"

"The guy really pressed me to come out," I said. "Apparently the vice president of marketing at Hunt-Wesson is an ex-P&G guy who knows me, or at least knows about me. If I go, I'd just look the situation over. It can't hurt to look."

"What happens if you like it and they offer you a job?" Sue asked. "What then? We'd have to move, wouldn't we?"

I took her in my arms and looked into her eyes. "Look," I said, "you're getting way ahead of things. I'm comfortable where I am. I don't have any idea if I'd like the people or the job, for that matter. And I doubt that they'll offer me a job. They've never met me and the job they're talking about would be a big step up from where I am. But I won't go out if you don't want me to."

"But you want to go," Sue replied. "I can't deny you that opportunity." She had tears in her eyes. "Just promise me that you won't take the job without us talking about it first. It would be so hard to leave here."

"I really don't think that I'd want to move to San Francisco even if they were to offer me the job, which is a long shot. I'm sure they're talking to a lot of people."

Sue looked up into my eyes. "Oh," she replied, "they'll offer the job to you. I just hope you won't want it."

On the way back from San Francisco, I took a limo from the airport and when I walked in our house, the expression on my face must have betrayed me. "They offered you the job," Sue said, "and you want to take it." She began to cry.

In March I moved to San Francisco and took an apartment on Telegraph Hill until Sue and the kids could join me when their school year ended in June. I searched for a house for us to live in and bought one without Sue ever having seen it. She didn't want to.

In the end, Sue learned to love the house I'd bought and found a new church that became even more central to our lives than the one we'd left. She established the first outreach programs for that church, founded a street ministry and attended the Church Divinity Schools of the Pacific Seminary in Berkeley for her Master of Divinity degree. She was one of the first women in the Episcopal Church to be chosen for the priesthood.

Two years after joining the San Francisco advertising agency that brought me from Chicago, I became its president. Taking nothing away from the things Sue and I lost in leaving job and friends and family in Chicago, we found a new, richer, more rewarding life on the West Coast.

****

Hiking Glacier's trails with a young family meant carrying kids too young to walk. As a result, during the first half-dozen trips we took to Glacier Park, our hiking was limited to day trips. The ultimate backcountry experience – backpacking – was our goal but that would have to wait until I could carry a backpack that didn't have another human being in it. Sue and the girls could not be expected to carry a tent, sleeping bags and all the stuff our family would need.

Our first extended trip into the backcountry of Glacier Park took place in 1976. Debbie, 16, was able to carry a pack and share the load with Sue and myself. Ever the good hiker, Heather, age 11, didn't want to be left out and insisted on carrying a small backpack. And most important, Patrick, at 6, could walk.

Sue and I had, for years, dreamed of backpacking from Logan Pass, in the center of Glacier Park, north along the farthest reaches of the Garden Wall to adjoining Waterton Lakes National Park in Canada, a distance of a little over 30 miles. What could be more exciting and romantic than trekking from the United States into Canada through remote mountain high country?

The route would take us on the now-familiar trail along the Garden Wall to Granite Park Chalet where we would spend the first night. We would proceed north and camp at Fifty Mountain Campground, twelve miles distant from the Chalet. The third day would take us another twelve miles down from the high country to Goat Haunt, the Glacier Park ranger station at the head of Waterton Lake. There, we would catch the regularly scheduled tour boat for the ten mile trip down the lake to Waterton Townsite where we figured we could get a motel. This scheme was, among other things, meant to lighten our load; we'd need to carry supplies for three days but just one night.

We checked in at the visitor center in Apgar to get the required backcountry campground permit that assured us of a campsite at Fifty Mountain. The ranger looked at us with a skeptical expression when I explained that we all – including Patrick – would be hiking to Canada. The weather, which had been hot and dry, would continue to be so, the ranger said. I'd heard that once before.

I grew more and more excited as we laid out the food, underwear, rain gear, backpack camp stove, fuel bottle, sleeping bags, tent and other assorted gear we would need on the three day hike. I calculated who could carry what load and divided it up into our four backpacks. I sensed that the emotions of others were somewhat different from my own; Sue seemed concerned about the prospect of heading so far into bear country where we would sleep on the ground, miles – and hours – from a road or telephone or – God forbid – help of any kind. Debbie was clearly reluctant to carry a pack all the way to Canada and Patrick wasn't sure he wanted to go at all. Only Heather seemed to share my exuberant anticipation.

We left Logan Pass for Granite Park early on a cool, sunny morning in late July. We'd made the hike to the Chalet enough times to know what to expect. As always, the views were spectacular, the bear grass was in bloom and the slopes were filled with wildflowers. To break the boredom of hiking that dogged the kids, Sue led is in song, singing "As We Go A-Wandering" from

90

the Sound of Music. Somehow that always put a spring in the step of tired legs. Despite the building heat of the day and weight of our packs, we arrived mid-afternoon in good spirits.

Getting to Granite Park Chalet had become like coming home to an old friend. It was good to see the old stone structure, to take the weight of our packs off our backs, check in with the manager, sit at a table, rest our hot, tired feet and have a cold drink. We chatted with other hikers in the dining room, asking where they were from, exchanging observations and generally regaling one another with tales of animals we'd seen or adventures we'd had – or claimed we'd had. I must admit that I took some pleasure explaining that we (the really adventurous hikers) were going on beyond the Chalet into remote backcountry, all the way to Canada. Life was good.

We were assigned a room on the second floor, off the balcony that runs along the front of the Chalet. Our windows looked out across McDonald Valley onto Heaven's Peak, a snow-covered eight thousand foot mountain scarred by a massive hanging cirque. We went out onto the balcony and leaned our elbows on the log-work railing, enjoying the view and warmth of a lowering sun in the cooling late afternoon mountain air. Below, hikers were looking through a spotting scope a ranger had set up, hoping to spot grizzly bears that frequently visited the meadow below. We speculated on what would be served at dinner; roast beef, baked ham or turkey? It would be one or the other, for, like Sperry, no choices were offered. And though we knew the meat and green beans were canned, we looked forward to six o'clock when the evening meal is served.

The night was cold, as it nearly always is at an altitude of seven thousand feet. Sue and I snuggled down beneath the thick comforter provided by the Chalet, snug and warm. I wondered about the next night. We'd be in sleeping bags on the ground inside our backpack tent at Fifty Mountain, approximately the same altitude as the Chalet. I hoped the backpack sleeping bags we'd bought would be warm enough.

At breakfast, we picked up brown-bag lunches the Chalet provided, wished our hosts a cheery goodbye and headed north, away from the Loop Trail that leads down to Sun Road. Each step forward was an adventure, a step into a place we'd never been before, a step farther from civilization. For the next two days we would be on our own. I could not help feeling a bit of trepidation about taking my young family so deep into remote wilderness.

The trail initially proved easy, gentle ups and downs at about the 6,800 foot level, hugging the rugged spine of the Garden Wall. I breathed a sigh of relief. Everybody should make it OK, I told myself. As the shadows of the mountains shrank in the morning sun, we found ourselves stopping to shed a layer of clothing. The day would be hot.

The trail was more or less level, but as the hours passed, our feet began to remind us that it was also long. After three hours of hiking, we swung sharply east around a shoulder of the Garden Wall. The trail descended several hundred feet to Ahern Creek. Based on my reading of our topographical map before we left, I figured we'd gone about four miles, eight miles to go. "Let's stop here," I said. The kids were again bored with hiking, we were all tired and everyone was happy to take a break. I swung my pack – which seemed to have gained weight – off my back, set it by the side of the trail and helped Sue and the girls with theirs. Everybody dove into the packs and grabbed water bottles. We were all thirsty, our mouths parched and dry. I sipped sparingly. Ahern Creek, I saw, had barely enough water in it to wet my hands and splash a little on my face. I'd hoped to refill our water bottles along the way, but that was not to be, not here anyway.

Sue and Patrick and the girls sat beside their packs, drinking water and munching trail snacks. A spur trail split off just beyond the creek. I squinted up into the bright blue sky at a gap in the Garden Wall high above. "Must be the trail to Ahern Pass," I said. "I think I'll climb up. It isn't far. I'll be back in a few minutes." I looked at Sue. "You'll be OK."

Sue, I could see, wasn't a bit happy with this idea. "How far is it?" she asked. "How long will you be gone? I don't like being here by ourselves."

We hadn't seen any bears or, for that matter, bear sign – scat – poop since leaving Logan Pass. In fact, we hadn't encountered bears in our many hikes over the years, at least not up close. "Don't worry," I replied. "I'll be back in twenty minutes, tops. Just to be sure, I'll turn around in ten minutes if I'm not at the Pass by that time."

As I headed up, I soon realized there was no way I could reach Ahearn Pass in ten minutes. If I busted my butt, I could probably get there in twenty. I virtually ran up the steep switchbacks, oblivious to the hot sun or the stress I was putting on my body.

Ahern Pass is a flat saddle of mixed scree and talus. The trail ends there. Beyond, a slope too steep to safely descend falls two thousand feet or more to bright blue Helen Lake. The view was breathtaking. After a few precious moments of gawking at the deep valley and astounding Ptarmigan Wall, a three-thousand-foot vertical stone precipice that rises from the shore of Helen Lake to the top of the Continental Divide a thousand feet above the pass, I reluctantly tore myself away. I ran back down the trail as fast as I could and arrived breathless and soaked in sweat thirty minutes after I'd left. To my surprise, Sue wasn't worried. "I figured it would take you longer than twenty minutes," she said with a wry grin.

We swung our packs on our backs again. From Ahern Creek, the trail swung back northwest and began to ascend moderately. Sensing that the kids needed motivation after more than three hours on the trail, Sue picked up our marching song, "As We Go A-Wandering." Grumbling mutterings stopped and our decidedly deliberate pace sped up a bit.

An hour later, the trail rounded another shoulder of the Garden Wall, reversed course to the northeast and leveled out. A few hundred yards beyond, a switchback dropped us a hundred vertical feet, at which point the trail began a long, shallow descending arc to the north. I could see in the distance a green slash dropping straight down from the naked flanks of the Garden Wall. I recognized it as a depression masked by brushy cow parsnip and guessed that it must be Cattle Queen Creek. I'd made a mental note of the creek when I saw it marked on our topographic map because it appeared to be about half way between the Chalet and Fifty Mountain Campground.

My reaction to spotting Cattle Queen was mixed; I was happy to see the half-way mark of this day's journey on the one hand. On the other, with the creek still almost a mile away, I was beginning to appreciate just how much distance still separated us from our campsite and – more – from Goat Haunt and Waterton Lake. I wondered if, in my enthusiasm for adventure, I'd again bitten off more than Sue and my kids could handle.

As the trail descended toward the creek, the light breeze that had kept the noon-day sun tolerable was blocked by steep flanks of the Garden Wall to our left and right. The air became still and the sun began to beat down without relief. By the time we reached the creek bed, the air felt stagnant. It seemed as though I had to gasp for every breath. I'd planned to stop for lunch and fill our water bottles, but the creek was dry. Head-high cow parsnip seemed to radiate heat and no one considered spending one moment more than was necessary in what felt like a suffocating hole.

After crossing the creek, the trail swung sharply west and began a moderate climb. Everyone was tired, thirsty, our feet hurt, and we were soaked in sweat. No one spoke. The kids, I knew, were suffering and I felt truly sorry and a little guilty. There was nothing to do but march on.

Forty-five minutes later, the trail rounded another shoulder and swung back north. The mountain breeze returned but, at the same time, the trail began to climb in earnest. I called a halt. It was time for a drink from our dwindling water supply and lunch, at least for those who had an appetite to eat it. Sue pulled out the brown bags the Chalet kitchen crew had packed for us. We found cheese and thick slabs of ham left over from dinner between generous slices of coarse whole-grain bread. We'd had these sandwiches other years and always found them delicious. This time I enjoyed mine but everyone else was too hot and tired and dry for ham and cheese. Sue took four oranges out of her pack and I peeled them. With a little encouragement, each of kids reluctantly took a piece and, when they'd taken a taste, began to devour them. The sweet, juicy fruit slaked our thirst and, at the same time, seemed to miraculously revive our energy. It was pure nectar. I think we could have eaten a bushel of oranges if we'd had them and from that day, we never hiked long distances without carrying a supply. (I never knew how heavy oranges could be.)

We hadn't seen another human being since leaving the Chalet in the morning. I was becoming concerned about the time and the distance we still had to go to reach Fifty Mountain. We couldn't afford to be on the trail after dark. There were wild animals out there, after all, and besides, one stumble over a rock in the dark 25 miles or more from the nearest help could spell disaster.

My eyes followed the trail ahead. We were faced with a daunting climb. It traversed steepening slopes, ascending hundreds of vertical feet to the base of sheer rock faces of the Garden Wall. I looked at Sue who was attending to the kids and hoped in vain that she hadn't seen where we must go, how high we must climb. But how could she not?

Where was Fifty Mountain? I asked myself, half angry but knowing that it must still be at least five miles off. With the sun beginning to move down toward the western horizon, I hurried us on. Up, up we climbed, for an hour, then two, a slow unrelenting uphill struggle under heavy packs. I marveled at Sue's strength and endurance and that of the kids. The whining and complaints we'd heard earlier in the day were now silenced by the effort it took to just keep going.

At last we reached the point where the trail leveled out about one thousand vertical feet above Cattle Queen crossing, very near to the vertical stone spine that marked the Continental Divide. I'd

never been more relieved to see anything than the end to that
climb, and I wasn't alone. None of us, I knew, would ever forget
the punishing trail out of Cattle Queen. We threw down our packs
and emptied what remained in our water bottles.

Nearby a faint spur trail lead steeply up toward another notch in
the Garden Wall. As we rested, I pulled out our topographical
map. The trail, I gathered, led to Sue Lake overlook, about which
I'd read. The guidebook said the notch provided one of the most
spectacular views in the Park. I thought about that and about the
toll the climb up from Cattle Queen had taken on me and about the
lateness of the hour. My body was tired and I worried about the
time but in the end, I couldn't resist. I had to try to make it up to
the overlook. How many more opportunities would I have to do it
in this lifetime?

Once again, I promised Sue I wouldn't be gone long. Once again,
she told me I must be crazy. Once again, I headed up. Even
without my pack, the ascent was tough. My feet slid backwards
on loose pebbles in the nearly impossible slope, but by scrambling
as fast as I could, within fifteen minutes I stood in the notch that
overlooked startlingly blue Sue Lake. The drop to the lake was
breathtaking; my heart beat fast and my spirit soared. More than
three thousand feet below, the lake looked like a tiny gem. Shaded
from the sun on the east side of the Continental Divide, it was
surrounded by snow fields. Little chunks of ice dotted its azure
waters. I lifted my eyes from the astounding depths to the jumble
of serrated peaks of the Livingston Range. Out to the east, far
beyond, the unending flatness of the plains stretched to the
horizon. My God, I thought, I must be able to see two hundred
miles! I turned to the West; below me lay aptly named Flattop
Mountain and to the north, high, wild peaks that dominate the
northwest region of the Park. The guidebook was right; the view
from the overlook is awesome.

But somewhere out there was Fifty Mountain Campground. We
needed to find it. I needed to lead my family to safety. I
scrambled down as quickly as I could and got everyone back on
the trail. We hiked an hour and then two. At some point, tired legs

and sore feet and the continuing march, march, march dulled my senses and I couldn't fully appreciate the magnificent country we were traveling through. All that mattered, all that existed in my mind was the need to get there.

The sun hung low over the western horizon when I finally spotted what I thought might be Fifty Mountain Campground. A brown thread of trail in the distance led to a cluster of alpine fir dotting a broad, flat, green meadow. Just to the north of the trees, a stream snaked through the meadow, a promising prospect for thirsty hikers. The high, remote meadow with its little cluster of trees formed, I thought, a thoroughly charming tableau. "I think that's Fifty Mountain," I said, pointing.

Sue followed my finger. "Do you think so?" she asked. "We're all about done-in back here." Everyone's spirit picked up at the prospect of finally "getting there", getting off the trail and off our feet, getting to a safe place where we could spend the night. As we approached to within a half mile or so, we came to a junction. A spur trail lead west to the campground, still, I thought, disappointingly far off. Things seem to look closer than they really are at the end of a long, hot, tiring day.

Ten hours after we left Granite Park Chalet, we arrived at Fifty Mountain Campground. I felt a tinge of disappointment - disappointment edged with foreboding. I'd hoped to find one or two colorful tents set up by other hikers, but all we found were empty tent sites scattered loosely among the copse of alpine fir. No one was there. We were alone. Worry niggled my brain. Night was not far off and I was concerned about bears and remoteness and distance. My wife and kids and I were in grizzly country, about to spend the night farther from any other human being than we'd ever been. That was exciting but also worrisome. I dropped my pack at the tent site we'd first come to, figuring the safest place was near the edge of the campground, in the direction of the main trail.

Sue and the girls began laying out our tent while I took our Pur water filter to the stream to fill empty water bottles. Everyone was parched. The steam ran full, its cold, clear water straight from heaven. Five minutes later I returned with bottles full of water so cold it hurt our teeth. When everyone had their fill, the kids took off their hiking boots to cool and rest their feet while I unrolled our sleeping bags and put them in the tent. Sue busied herself with lighting our camp stove, boiling water and laying out packages of freeze-dried food, entrees we had each chosen. One by one, she filled the foil pouches that contained our dinners with boiling water and handed them to us. It took, the directions said, three minutes to rehydrate the stuff which produced surprisingly good-tasting lasagna and stew and beef stroganoff. What an experience! It was exciting to be eatingt dinner beneath the great dome of sky near the top of the world, miles and miles from another human being. I felt free, unburdened by the mundane cares of life back home, as close to mother earth and the natural world as one could get. The heat and exhaustion and tired legs and blistered toes we'd experienced that day were, in the darkening coolness, forgotten, at least by me. I smiled over at Sue who sat next to me. "No pain, no gain," I said. She smiled and took my hand. "I wouldn't have missed this for the world," she replied.

When dinner was finished, I went to the stream for water so Sue could wash up the forks and spoons we'd dirtied. "Gather up some firewood," I said to the kids. "We'll have a fire after dinner." I figured a fire might discourage bears, if there were any around, as well as add another delight to this wonderful adventure. The kids groaned. After a little prodding, they rose to their tired, sore feet and went off in stocking feet to gather loose deadwood on the ground.

A sign a short distance from our campsite indicated where we should hang our food to keep it out of the reach of bears. A wire about twelve feet above the ground was strung between two trees. I put all our food and garbage into a black plastic bag, tied a rope around its neck, threw the rope over the wire and hoisted it up. I tied the rope to one of the trees and hoped the smell of the food wouldn't bring a bear into the campground. We'd never done this before.

Sitting around the fire in the failing light, miles from anyone, I was conscious that our fate depended solely on ourselves and the vicissitudes of mother earth. Few people ever experience this sense of freedom and independence, vulnerability and self-reliance. It was magical. Sue and I had been right; backpacking is the ultimate experience. I felt, at that moment, deep gratitude; gratitude for the existence of such a place and for my family's ability to reach it, to experience it. Though the trail tested the kids' toughness and endurance, I felt it would provide a perspective to life they otherwise would never have. How few people, I thought, would have this chance.

At latitude 49 degrees north, only twelve miles south of the Canadian border, summer days are long and nights are short. When the embers of our fire had just about died, the sun behind the western mountains still lit the sky with a roseate glow. The naked stone of the Garden Wall and lush grasses of the campground were bathed in an ethereal light. But nobody minded crawling into our tent before dark.

The last one in, I looked about, secretly anxious about bears. Three does stepped out from behind nearby trees. They stood silently watching me, perhaps wondering what I was and why I was there. I breathed a sigh of relief. I figured deer wouldn't be there if bears were around. I hoped I was right.

The morning dawned bright and cold and early. When the sun lit our tent, it woke me. I looked at my watch; it read six AM. I wanted to roll over and go back to sleep but instead, I sat up, rubbed the sleep from my eyes and woke everyone else. We needed to be up and on our way. The last tour boat to Waterton Townsite leaves Goat Haunt at five PM. If we missed the boat, we'd either have to hike another ten miles to town or sleep in the campground at Goat Haunt, neither option attractive. Five o'clock, I realized, was only eleven hours away. It had taken us ten hours to hike twelve miles from Granite Park. The guidebook said the distance to Goat Haunt was about the same. There was no time to lose.

We could see our breath as, one by one, we emerged from our tent, toddled off to the small wooden outhouse fifty yards away, splashed water on our faces in the frigid stream and brushed our teeth. I brought water to the campsite for Sue to heat for instant oatmeal. It didn't taste half bad and I ate two packs.

It took a frustratingly long time to get everyone organized, cook and eat breakfast, take down the tent, roll up the sleeping bags and pack everything in the packs. I itched to be on the trail. I'd hoped to be gone from Fifty Mountain by seven o'clock but we didn't hit the junction with the main trail until nearly eight. We had twelve miles to cover in just over nine hours. There would be no side trips for me today.

The trail began a fairly steep descent as it cut across the north end of Flattop Mountain to descend into the valley through which Waterton Creek flows. Within a mile, our view of the Garden Wall was gone. I checked my watch. We hadn't been on the trail more than a half hour. I judged we were making good time, probably better than two miles an hour. After descending five hundred vertical feet in perhaps two miles, the descent became gradual and, when we reached the creek, the trail was nearly level. Our pace was faster than the previous day, fast enough, I judged, to get us to the boat dock at Goat Haunt in time.

That was the good news. The bad news was that the trail entered a dense forest. There was nothing to see except trees and more trees. By the time we stopped for lunch, our feet were sore, our legs tired and our minds numb. The exhausting rigors of the high country we'd experienced the day before were forgotten and somehow a flat trail was no big relief. On we trudged, straight north through the valley. Nobody worried about bears or even whether we'd be on time to catch the boat. Numbed minds don't worry much. Would this trail never end? I wondered.

When we thought, perhaps, that we could walk no further, we came to where the trail broadened out into a lane wide enough for a vehicle and two bare tracks. Everyone's spirits picked up. "We must be close," Sue said. My watch read three-thirty. We'd made really good time; twelve miles in less than eight hours. Downhill is definitely faster than uphill.

Soon a squat, oddly modern structure came into view and behind it, the grand sweep of Waterton Lake, mountains soaring once again into view. We climbed steps to the deck that surrounded the ranger station and looked in its large picture windows. No one was there, though a two-way radio crackled with Park Service chatter. The boat dock two hundred yards to the east held several people, one of whom wore a Smokey Bear ranger hat. We headed for the dock, anxious to relieve our backs from the weight of our packs and end the pounding pressure we'd put on our feet. The ranger we met seemed scarcely older than Debbie and we wondered that a fellow his age had responsibility for this remote Park outpost. With him were two girls and a guy who, we guessed, were in their early twenties. After asking us about our route through the Park and if we'd had any bear encounters, the ranger and his friends climbed into a National Park Service boat that was moored at the dock. He fired up the powerful outboard engine and off they sped in the direction of Waterton Townsite.

Sue and I reclined against our packs on the pebbly beach and the kids waded in the water. A cool breeze caressed our bodies while we exposed our sore feet to the air and eased tired muscles. Few pleasures exceed the relief of rest for a body stressed to the limit. I was filled with a variety of emotions; relief at having taken my family safely through thirty miles of remote wilderness, pride at having done something daring and exciting and rewarding; joy in replaying the things we'd done and seen; love for Sue and the kids who had shared my pain and pleasure; and gratitude. Oh, the feeling!

Almost too soon we spotted a white hull far off across the water. We called to the kids to put their boots on and get their things together. I struggled to get to my feet. My muscles were not only tired, they were also stiff and objected to this new call upon them. As I helped Sue with her pack, I marveled at her strength and endurance. And patience. How lucky I was, I thought, to have a wife like Sue!

The Waterton tour boat slid majestically across the water toward the dock. It was a handsome vessel, perhaps sixty feet long, a closed cabin below, upper deck open to the sky. Tourists crowding the rail waved while a crewman jumped from the boat to the dock and tied it up. The tourists clambered off the boat for a brief stop and look-around, now able to say they'd sailed into the United States. Several people made their way over to us and asked where we'd been. We, of course, were delighted to recount our adventures which were met, for the most part, with amazement and unconcealed admiration.

The smooth trip down the lake was wonderful. We sat on the upper deck, marveling not only at the towering American and Canadian mountains that rose from the waters to the sky, but also at the luxury of resting our weary bones on a real seat with a real back. A half hour after leaving Goat Haunt in the U.S., the boat rounded a curving spit of land that sheltered Waterton Lakes Harbor from Emerald Bay and pulled up to its dock. Somewhere on our journey down the lake we'd crossed the 49th Parallel, the US border with Canada.

We allowed the tourists to get off the boat before retrieving our backpacks in the bow where we'd left them. To my surprise, I found that it took real effort to get to my feet. My body wanted to stay just where it was and resisted my attempt to move it. Despite its protest, I got my stiff limbs moving and stumbled down the ladder to the main deck. Lifting Sue's and the kids' packs onto their backs reminded me how tired I was. They, I knew, were equally exhausted. We labored down the gangplank and found ourselves standing in a parking lot next to the tour boat ticket window. A grassy, tree-shaded park ran south from the boat dock out onto the curved breakwater that sheltered the harbor from the main body of the lake. More grass and trees ran north. Across the parking lot we could see a single street lined with cute little shops and restaurants, anchored by a modern-looking motel. Debbie yelled and pointed to the park. "Look!" she cried. Two does were walking calmly across the grass, oblivious to nearby tourists. Sue looked at me with a grin. "Brigadoon!" she said. "This reminds me of the little Scottish village that comes to life every hundred years."

We headed for the motel. anxious to get a room where we could shed our packs, lie on a soft bed and, when the spirit moved, take a shower. Entering the lobby, I was a little self-conscious, for we looked – and probably smelled – like vagabonds. The kids took off their packs and flopped down on cushy chairs while Sue and I approached the clerk at the counter. "I'm sorry," she said, "we are full up. This is the height of our season and we're booked."

This was something we hadn't anticipated. "I assume there are other motels in town," I said.

"Yes, there are several, but I know for a fact that they're booked as well. I'm sorry."

"What about the Prince of Wales?" Sue asked. We'd seen the magnificent five-story hotel that looks like an oversized Swiss chalet poised high on a point overlooking the lake when the boat approached the harbor.

"Oh, they fill up first," the clerk said. "There wouldn't be anything there. I am sorry."

Sue and I looked at one another, wondering what we would do now. We supposed there was a campground in town but nobody wanted to spend another night in a tent.

"You might check with the RCMP," the clerk said. "Sometimes they are aware of rooms for rent. We have a few bed-and-breakfasts here in town. Their station is just down the street at the end of the block. It looks as if you've come from the States so at any rate, you'll need to check in with them."

"OK, kids," I announced, "Pick up your packs." My announcement was met with a chorus of groans. "We're going to see if the Mounties can rescue us. This lady says all the motels in town are full."

The route to the Royal Canadian Mounted Police station seemed to span the longest block in the world. Every jolting step under our heavy packs was painful and when we reached the end of the block, I felt as though I couldn't take another. Across the street on a shady corner lot we found a small stone building that might have been straight out of Snow White & the Seven Dwarfs. It was, perhaps, the most charming structure in a village full of charming structures. A wooden sign in the yard read "RCMP."

The kids threw down their packs and lay on the grass while Sue and I went inside. An officer in a gray uniform asked where we'd come from, looked at my ID, questioned us about contraband and officially welcomed us to Canada. "We need a place to stay," Sue said. "Do you know of any place that might have a room available for us and our three children? You're kind of our last hope." The officer's eyes narrowed. He turned his back and picked up a phone. He spoke softly into it for a few moments and hung up. He turned back to us and announced, "There just happens to be two rooms available at Mountain Haven. It's a bed and breakfast on the west end of town. It's a decent place. I can direct you, if you like."

Sue's eyes brightened. "That's wonderful," she replied. "How far is it? Quite frankly, we're exhausted. I'm not sure the kids can carry their packs much farther."

The officer frowned and turned back to the phone, dialed, spoke into it and turned back to us again. "The woman who runs the place where you'll be staying will be here with her car in a few minutes. She says she'll be happy to give you a lift."

"Thank you so much," Sue said. "You're a life saver."

We had hardly left the police station when an old, weather-beaten station wagon pulled up and a lady with a head of thick, long gray hair got out. "You must be the folks who are looking for accommodations," she said, a welcoming smile on her face. "Put your packs in the back. My place is just a few minutes from here."

We expressed our gratitude for her kindness, loaded up her station wagon and climbed aboard. What luxury! The short ride in her old car could not have pleased us more if she'd had a brand new Rolls Royce.

Mountain Haven was located on a shady street lined with modest but attractive houses. It was just a half block from Cameron Falls, a two hundred foot high cataract that roars brashly and unexpectedly into the heart of the Townsite from Cameron Lake, far above and fifteen miles distant. We pulled our packs from the back of the old station wagon and lugged them up a dozen concrete steps to the house. The owner held the door open for us as we clambered into a windowed sun porch spanning the front of the house. The large windows looked down on the street and the Townsite in the distance, affording a fine view. The B&B was small and somewhat crowded, but it had the pleasant, comfortable feeling of a home well-used. We immediately felt welcome.

The owner showed us to two small rooms upstairs and said that we could take dinner with her and her husband if we liked. Sue immediately accepted her kind offer. Nobody considered venturing out of this cozy haven if we didn't need to. "Come down whenever you like," she said. "We've got the Olympics on. Everybody in town has been glued to the television this past week. You're welcome to watch with us." I'd completely forgotten that the Summer Olympics were taking place in Montreal. This was a Canadian event. No wonder the folks of Waterton were excited. Sue and I had always been sports fans and we looked forward to the diversion of lounging in cushy, overstuffed chairs to watch world-class athletes compete. Even the girls, who weren't much for spectator sports, joined us on the sofa after showering and – most important – washing their hair.

We enjoyed a delicious dinner and pleasant evening with our friendly hosts before turning in for the night on wonderfully soft beds. We were thankful that the motels in town were full. Mountain Haven was definitely better.

After breakfast the following morning, I turned my attention to our next objective; getting back to Logan Pass where we'd left our car. I'd planned to take a Red Bus – one of the 1930's era tour busses that were everywhere in the Park. The brochure we'd read indicated that a Red Bus ran from the Prince of Wales Hotel to Glacier Park morning and afternoon. We declined the offer of our hosts to drive us to the hotel, preferring instead to explore the charming village of Waterton as we went.

When we reached the Prince of Wales, we were shocked at what we learned from the clerk behind the transportation desk. The Red Busses, he said, no longer ran between Waterton and Glacier Park. In fact, there was no public transportation to Glacier save for the Greyhound that came by once a week and he had no suggestion as to how we might retrieve our car. This was a problem. Our car was nearly one hundred miles away with no way to get there. We were stuck, it seemed, in Canada. Alarmed and dispirited, Sue and the kids and I headed back to Mountain Haven. We hoped the rooms we occupied would continue to be available until we could figure out how to get to our car.

Fortunately, our hosts were delighted that we weren't leaving immediately. They enjoyed our kids and our company as we enjoyed theirs. We suspected they could use the money as well.

That afternoon, Sue and I discussed the alternatives available to us. There weren't many. Hiking back to Logan Pass was out of the question. We couldn't ask our elderly hosts to drive us that distance in the vehicle they owned and they didn't offer. The Greyhound Bus had come and gone the day before and wouldn't be back for a week. The only alternative open to us, it seemed, was to catch a ride with someone. "I'll have to hitchhike," I said. "You and the kids stay here. You'll be just fine until I get back."

"But how long will that take?" Sue asked. "I'll be worried about you the whole time."

I had no answer for her, nor did I know if I could actually get a ride all the way to Logan Pass, but I had to try. Sue reluctantly agreed. We decided that I'd wait until the next morning to start out. We figured that would give me the best chance of getting to our car in one day. I didn't want to spend the night by the side of the road somewhere.

The following morning Sue and I headed for the Prince of Wales. I took a backpack with me, figuring that would identity me as a hiker needing a ride. Besides, I wasn't sure how long I'd be on the road. I needed to carry enough food and water to get me by for at couple of days.

Having Sue with me in the parking lot of the Prince of Wales proved to be a good idea. She approached a family coming out of the hotel carrying bags and explained our difficulty. She disarmed them as I never could and they offered me a ride as far as Babb where the road turns off to Many Glacier. I thought for a moment. What was the chance that I could find someone willing to give me a ride all the way to Logan Pass, nonstop? Not too likely. I decided to seize this opportunity and take my chances on hitching a ride the rest of the way at Babb. I gave Sue a goodbye kiss and headed across the parking lot with my benefactors.

I was grateful for the ride back to the United States and gave my sincere thanks to the folks who drove me when they dropped me off at the Babb Bar. Babb sits in the shadow of the mountains on the cusp of the great plains that spread out from there over the Blackfeet Reservation. It wasn't yet noon and there were no cars in the bar parking lot. The land was flat, barren, empty. The wind blew and I felt very alone. Traffic on Highway 89 was sparse. I picked up my backpack, headed for the side of the road and waited. It wasn't long before several cars buzzed by without so much as a look. I became worried. A few minutes later an old red pickup came into view. I stuck out my thumb and the pickup slowed and pulled off the road. The truck, I saw, bore Montana plates. I ran to it as fast as I could. The driver rolled down his window. "Where ya' goin' young fella?" he asked. I explained. "We ain't got any room inside here but you're welcome to crawl in back. We're headed for Great Falls. We can drop you off at St. Mary if you like. Best we can do." I gladly took him up on his offer and climbed into the bed of the truck. Fortunately, it had a topper. It leaked wind but it was better than no topper at all.

The little village of St. Mary appeared eight miles later and the Montana folks dropped me off. I felt better there, at the junction of 89 and Going to the Sun Road. A gas station and restaurant were nearby along with a couple of run-down motels across the road. At least I wouldn't starve or freeze to death. The traffic going into the Park was heavier, too, and I was soon throwing my pack into the trunk of a car with a couple of tourists heading up to Logan Pass for their first visit. Naturally, the folks stopped at every turn-out and vista along the road, turning a half-hour drive into a two hour sightseeing tour. Anxious as I was to get to our car and return to Waterton, I couldn't blame them. I remembered how excited I had been on my first trip up Going to the Sun Road. I enjoyed being their tour guide, telling them things I'd learned about the Park over the years.

We rolled into the parking lot at Logan Pass about three thirty in the afternoon. When my tourist friends dropped me at our car, I fished the keys out of my pocket, unlocked the car door and threw my pack in the back. I'd been incredibly lucky. I'd made the hundred mile trip in other people's vehicles in less than six hours. I couldn't have hoped for more. I sat back in my seat, gave a sigh of relief, and hoped the car would start. It seemed as though we'd left it weeks ago. In fact, our Ford wagon had only been in the lot four days and of course, it started right up. I'd be back at Mountain Haven with Sue and the kids by dinner time. Real happiness filled my heart as I started down from the Pass, back toward St. Mary and Babb and Waterton Lake. How few, how very few people would ever experience the adventures we'd shared during the past four days. My God, I thought, what a lucky man I am.

****

With my new job came an extra week of vacation. We now had three weeks and when we returned from Waterton, ten days remained before we had to return to the Bay Area. Sue and I decided to camp at Swiftcurrent campground as we'd done during several previous visits. The weather had been hot and dry and we didn't expect to encounter anything like another tent blow-down.

We took day hikes in Swiftcurrent Valley and on the Saturday before we needed to leave the Park, we decided to drive up to Logan Pass and hike to Hidden Lake, one of our favorite places. On the hike up from the parking lot, we encountered a small herd of Bighorn Sheep grazing placidly on fields of wildflowers and tundra grass by the side of the trail. We had a picnic lunch on a stone bench overlooking the lake, snapped pictures of brazen mountain goats and their kids and tried to imprint the image of that amazingly beautiful place in our memories.

As we returned to our car in the parking lot, we all agreed we'd had a wonderful day. We headed down Sun Road toward St. Mary and our campsite at Swiftcurrent about six o'clock in the afternoon. When we reached Two Dog Flats and St. Mary, the sun was still high in the summer sky, the air hot. We turned north toward Babb and Swiftcurrent. When we reached the junction, I decided to pull into the Babb Bar parking lot. A beer, I thought, would taste mighty good when we got back to our tent.

"Wait here," I said to Sue. "I want to get a six-pack of beer. I'll be right back." The large parking lot was filled, mostly with pickup trucks. It was, after all, Saturday night. I didn't give it a thought. I walked up to the building, pulled open the heavy wooden door and went inside. The place was packed with dark-skinned men wearing cowboy hats and plaid shirts. There wasn't an empty barstool anywhere in the noisy bar. Patrons stood shoulder to shoulder, talking and laughing and gesticulating with beer bottles. A moment after I stepped in, heads snapped around toward where I stood, every eye focused on me. The place went quiet. I was startled. It took a moment to realize that everyone in the bar was an Indian. Except me.

I wasn't quite sure what to do. I felt anger and challenge in their unfriendly eyes. The thought of flight crossed my mind but my manhood wouldn't let me slink out of the bar in fear of some

109

ignorant Blackfeet. Besides, I thought it unlikely that, in 1976, anybody would cause trouble for someone just buying beer. Ignoring their hostile stares, I pushed my way through the crowd to the bartender. He was in the process of taking a bottle of beer from a cold case beneath the bar, opening it and setting it in front of his customer. He pulled out another bottle and served another customer at the end of the bar. Then the bartender turned to the back-bar, mixed a drink and served a third customer. I figured I'd better speak up. "I'd like to get a six pack of beer," I said. The bartender ignored me and took orders from the crowd. I waited, thinking that he would get to me at some point, but he didn't. It was obvious that he had no intention of serving me. I raised my hand and my voice. "Hey, I'd like to buy some beer here," I said. In the strangely quiet bar, I felt the eyes of the Blackfeet crowd burn into my back.

The bartender continued to ignore me, working his way up and down the bar, taking orders, opening bottles, pouring drinks and making change. Finally, I'd had enough. "I want a six-pack of beer," I shouted. A moment later I felt a hand grab my shoulder and spin me around. I was suddenly face to face with a young Indian with fire in his eyes, an eight inch Bowie knife in his hand. He thrust the knife toward my throat. Nobody spoke. I was terrified. An old man suddenly appeared out of the crowd. "Leave the white man alone!" he growled. He pushed the Indian with the knife away and looked hard into my eyes. Then he turned to the bartender. "Get this man what he wants," he ordered. Then he looked at me again. "You take your beer and get out, white man. Don't come back. You don't belong here." The old man dissolved back into the crowd, the bartender went to a glass case at the end of the bar, pulled out a six pack of Coors and slammed it down in front of me. Still nobody spoke. I paid for my beer and, on rubbery legs, beat a hasty retreat.

Sue looked startled when I returned to the car. "What's wrong?" she asked. "You're white as a sheet."

"An Indian with a knife nearly killed me," I said. Still shaking, I started the car and we shot out of the parking lot toward the safety of Swiftcurrent Campground. That was my last visit to the Babb Bar. I took the words of the old Indian to heart. Since that day, we've driven by countless times but never stopped.

****

We returned to Glacier Park in 1978, starting as was often our practice, at Two Medicine, the name of which had been changed by the Park Service. The "Lodge" in Two Medicine Lodge Lake had been dropped. We weren't pleased with the change because we liked the Park exactly the way it was.

Sue had given me an ice ax for Christmas the previous year and I was anxious to try it out. But to use an ice ax one must have ice – or at least snow. That was in short supply at Two Medicine so we decided to drive up to Many Glacier and hike to Iceberg Lake. It is nestled in a tight cirque on the west side of the Garden Wall, sheltered from the sun most of the day. We'd been there before and found snowfields on the surrounding slopes.

We took familiar Highway 89 north toward St. Mary. As we were coming down the long, steep hill that leads into the village, we saw something unusual by the right side of the road. I slowed down and a moment later Sue yelled for me to pull over and stop. A large, heavy-set man lying on the ground was extending his arms out toward a boy who appeared to be submerged up to his waist in the middle of a small pond. When our car came to a stop, the man jumped to his feet and ran toward us. When I got out, I could see he was frightened.

"Please help me," the man cried. "I can't reach him!"

"What's wrong?" I asked.

"He's sinking!" the man replied. "I need to get him out! It's quicksand!"

I ran to the edge of the pond and saw that the boy was submerged in something other than water. I'd never seen quicksand before, but I could see that he was definitely sinking. The liquid was nearly up to his chest. I put my foot into the liquid at the edge of the pool. The stuff was soft and it was obvious if I went further, I too would be stuck. My heart began to race. "Stay back!" I called, as Sue and the kids followed me out of the car to the pond. "It's quicksand!"

The boy was an Indian lad of perhaps 8 or maybe 10. He was crying and screaming for us to get him out. The boy was large and I suspected he weighed as much as I did. As he continued to sink, I, too, came close to panic. How could we reach him? I asked myself. I cast around for something to stand on, anything, but the roadside held only rocks and weeds. On the opposite side of the road, just at the edge of the village, was a gas station. "Maybe somebody over there can help," I yelled. I dashed across the road and found there was no one there minding the filling station. I guessed the man trying to save the boy worked there. I frantically looked about for something that might help us, anything. A large piece of plywood was lying by the side of the building. I grabbed it up and ran back across the road with it. "Here," I said to the man, "let's put this down on the quicksand and maybe he can pull himself up on it. We put the plywood down and it reached to within a foot of the boy but by this time, he had sunk up to his armpits and he could not do more than reach for the plywood. There was no way he could pull himself out.

I looked hard at the man who was, by this time, overtaken by panic. I took his arm and made him look at me. "I'm going to try crawling out on the plywood," I said. "You need to hold onto my ankles in case I begin to sink." The man's eyes widened and he nodded. "OK, I'll hold onto you," he replied. "I won't let you sink. Just get him out!"

I inched my way onto the plywood. It seemed to hold my weight. It didn't sink more than an inch or two. The man held onto both my ankles as I lay out prone on the plywood. I was just able to reach the boy. The liquid was above his armpits and his eyes were round and wild. He grabbed onto both of my outstretched hands. "Let go," I said. "Let me grab onto you." The boy held on but looked into my eyes. "I need to hold onto you," I said. "I won't let you sink. But you've got to let go." He released his grip on me. I grabbed his wrists, one in each hand and pulled. Instantly I knew there was no way I could get him out on my own. I looked back at the man holding my ankles. "Pull me back!" I yelled. "I've got him but I can't get him out." The man pulled on my ankles and I pulled on the boy in the quicksand. At first, nothing happened. "Pull harder!" I yelled. The boy cried out in pain as the pressure we put on his arms and body increased. Slowly he began to move in the quicksand. His submerged body began to slide toward the end of the plywood but he wasn't coming out of the quicksand. "Pull!" I cried. The man kept pulling on my ankles and slowly the plywood, me and the terrified Indian boy inched toward the edge of the pond. As we got closer, the boy began to emerge from the pit, first his chest, then his torso and finally his waist. When I was back on solid ground, the man and I were able to wrench the boy clear of the quicksand.

He cried out in pain as we laid him on the ground. The effort to remove him from the quicksand had apparently injured his back. At that moment, a large Indian woman ran screaming across the road from the direction of the village. Tears ran down her cheeks as she knelt down and cradled the boy. Moments later an ambulance from the Blackfeet Indian Reservation arrived with siren screaming and red lights flashing. The emergency medical technicians put the boy on a gurney and into the ambulance. The woman turned to the man and me, tears still streaming from her eyes. She grabbed my hand. "Oh, thank you, thank you," she cried. "I can never thank you enough!"

My pants were covered in dark gray muck. To the astonishment of everyone, it dried quickly, leaving a fine, powdery sand residue. When I brushed my jeans, the sand instantly fell away, leaving the fabric as clean as if it had never been soiled.

We drove to the nearby entrance station to Glacier Park and reported what had happened. I told the rangers about the dangerous pool of quicksand by the side of the road and asked that they do something to prevent another situation like this. They told me this was a State highway on Reservation land and that they would report it to the State highway department.

More than a little shaken, we continued on to Swiftcurrent Campground where we set up camp. All we could talk about that night was the boy, his mother and quicksand. I felt very lucky to have come along when we did.

****

The next day we set out in early morning sunshine for the five mile hike to Ice Berg Lake. I was eager to try out my ice ax. The trail, beginning at the west end of the campground, proceeds west toward the Garden Wall, traversing the lower slopes of Mt. Henkel. It climbs gradually but steadily and in three miles, reaches a junction with the steep trail to Ptarmigan tunnel. We proceeded across Ice Berg Creek, following it two miles up the valley through which it runs.

Ice Berg Lake, twelve hundred vertical feet above Swiftcurrent Campground, is nestled in a deep cirque, surrounded by near vertical walls of Mt. Wilbur to the south and Ptarmigan Wall to the north. The beautiful circular lake looked as if it lay in a hole bored down into the mountains, stone walls rising up from beneath its waters.

The narrow, grassy northeast shore where the trail terminates is littered with large blocks of stone which the glacier that carved the cirque plucked from walls high above. Everyone was happy to get there. The hike was not demanding, the setting gorgeous. The sky was blue, the sun warm, wildflowers grew in profusion. I removed my pack which held our lunch and walked to the waters' edge. Dozens of white icebergs floated in the lake. Heather pointed. "Look," she cried, "it looks like a swan!" To everyone's amazement, the summer sun had carved the floating chunks of ice into fantastic shapes, some of which looked like professional ice sculptures. We pointed to first one, then another, everyone finding an iceberg that looked like something else. It was wonderful fun.

During our picnic lunch by the lake, I scanned the stone walls surrounding it. I'd read about Iceberg Notch in our guidebook, a treacherous, near vertical climber's route from the Ptarmigan Wall down to Ice Berg Lake, a drop of nearly two thousand feet. Few climbers, the book said, attempt it. I examined the outline of the rocky walls against the sky, attempting to identify the notch and the route climbers might take. It was tough to tell because there were several "notches" looking down from the Garden Wall. I finally settled on one that seemed most likely. Then my imagination began to work on how one might get down from – or up to – the Notch. Snow fields rose from the grassy shore where we sat to the vertical face of the Ptarmigan Wall. As I lay back, enjoying the sunshine and the antics of the kids, I wondered how far I might get if I were to climb toward Ice Berg Notch. The more I thought about it, the more I itched to find out.

I got up, picked up my ice ax, and said, "I'm going to do some exploring. I won't be gone long."

Sue looked worried. "Where are you going?" she asked.

I pointed to a snowfield on the north side of the lake. "Over there," I said. "I'll see how my ice ax works."

"Just be careful," she advised. "And don't be gone too long."

With that admonition and my promise to be back soon, I started out. I was happy that a copse of alpine fir near where we'd had our picnic blocked Sue's view of the snowfield I planned to climb. It seemed the perfect place to try out my ice ax. I started up, first digging the pointed pick of my ice ax into the hard, almost vertical snowfield, and, once anchored, kicking in toe holds. Up I climbed, one toe hold above the next. It was tough going but safe enough, I judged. Concentrating on the task at hand, I lost track of both time and height. When I reached naked stone at the top of the snowfield, I was surprised how high I'd climbed. The view to Ice

Berg Lake directly below was exhilarating. I grabbed a rock outcropping to steady myself and looked east, down the valley toward Swiftcurrent Lake. I could see it and Shurburne Lake and the plains beyond. I felt the thrill that gripped me whenever I looked down from a high place.

I looked up at the rock wall above me, wondering where, exactly, the climbers' route down from Ice Berg Notch might be. It was difficult to tell. I spotted what I thought might be a route to a stone ledge twenty feet above me. Perhaps if I climbed higher I would be able to identify the route to the top, I thought.

Ice ax in one hand, I used the other to grab onto a stone outcropping and leveraged my way up. It was easy enough and didn't seem that dangerous. I looked up again. Just above me was another outcropping I could grab to get higher. The ledge I'd spotted was wide enough that it provided a secure vantage point. I scanned the wall above but still couldn't see a clear way all the way to what I'd decided was Ice Berg Notch. I spotted another ledge higher up and, since the climb from the snowfield had been manageable, I decided to move higher. Up I climbed, using outcroppings and footholds to pull myself up from one ledge to another, higher and higher. Finally I came to a ledge so small that I needed to pull myself hard into the rock face just to keep from falling off.

I looked over my shoulder, down to the lake. It was a long way down, farther than I expected. The top of the snowfield was a good hundred feet below me and, from my precarious perch, its slippery slope appeared nearly vertical. I scanned the rocks above. I couldn't see a safe route beyond me and figured it was time to turn around and head down. But my desire to keep going was strong. If I turned back now, would I be a wimp? I wondered. Wimp or not, it was clear that climbing higher just wasn't smart. After all, I had Sue and the kids to think about. It was time to start down. I felt exhilaration on one hand and a sense of failure on the other.

I discovered that climbing down was more difficult than climbing up. I'd been able to spot handholds and ledges on the way up but that was difficult on the way down. To compound my problem, I couldn't remember exactly which way I'd come up. I moved to my left but there were no footholds that way. I was stuck, it seemed. How was I going to get down? I wondered. Nervousness began to flutter in my stomach. Clearly I'd gotten away from the route I'd taken up. I moved back to my right and found a small foothold below me that I hoped would hold. I had to take that risk. I stretched a leg out, felt for the foothold, and eased myself down, holding as tightly as possible to my handholds. I inched my way down from ledge to ledge, feeling with my feet for places to stand. It was slow going but I was making progress, coming closer to the top of the snowfield and safety.

I began feeling confident. Perhaps that's what caused my fall. I edged myself down to a toehold about fifteen feet above the top of the snowfield. I transferred my weight to my lower foot. An instant later I felt it slip off. I tried to clutch the rocks I'd been holding onto, but my grip wasn't secure. I fell, bouncing off a rock outcropping before landing on the snowfield. Suddenly I found myself on my back, shooting down the snowfield toward large boulders at the bottom. Somehow I remembered what I'd read about using an ice ax. I pressed the sharp pick end of the ax into the blur of snow that was rushing by my right shoulder. As the ax dug in, my descent slowed. I rode the ice ax all the way to the bottom in good control and landed on my feet, shaking like a leaf. I realized that I'd just escaped serious injury or worse.

Without looking at my watch, I knew that I'd been gone a long time. Sue would be worried – and pissed. Ice ax in hand, I began to run back to where I'd left her and the kids. When I burst around the copse of trees where they were sitting, I saw fury on Sue's face. "Where have you been?" she demanded. "You've been gone two hours." Suddenly her expression changed from fury to shock. "What happened to you?" she cried. She jumped up and ran toward me.

"What do you mean?" I asked.

"My God, your head! You're hurt! You're all bloody!" She reached out and touched the side of my forehead. Her touch felt sticky. I reached up and touched the spot and looked at my fingers; blood, quite a lot of it. "How did that happen?" she demanded.

I dreaded telling her the truth, but I had no choice. "I fell," I said. "I didn't realize I'd hit my head. I'm OK." In truth, I hadn't felt any pain until Sue called my attention to the wound and even then the pain wasn't bad.

Sue's fury returned. "How could you do that, Don? Go off for hours, leaving us alone all this time. I've been worried sick. And now you turn up with blood all over you!" She looked at for a moment, sighed and turned to the kids. "Come on," she snapped, "pick up your stuff. I'll carry the pack." She looked at me. "You're in no condition to carry it. We've got to get you down." She shook her head. "I can't believe you'd do a damn fool thing like this. Let's get you down so we can get you some help."

"I'm fine," I insisted, but didn't argue. I knew when not to argue with Sue.

Sue put a handkerchief to the gash in my head, wiped the blood and we headed down the trail. Suddenly I felt an urgent need to get down as quickly as possible. I couldn't say why, exactly, but a kind of panic gripped me. Perhaps I was in shock. At any rate, I needed to get down. I started to run down the trail and everyone else followed as fast as they could. We ran nearly the entire five miles back down to the trailhead and our campground. When we got there, Sue wanted to find a doctor to treat my wound, but where? By that time, the bleeding had stopped and the pain was diminished. "Put a bandage on it," I said. "I'll be fine."

Challenging the Ptarmigan Wall above Ice Berg Lake represented, perhaps, a foolhardy adventure that fell short of the responsibilities I had to my wife, my children and myself. I was fortunate to have escaped serious injury. Recognizing and respecting my responsibility to avoid dangers one might encounter in the backcountry was a part of my growing up in Glacier Park. That's not to say that I would no longer venture into the wilderness or challenge the heights of the Livingston Range. Not at all, for I'd found that in doing so, my soul is nourished, my spirit buoyed, my zest for living enhanced. But I would strive to be more thoughtful, more careful, more respectful of the possibility of danger. I had yet to discover that, when venturing into Glacier Park's backcountry, one might encounter life-threatening dangers that cannot be anticipated or avoided.

CHAPTER 3

THE HERMIT

Sue's and my 14th wedding anniversary occurred on February 1, 1978. I'd promised her that I'd take a day of vacation from the job which occupied me twelve hours a day, sometimes six days a week and go somewhere nice. The phone rang in my office on January 28. This was a Thursday. "Where have you decided to take me?" she asked.

Quick on my feet, I said, "It's a surprise." In the course of my new job as president of a growing ad agency, I'd completely forgotten – not only my promise but our wedding anniversary. I'm confident I didn't fool Sue for a moment. When she'd hung up, I called to my secretary to get a map of California, quick. Though we'd lived in California for nearly three years, we'd had little time to go exploring so I didn't know much about what the state had to offer.

Mendicino on the coast looked nice. After making a half-dozen calls on my behalf, my secretary reported that the good resort hotels were booked. Panic set in. My eyes searched the map. If the coast wasn't going to work, how about the Sierras? Mountains sounded good. I had no idea where, in the Sierras, we might go. I spotted a blue line on the map that ran through the mountains. California Highway 108. My eyes followed the line to a lake. A lake in the mountains sounded real good. I summoned my secretary again and in minutes she reported that she'd found only one place on the lake, a condominium. One suite was available.

As we drove up 108, we found the Sierra Mountains and Pinecrest Lake to be stunningly beautiful. Tuolumne National Forest which surrounded the lake consisted of giant sugar pine, three and four feet in diameter and two hundred feet high. Deep valleys and towering mountain faces were carved out of white speckled granite that formed the foundation of the mountains.

The condo was great and, best of all, when we awoke Saturday morning we found the ground covered with snow. We hadn't seen the white stuff since leaving Chicago and we'd missed it. That afternoon we got in our car and went exploring. On the way, Sue spotted a small sign on a tree. "For Sale." We pulled into a driveway and far back in the towering trees stood a small cabin. We couldn't resist. We got out and looked in the windows. It was small and old and run-down but the setting was gorgeous. Besides, we could expand it and renovate and turn it into whatever we wanted. We called the telephone number on the sign and within two hours had bought ourselves a cabin.

When we returned home, I said to the kids, "We bought something and it's bigger than a breadbox. Guess what it is."

The three kids answered almost in unison. "You bought a cabin in the mountains!"

"How did you know that?" I asked.

"You've been talking about buying a cabin in Montana for years," Heather replied.

Indeed we had. Over the years, Sue and I had said to one another, "Wouldn't it be great to have a place of our own where we could put our feet up on the porch and look out into Glacier Park?

Our cabin at Pinecrest turned out to be one of the best purchases we ever made. We drove up into the Sierras nearly every weekend. When I opened the door Friday nights, I felt like I was on vacation. It proved to be a sanctuary from the hectic life I led during the week.

We didn't learn about the ski area three miles away until it opened in November. "You didn't know about Dodge Ridge?" our neighbor asked, a bit incredulous. "And you bought the place anyway?" We all took skiing lessons and skiing became our passion. Patrick joined the Dodge Ridge junior race team. I joined the senior race team. Heather worked as hostess, helping kids on the slopes and folks new to skiing. Over the years, we took winter vacations in Austria, Switzerland and Italy. Skiing was, without doubt, one of the most enriching experiences to come out of our move to California.

Patrick took ski racing seriously, practicing every winter weekend and travelling with his team all over the Sierras to race events. In the spring of 1981, he asked if we would send him to Bob Beattie's National Ski Racing Camp at Mount Bachelor, Oregon, and we agreed. The organizers required that we drive him to Bend Oregon and drop him off at the ski camp since this was his first trip and he was only eleven years old.

From our half-dozen summer trips between the Bay Area and Glacier Park, we knew that Bend Oregon was about half way. We realized that if we drove Patrick up to Bend and returned home to the Bay Area, we'd just have to turn around and drive back when ski camp was over ten days later. Why not continue on up to Glacier Park instead? However, we weren't certain this was a great idea. Early June weather in Glacier Park is often cold and rainy and most years snow still covers the high country. What would we do with ourselves?

"We could go up and look at property," Sue said. "We're not ready to buy, but it would be fun to look. We can get an idea about property values and what's available."

That sounded like a better use of time than driving back and forth to Bend Oregon. "OK," I said, "why don't you call a real estate agent up there and see if you can set something up?"

Sue called one of the nationally advertised real estate companies in Kalispell, the largest town near Glacier Park, and told Bill Nauman, the real estate agent who answered the phone, that we were interested in property near Glacier Park with a view of the mountains. We were looking, she said, for a vacation place with, perhaps, a few acres. Bill said there was a property for sale that, according to the listing, had a good view of the Park. It was on a gravel road, close to the western boundary of the Park. But, he said, there were many beautiful properties for sale as well. The man said he'd love to show us around.

The more Sue and I talked about the possibilities, the more enthusiastic we became. She called Nauman and made a date to get together. We drove up to Mt. Bachelor, dropped Patrick off at the ski racing camp, and continued on to Kalispell.

We met Bill at his office the morning after we arrived in Kalispell,. He was young and enthusiastic, eager to please. We were excited to be back in Montana and to begin the process of looking for a vacation place close to the park we loved. Expectations were high, even though we knew we wouldn't buy anything, not at this point.

Bill drove the back roads of Flathead Valley, showing a variety of small farms and working ranches to us. Many were charming, in beautiful settings with grand views of mountains, but none had a view of Glacier National Park. We spent two more days touring rural properties with the same result. Sue and I had become discouraged and at four o'clock on the third afternoon, all I wanted was to go home.

"What happened to that listing you told me about the day I first called," Sue asked. "You said it was close to the Park and had a view of the mountains."

"Oh," Bill replied, "the day you called was my first day on the job. You were the first customer I talked to and I was really nervous. I opened a file drawer and just happened to pull out that listing I told you about. The people in my office said that people from California wouldn't like a place like that. It's way up a dirt road and doesn't even have electricity. Nobody up there does. And the piece of property is big, probably bigger than you want. It's an original homestead of a hundred and sixty acres. Besides, the old man who owned the property has the right to continue living there for the rest of his life, even after it's sold."

"But you said it has a view of the mountains in Glacier Park," Sue replied.

Bill nodded. "Yes, but it's way off in the woods on a gravel road. I really don't think you'd like it.

"Something in here," Sue said, pointing to her stomach, "says we should see it."

It was getting late and I was tired of riding around looking at real estate. "How long would it take to get there?" I asked.

Bill frowned and consulted the listing, then scrutinized the road map he had. We were near the town of Columbia Falls. "I'd say it's a good two hours from here, maybe more."

I looked at Sue. "Let's forget it," I said. "That's a four hour round trip. It's late and frankly, I'm tired of riding."

"I've got this feeling we should see it," Sue said. "I'd really like to go. Would you do that for me?"

I could see that Bill Naumann wasn't enthusiastic about a four or five hour round trip on a gravel road to see a property that wasn't at all what he thought we'd want. Still, Sue rarely asked me to do something for her, especially something that she knew I didn't want to do. This was important to her. "OK," I said, "if you really want to see it, let's go."

We sped north from Columbia Falls on a good blacktop road. After a few miles, however, the pavement ended. Our pace slowed. We bumped along at twenty miles an hour over hard-packed dirt that contained rocks as big as breadboxes and potholes the size of grizzly bears.

The road wound through a deep valley, emerging out onto a mountainside above a river flowing with whitewater. "That's the North Fork of the Flathead River," Bill advised. The scenery was the best we'd seen this trip and getting better with each mile. The road, however, was getting worse. It narrowed to a lane-and-a-half as it climbed across a steep slope high above the river. Lacking guard rails, the long drop to the river bottom got Sue's attention.

124

As we rounded the shoulder of the mountain, the road emerged from the shade of the valley we'd been in and a startling view opened up. A wide, lush valley blanketed in green-black conifer forest spread out below us. Far across, on the east side, snow-topped peaks of the Livingston range thrust up dramatically. "This is it!" Sue exclaimed. "This is what we've been looking for! Something told me we should drive up here!"

I sat up straight, gawking at the spectacular wall of peaks that stretched north as far as the eye could see. My fatigue was forgotten. "You were right," I replied, "this is awesome!"

The road left the open slopes and climbed gradually through stands of tall trees. Save for brief glimpses here and there, the view to the mountains was gone. As we bumped north, we didn't encounter another vehicle. We saw no cabins or even tracks into the trees that might lead to cabins, only vast forest lands covering high, rounded mountains to the west and, to the east, more trees. This was wilderness, the kind of country we sought. I was excited. "There doesn't seem to be any private property here," I said.

"This is the Flathead National Forest," Bill explained. "The government owns almost all the land up here, I'm told."

To everyone's surprise, we suddenly found ourselves back on blacktop. "What's going on?" I wondered. Bill shook his head. "I have no idea. I sure didn't expect a paved road up here." Our speed increased on the mostly smooth asphalt. I wondered how far the pavement might go, glad for relief from the agonizingly slow crawl over the terrible road but also hoping we weren't getting back to "civilization." A large, exquisitely beautiful haying meadow spread out on both sides of the road, allowing wonderful views of Glacier's mountains to the east and the Whitefish Range to the west. An authentic-looking ranch house stood far back from the road behind a picturesque stand of pine. This was the epitome of the Western idyll sketched by A.B. Guthrie and Ivan Doig in their celebrated novels about the West, the epitome of what we sought.

The pavement entered dense forest again and, in about three miles, ended as suddenly as it had begun. We crossed a creek, rounded a corner and were once again crawling along the dirt road, dodging stone breadboxes and grizzly-sized potholes.

A half mile on, we came to a sign that read "Polebridge" with an arrow pointing east, down an intersecting road. A log house stood to the west of the junction with several derelict barns on the other side of the road, the first sign of habitation we'd seen, save for the ranch house. Bill stopped to consult his map and, reassured that we hadn't passed our destination, continued north up a steep hill, deeper into the wilderness. The road twisted and turned as it climbed. Trees crowded closer. From time to time, we'd come to a bend or a creek where the view opened up, providing stupendous views of craggy peaks, seemingly so close, so high that we could only gasp and point.

More than two hours after leaving Columbia Falls, we came to a halt at two ruts that cut west off the road and disappeared into the forest. A large mailbox on a red stand had the word "Reynolds" written on it. "This must be the place," Bill said. "It was owned by Mr. Reynolds."

"What do you mean 'was owned,'" I asked. "Doesn't he own it now?"

"No, someone else has it listed," Bill replied. "Mr. Reynolds still lives here, though. Apparently he's a recluse." Bill turned off the road, following the twin ruts up through a dense forest of lodgepole pine. I was excited to be there, surrounded by wilderness so near to Glacier Park, wilderness that was for offered for sale.

Two hundred yards in, we came to a camper trailer parked by a cabin. Bill stopped the car, we unwound our stiff legs and got out. No one was around. "The listing says the old man lives in a second house," Bill explained. The scruffy trailer and decidedly rustic cabin weren't much to look at, but that didn't dampen Sue's and my enthusiasm one bit. The cabin at Pinecrest hadn't been much either when we'd first seen it. We both agreed the cabin had character and potential, but the trailer would have to go. The presence of a camper trailer violated our sense of what was appropriate on this old homestead in the wilderness. "Modern" just didn't fit.

In truth, what was on the property wasn't that important. Our primary interest was the land. The forest in which we stood was gorgeous, the remoteness thrilling, its proximity to Glacier Park intriguing. But there was a problem; the forest was so dense, the trees so tall that, where we stood, we couldn't see the mountains. That was part of our dream.

"Let's do a little exploring," Bill said. "Let's take a walk around. We can follow this road and see if it leads to a place that has a view. According to the listing, we are standing just a mile from the Park boundary. There should be a good view here somewhere."

We headed up the primitive road that cut through the property. In about a quarter of a mile, the twin ruts that had led us in came to a junction with what appeared to be a logging trail. Stumps here and there indicated that at least a portion of the property had been selectively logged, though the beauty of the forest remained unspoiled. Huge spruce and fir and pine interspersed with aspens larger than we'd ever encountered combined to form a forest as majestic as any we'd ever seen.

"Let's follow the main road," I said, the spring in my step betraying, perhaps, the growing excitement I felt. The ruts began to climb steeply up a hill. As we were about to crest the hill, I caught sight of a log house standing in a clearing and stopped short.

"That must be where Mr. Reynolds lives," Sue said. "Let's not disturb him."

We peered cautiously over the top of the hill, careful not to be spotted. Mr. Reynold's dwelling didn't look like any log cabin I'd ever seen. Its roofline was unusually steep. Large multi-pane windows looked out from the front. The center section was constructed of logs with two smaller shingled sections to either side. A log porch thrust out from the center of the house, its upper section having a European half-timbered appearance. A small portico supported by rustic logwork sheltered a door at the end of the house. To top it off, the house was painted red! It was, we thought, utterly charming.

"We could go up and see if there's a view to the mountains," Bill said. "At this elevation, there ought to be."

"No," I replied. "Sue's right. Let's not disturb Mr. Reynolds. Let's see where that logging road leads."

We retreated back down the hill and followed the logging trail north. The trail descended steeply to a small creek, crossed the creek and headed up again, traversing a slope to the north. The property was, we saw, a series of steep hills, deep ravines and high benches. Wonderful! The logging trail took us to a promontory that afforded a view more grand than ever we expected. High above the road we'd travelled from Columbia Falls, we looked east, out onto the wide, forest-clad valley we'd followed, cut-banks of the North Fork River visible to the north. Beyond, stretching north and east and south ran a solid phalanx of peaks thrusting up abruptly from the valley floor. The Livingston Range, Glacier Park! The view was breathtaking. I put my arm around Sue.

She looked up at me. "This is it," she said. "This is what we've been looking for."

On the way back to town, neither Sue nor I talked much. I was reluctant to share my feelings about the property with anyone but her and perhaps she felt the same. My feelings were too elemental, too strong for anyone but Sue to know. I sensed they were a tad irrational, as well, and didn't want to risk the appearance of being impulsive or overly romantic or foolish to anyone but the woman I loved. The truth was, I hungered to own that land.

Alone that evening in a rental cabin on the shores of Lake McDonald, Sue said it first. "This might sound crazy, Don, but I think we should make an offer. I know we can't really afford it and we only saw the property today, but I have this feeling; that's where we belong."

We put a call into Bill Naumann about eight o'clock that evening. "We'd like make an offer for the property you showed us this afternoon," Sue said.

Bill was more than mildly surprised but he didn't mind being called after hours one bit. This would be his first sale. "Do you want the whole 160 acres?" he asked. "That's what's being offered, but if you want just a portion of it, I think it could be split."

"Oh, no," Sue replied, "we wouldn't want to split up the property. We'd like to make an offer on the whole 160 acres."

Bill said he would call the seller's real estate agent and try to get some sense of what kind of offer we should make. He promised to get to us the next morning and bring paperwork for us to sign.

When we woke, the enthusiasm we'd felt the previous day was dampened, perhaps by the weather. Clouds had rolled in over night and morning held only the promise of a dark, dreary day. A steady rain drummed down on the metal roof of our cabin, trees dripping, pot holes in the parking lot filling. Excitement and enthusiasm were elbowed aside by an indistinct feeling of anxiety and trepidation that we might not be able to possess something we had both come to want very much.

We waited impatiently for Bill, who showed up around eleven o'clock. To our surprise, Lynette Berg, the seller's real estate agent, was with him. We thought that unusual and were reluctant to talk about an offer until Bill explained that Lynette was anxious to help transfer ownership to someone who appreciated the property and would keep it in one piece. Lynette owned property in the area herself.

"Tom Reynolds has lived up there for fifty years," she explained. "He doesn't want to see it split up. Neither do I. Based on what Bill tells me, you sound like the kind of people who would keep it in one piece and take care of it."

After talking with Lynette and Bill, Sue and I decided to put in an offer to buy the 160 acre piece of property for close to what the seller was asking. Lynette was pleased and excited. She and Bill said they would take the offer to the seller immediately. He lived only a short distance away– by Montana standards – and we should have his answer in a couple of hours. Lynette was optimistic.

Those were among the longest two hours of Sue's and my life. When Lynette and Bill returned, we immediately saw there was a problem. Both were downcast. "The seller has made a verbal agreement to sell 60 acres to someone else," Lynette reported. She was upset and sad. "I'm sorry. I didn't know anything about this."

This news came as a real blow. I felt sick. I felt loss, almost as if someone had died. Sue, I could see, was equally upset. I don't know how we could have become so emotionally involved in a piece of land in such a short time, but we had. Bill Naumann looked completely disheartened.

"Is this a done deal?" I asked.

"Apparently it's just a handshake at this point," Lynette replied. "No money has changed hands."

"Have papers been signed?"

Lynette shook her head. "No, the owner says the papers will be signed in a few days.

"Is there a possibility the seller might change his mind?" I asked. "Is there anything we can do?"

"I don't know," Lynette replied, but her tone and expression did not reflect optimism.

"What kind of guy is he?" Sue asked. "How did he come to own the property?"

"That's a long story," Lynette replied. "It seems that Tom Reynolds deeded the property to a relative in Australia about three years ago and told him it was OK if he sold it so long as the property wasn't split up or clear-cut. Tom also wanted to get any real estate commission that resulted from a sale. Before Tom signed the place over to his relative, he went down to the county courthouse and had a life estate recorded on the deed so, regardless of who owned it, he could continue to live out his life in his house. That was a shrewd move on Reynolds' part because promises aren't always kept. The current owner bought the place and, from what I'm told, kept the real estate commission that was to go to Reynolds for himself. Then he hired a logger to log the property. The logger, apparently, was told to basically take every merchantable tree on the place. Well, the logger had known Tom Reynolds for years. Tom, you see, worked for the Forest Service and had worked with all the loggers. Anyway, the logger told Tom what the owner planned and Tom was furious. He told the logger to stop what he was doing and get his equipment off the property. That's why only a small area was logged. And of course Tom is furious about not getting the real estate commission he'd been promised. Now, to top it all off, it seems that the property is about to be split. It's a real shame."

"Why did the current owner buy the property in the first place?" I asked. "To sell the timber, or what?"

"The seller has been speculating in land up here in the North Fork for a few years," Lynette replied. I hear that he's over-extended. He needs to sell the Reynolds place because he's cash poor. That's the rumor, anyway. He and his friends have used the trailer he parked up there as a hunting camp the past couple of years. Apparently they get pretty liquored up. They've shot up a number of the trees on the property. Tom Reynolds has been upset about that, but there's nothing he could do."

The story Lynette told made me both sad and angry. Even though I had never met him, I felt sorry for the old man who had given away land he'd lived on most of his life and then been treated so shabbily. I suspected that Sue did too. Losing the opportunity to buy the property and make things right for Mr. Reynolds was distressingly painful. "There must be something we can do to convince the owner to sell the whole property to us," I said.

Sue and Lynette and Bill and I sat silently around the kitchen table in our cabin, thinking. Our spirits were as dreary as the weather outside. Suddenly Sue brightened. She looked at Lynette. "You said the owner is a land speculator who is over-extended and cash poor." Lynette nodded. "That means he wants to make money on the sale and needs cash right now. So let's offer more than the asking price for the whole 160 acres and give him ten thousand dollars cash up front. That way he'll turn a profit better than he'd expected on the deal and get the cash he needs." She turned to me. "What do you think, Don?"

I jumped to my feet, totally surprised by Sue's amazingly creative idea. "I think that's a great idea!" I exclaimed. "What do you think, Lynette?"

"It just might work," she replied. "My guess is that he'll go for it."

Bill was a bit incredulous. "Even though he's made a commitment to sell 60 acres to somebody else?" he asked.

"I think an offer above his asking price and cash up front will prove to be more important to the seller than a hand-shake," Lynette replied. He doesn't have the best reputation." She turned and looked squarely at Sue and me. "If he takes the bait," she said, "you'll need to go into Kalispell and get the best lawyer in town to draw up an iron-clad contract that would make it impossible for him to change his mind before you give him the ten thousand. My guess is that, in a couple of weeks, the seller could very well change his mind again and renege on our deal."

Bill brought forth a clean set of papers and drew up a new purchase agreement. Sue and I put our signatures on an offer to buy Mr. Reynolds' 160 acres for more than the seller was asking, including ten thousand dollars cash up front. That agreement required the owner to sign a separate contract to sell before we transferred the cash to him. Bill and Lynette departed for a second meeting with the seller and we were left to wait.

I paced, as was my habit when something was on my mind. Sue fidgeted and looked for things to do. Rain continued to come down. The dreary light of a cloudy afternoon faded into darkness.

Suddenly the door opened and Bill and Lynette, round-shouldered and dripping from the rain, stepped inside. Their faces told the story. They looked more dispirited, even, than they had the first time. My heart sank into my shoes. Then, almost as one, they straightened up and the expressions on their faces were transformed; from defeat into victory, sadness into joy. "Well," Bill said, "it looks as if you've bought yourself a piece of property!"

"He took the bait!" Lynette said.

Anxiety and sadness were swept away by the most wonderful feeling of excitement and joy. Sue jumped up from the table and threw her arms around me. "Oh, my God!" she exclaimed. "That's wonderful!" She went to Lynette and gave her a big hug, then to Bill, hugs and tears of joy and excitement all around.

Bill brought out our copy of the purchase agreement and proudly pointed to the seller's signature. "Here it is," he said. "You are about to be the proud owners of a full quarter section! Congratulations!

"I'd say congratulations are in order for you and Lynette," I replied. "You did it!"

"No," Lynette replied, "Sue did it. It was her idea that did the trick. Now, you need to get yourselves into town right away. I suggest you see Charles Hash. He's the best lawyer in Kalispell. If anyone can draw up that iron-clad contract I mentioned, he can."

When Bill and Lynette had left, Sue looked at me and said, "So, where do we come up with the ten thousand?"

"Hey, that was your idea," I replied. "I figured you had ten grand stashed somewhere."

Sue gave me a playful frown. "Oh, you did! Well, I guess the deal will just have to fall through, then."

"I'll sell some company stock," I said. "I just bought it but my boss will understand. We'll do what we have to do."

We met Charles Hash the following afternoon in his downtown Kalispell office. He was a white-haired gentleman with a soft voice that, we soon learned, belied a strong character. When we explained our situation, Mr. Hash nodded, his expression betraying no emotion. "I know the seller," he said. "You've been given good advice. Give me two days and I'll have something for you to look at."

Sue and I checked into the City Hotel in Kalispell, an historic hotel dating to the late 19th Century when cattle was king and the railroad had only recently come to town. On the corner of First Avenue East and Main St., it retained much of its charm while still affording the comforts we latter-day travelers expected. It felt right.

And we needed a rest. Three days of running around Flathead Valley in fruitless search of our dream followed by the excitement of finally finding it was exhausting, to say nothing of the roller coaster ride we'd been on in trying to buy it. Two days of down-time, we figured, would be about what we needed.

In talking with the owners of the hotel, we learned that Charles Hash was one of the most respected attorneys in Montana. He had been head of the Montana Bar Association and had received numerous awards for his work, including Montana Attorney of the Year. Indeed, we had been given good advice - on two counts, it seemed. We were grateful to Lynette – the seller's real estate agent!

When we met again, Mr. Hash reviewed the purchase contract he'd drawn up. "Breaking this contract will be so expensive that the seller could never afford to do it," he said. "You get him to sign this contract and you'll own that property." Sue and I affixed our signature to it, wrote a check for ten thousand dollars and gave our heart-felt thanks to Mr. Hash.

We returned to our hotel and called Bill. He and Lynette would present the contract to the seller, he said. Lynette thought it important that she be there to encourage her client to sign it. That afternoon we entrusted the contract to our two new friends and once again held our breath.

When Bill called after presenting the contract to the seller, he was bubbling with excitement. "He signed it!" he exclaimed. "It was the ten thousand that did it. It's a done deal!" We met Bill and Lynette that night and treated them to a celebratory dinner. Mr. Reynolds' property would remain whole, there would be no more logging and we would own our dream.

Sue and I returned to Bend, picked up Patrick at the ski racing camp and headed back to the Bay Area. When we got home, we assembled the kids. "We bought something that is bigger than a bread basket," I said.

"Another cabin?" Heather exclaimed. "You didn't!

"In Montana," Patrick said. We couldn't resist tipping him off on the drive back from Oregon.

Two weeks later my secretary stuck her head in my office and said there was a call I should take. It was Bill Naumann. "Lynette was right," he chuckled. "The seller wanted to get out of the contract. She got a call this morning. When she sat down with him this afternoon and explained how much it would cost him to get out of the contract, he had no choice but to back off. Everything is a go! The deed will be recorded in your name at the county court house next Monday."

I breathed a sigh of relief and called Sue. "It's a done deal," I said. "The deed will be recorded next week. Believe it or not, we have become owners of Mr. Reynolds' 160 acres!" Little did we know that this was another watershed moment that would change our lives.

That change began in July when we headed north from the Bay Area on our summer vacation. This time our destination wasn't Glacier Park; it was the North Fork of the Flathead River Valley. Sue, Heather, Patrick and I were excited to take possession of our Montana dream that looked out onto Glacier Park. Debbie, now 23, had found other interests and would not return to Montana.

When our heavily loaded top-of-the-line Oldsmobile Vista Cruiser station wagon slowly bumped past the sign to Polebridge, Patrick had already asked "How much farther?" at least a half dozen times. We'd been on the incredibly terrible North Fork Road for what seemed like forever and still we weren't there. On and on we went, crawling along to avoid tearing our car apart, our speed sometimes down to five miles an hour. My nerves were rubbed raw. In truth, neither Sue nor I remembered just how bad the road was or how far up Mr. Reynolds lived.

The farther north we proceeded, the more the road narrowed and the closer the trees pressed in upon us. Suddenly the realization that we had immersed ourselves into really remote wilderness dawned on our teen-age daughter. Heather sat up straight. "Where can I plug in my hair dryer?" she exclaimed.

At last the mailbox on the red stand came into view. "This is it," I said proudly. "This is our property, on both sides of the road." The kids looked out at the same dense forest they'd been looking at for the past two hours and didn't seem all that impressed. I turned onto the twin ruts leading to our cabin, the pathway so narrow that lodgepole branches brushed both sides of our car.

When the cabin came into view, we were pleased to see that the seller had removed his camper trailer as agreed. I stopped the car and everybody got out, anxious to see what we'd bought. What we saw shocked us and the four of us stood rooted to the ground, speechless. The cabin wasn't at all what Sue and I remembered.

Scraggly bushes nearly obscured a small, poor, thoroughly dilapidated cabin. The ground around it was littered with every imaginable kind of junk. The structure didn't even stand straight; the large logs of which it was constructed leaned to the south. Window panes were broken out. Its low, crude gabled roof, which was covered in tattered green rolled roofing, sagged. Perhaps most distressing, unpeeled half-rounds of small lodgepole logs had been haphazardly fitted into the front of the cabin to plug a section that had evidently been cut out of the building. And the door consisted of a piece of plywood.

A flurry of thoughts bounced around in my head. How in the world could our memories be so at odds with what we saw? What do we do now? Our plan had been to stay in the cabin during our vacation, but from the looks of it, that was out of the question. Thinking that we wouldn't need it, we'd left our large car-camping tent at home and had only our backpack tent with us. The four of us couldn't spend three weeks in that. We obviously couldn't stay in the house at the top of the hill. The old recluse lived there and we hadn't even met him. I was at a loss.

Sue looked at me. "It's not exactly the way I remember it," she said. "It's messy, but remember, it's ours. It can be cleaned up."

"Where's the bathroom?" Patrick asked. "I have to go."

I remembered having seen the outhouse when Sue and I first looked at the property and thinking that it needed work. I walked around the cabin and looked into the small clear-cut to the west. The outhouse was about thirty yards away and by comparison, it made the cabin look pretty good. The tiny outhouse was literally falling down. It consisted of a pile of sun-bleached logs thrown together decades earlier. It had no door; the roof– which was partially missing - had two inch gaps between the boards.

"Come on," I said, "let's take a look." Patrick and I marched through the clear-cut to the bathroom. I pulled out several logs that had fallen across the open door and looked inside. There was no toilet seat, just a hole. "Go in there," I said. "Just be careful not to fall in."

When I returned to the cabin, Sue said, "Let's take a look inside. Maybe it's not as bad inside as it looks outside." Sue always saw the glass half full even when there wasn't any water in it! She marched toward the door. "Come on," she said, "let's see what we've got here."

Sue reached for the rough metal handle on the plywood door. It resisted her pull. She looked back at me. "It's stuck," she said. I came up behind her and yanked hard. The plywood held fast for an instant, then popped open an inch. I pulled harder and the makeshift door reluctantly shuddered open. It hung loosely on cheap metal hinges that allowed the bottom edge to scrape the ground.

We stepped inside and were even more surprised at what we saw there. The cabin floor was nothing but hard-packed dirt. Scattered everywhere on it was the most disgusting jumble of filth and junk we'd ever seen, including two soiled mattresses. The mattresses were covered with mouse fluff and animal droppings and showed large dark stains of unknown origin. Broken chairs were scattered around an overturned table. Cobwebs curtained the windows and hung down from the rafters, snatching at our hair and faces as we moved inside. The place smelled terrible. Empty and half-empty whisky bottles lay scattered among discarded food packages, garbage and every imaginable kind of discard. "My God," I exclaimed, "this is impossible! We can't stay here!"

Sue looked at me again. "What do you suggest?" she asked. "We have to stay here. We don't have a choice." She went back outside and called to Heather and Patrick. "Come in here," she said. "Let's see what we can do to make this place livable. Everybody is going to have to pitch in to get it cleaned up."

"We can't clean this place up," I objected. "There's no way we can stay here tonight." Sue didn't reply. She had returned to the car and was opening suitcases. "Get into some old clothes," she said to the kids. She stripped off the clothes she was wearing, put on a pair of old jeans and a shirt and went to work. I just stood there, my mind not at all in gear.

Sue went back inside the cabin and called to me. "Give me a hand with this mattress. We've got to get the mattresses out before we can do anything." I dutifully went inside and approached a mattress. It was so filthy I was reluctant to touch it. I didn't know what might have made the dark stains and hated the thought of touching animal droppings. Sue grabbed a corner. "Come on," she ordered. "I can't do this by myself."

Sue and Heather and Patrick and I held our noses, gritted our teeth and, from time to time, closed our eyes as we worked to remove the mounds of junk and layers of filth that filled the cabin. Fetid mattresses were dragged outside, grimy, half-filled liquor bottles were thrown out and gingerly turned upside down. Broken furniture blackened by ancient grime was removed, shards of broken mirror, rusted tools, pots and pans coated in dried food, cardboard food containers, broken porcelain, everything was pitched out. By late afternoon, the detritus that had littered the inside of the cabin lay in a pile outside.

Then the real work began. We had to clean the filth that coated the dirt floor, walls and windows, everything before we could even think of spending the night in our newly purchased cabin. Fortunately, Sue had brought brooms and the cleaning materials we figured we'd need in anticipation that the cabin we purchased might need a little sprucing up.

By early evening, we were all coated with the grime we'd removed from the inside of the cabin. Fortunately the summer sun was still high and the air warm. I went to the car and retrieved one of the five gallon jugs of water we'd brought so we could wash the grime from our bodies and feel clean once more.

While Sue and Heather prepared dinner from the back of the car, Patrick and I carried the green canvas army cots we'd thought to buy before we left home into our reasonably clean cabin. I climbed a makeshift ladder that lead to a loft above the back half of the cabin and Patrick passed the cots up to me. The cots would keep us off the rough unpeeled logs that formed the floor of the loft and we should be able to spend a pretty comfortable night in our sleeping bags. I went downstairs and set up a collapsible metal table and canvas camp chairs we had brought and concluded that Sue was right; the old place needed work but it would be just fine for now.

Sue and Heather finished cooking our dinner and brought it in. Tired but happy, we sat down to our first meal on our new property. As the sun moved below the large mountain behind our cabin, the old thrill of the wilderness returned. After dinner, we took a walk up our lane to show the kids the land we'd bought. With the long ride, dilapidated cabin and afternoon's hard work behind them, they were now surprised by the sheer size of the place and excited that this forest was their very own. We poked around the fringes of the twin ruts that led from the North Fork Road up the hill to Mr. Reynolds house until light faded and the woods threatened to turn dark. Bears, we assumed, were out there somewhere and we chose to avoid the possibility of encountering one by retreating to the cabin. I lit our Coleman lamp and everyone climbed the ladder to the loft and our cots. The day had been a rollercoaster of thrilling highs, dispiriting lows, hard work and finally, peace. We were exhausted and I, for one, fell asleep as soon as my head hit my sleeping bag.

Sometime in the night I woke with a start. Cold water was dripping on me. At virtually the same moment, everyone else woke also. The sound of pelting rain surrounded the cabin. "The roof is leaking!" Sue exclaimed. I rolled off my cot and reached for the matches to light the Coleman.

"Oh my gosh," Patrick exclaimed. "I'm getting wet.

Everyone was on their feet, unsure just what to do. I considered the possibilities. "OK," I said, let's put the cots downstairs under the loft. I'll go out to the car and get a plastic tarp to lay on the logs up here so the rain doesn't leak through. I put on a jacket, grabbed a flashlight and ran out the door. The rainy night was as black as any I could remember and it was a little scary. I played the flashlight all around – in case there might be a bear out there. There wasn't.

Soaked to the skin, I brought the tarp up into the loft where Sue helped lay it out. The sound of water dripping on plastic began immediately. The incessant drip, drop, drip reassured us that we'd made the right decision to go below. We all got back onto our cots and into our sleeping bags. As I turned out the Coleman lantern, I was feeling pretty smug about my solution.

Getting back to sleep was another matter. A new sound joined the dripping noise above our heads. It sounded like something scurrying across the tarp. Then there were two scurryings. Then more. Soon there was a real racket in the loft. "Mice?" Sue asked. "I really don't like mice." Suddenly I felt the light touch of something falling on me. I sat up straight. Then Heather screamed.

"Turn on the light, Don!" Sue cried. "Something's falling on us!"

I grabbed for the matches again and lit the Coleman. At first we didn't see anything; no mice, nothing, just the sound of creatures scrambling around on the wet tarpaulin. A faint noise drew my attention to our camp table. I got up to see what it was. I shined the light on the table. It was covered with little pieces of bark and scale. I looked up at the logs that formed the loft. I breathed a sigh of relief. "It's only the stuff from the unpeeled logs," I said. "I guess our moving around up there must have loosened all those little pieces of bark."

"Great," Heather said, "now we're getting covered with gunk from the logs. What do we do now?"

"There's nothing we can do unless you want to sleep in the car," I replied. "But let me tell you, it's wet and dark out there."

"At least it isn't mice running all over us," Sue said.

I got back onto my cot. "Crawl down in your sleeping bags and pull the covers over your head," I said. "That way you can kill two birds with one stone. You won't hear the mice upstairs or feel the stuff from the logs falling on you." Had we not been so tired, I doubt that any of us would have gotten much sleep that first night in our "new" cabin.

The next morning dawned bright as a penny, not a cloud in the sky, not a mouse to be heard. Where had they gone? I wondered. The air was crisp, pure, a great day to be alive. When I stepped outside, the smell of pines was in the air, freshened and heightened by damp needles drying in the sun.

It was time for Sue and me to figure out a plan, now that we knew what we were dealing with. "I think we need to go into Kalispell and rent a trailer to haul all this junk to the dump," I said. "We have to get the place cleaned up. And I've got to get some tools at the hardware store, as well."

Sue nodded. "And we need water." We used nearly all of what we brought with us."

We both knew that a trip to and from town would be a major undertaking, considering the distance to be covered and the condition of the road. But it had to be done.

"I think it's time we go up and meet Mr. Reynolds," I said. "It's only right." Both Sue and I were apprehensive about meeting the "recluse," as he'd been described. We had no idea what kind of man he might be or how he might feel about us, the new owners of the property he'd lived on so many years.

"Yes," Sue replied, "we should go up and introduce ourselves. Give me a minute. I'd like to put on something nice. First impressions are lasting ones."

We left the kids at the cabin, figuring that a recluse probably wouldn't like kids. We climbed the hill and this time, when we reached the crest, we continued on into the cleared area, in full view of the house. I was nervous as we approached the covered portico. I stepped up to the door. An elderly man was sitting at a table in a small kitchen, facing the door, but he didn't see me. He wore old-fashioned round wire-rim glasses and was absorbed in a book. Two perky light blue parakeets hopped about in a large birdcage that sat on his kitchen counter by a window. I knocked on the door but he didn't stir. I knocked again, louder. This time he looked up from his book and sat back in his chair, a momentary look of surprise on this face. He removed his glasses in an unhurried, deliberate manner, pushed his chair back, rose from the table and came to the door. He opened it and said, in a not-unfriendly voice, "You must be the new owners." His astute declaration surprised me. We had no idea he knew the property had been sold again.

"Yes," I said, "I'm Don Sullivan and this is my wife Sue. I hope we're not disturbing you. We just wanted to come up and introduce ourselves."

"I'm Tom Reynolds," he replied, holding out his hand for me to shake. He stood in the doorway and did not invite us in.

Tom Reynolds, despite his advanced age, was an imposing man. He was tall, rail-thin, neatly dressed and held himself erect, ramrod straight. We could see that, in his younger days, he would have been a handsome man. His clean-shaven face was thin, head

143

covered with strands of neatly combed hair, a clean black and red plaid shirt buttoned tight around his neck. But it was his eyes that held our attention. Deep set, they were bright, alive, with an unexpected intensity and intelligence that said this was a man to be reckoned with.

His expression was sober. "I understand you don't want to split up this place like that other fellow."

"No," I replied. "We won't ever split this place up. We want to keep it just the way it is."

"I don't know why you'd want this place," Tom said. "You're from California, I hear. What do you plan to do with it?" More surprise; Tom Reynolds knew where we were from.

There was a formality and correctness about Tom Reynolds that didn't fit a man who had spent his life alone in the wilderness. He was polite and his grammar was impeccably correct. He spoke with what might have been a faint accent or perhaps the syntax of an earlier era, I couldn't tell, but his speech was certainly refined, like one might encounter in a college professor.

Sue stepped up closer to the door. "We want it to be our vacation place," she said. "We understand that the man we bought it from did things with the property that you didn't like. We won't do that. We don't want to do anything that you don't want done. You've lived here a long time and we don't want to upset you in any way."

Tom's sober expression never changed, but I could tell he was listening closely. He bent his head down slightly. "I'm hard of hearing," he said, "and I'm not certain I caught all of that."

Sue repeated her remarks, this time louder, and I thought I saw Tom's expression soften, but he made no comment. "Where do you plan to stay?" he asked. "Did you bring a trailer? I see that other fellow removed his trailer."

"No," I replied, "we don't have a trailer. We don't think a trailer belongs on this property."

"Well, where do you plan to stay, then?" Tom demanded. "You can't stay here. I live here, you know."

"Yes," Sue said, "we know and we're glad you will continue to be here. This is your home and we don't plan to bother you at all. We're staying in the cabin down the hill."

Tom's expression changed for the first time since coming to the door. His eyes widened in surprise and he rocked back on his heels. "Did you say you're in the old cabin? Why, that place isn't fit to live in. It never was much and what with the mess that other fellow made of it, I wouldn't think it at all suitable."

I grinned and nodded. "Yes," I said, "it was a real mess. We arrived early yesterday afternoon and spent the rest of the day cleaning it out. It needs a lot of work but it'll have to do for now."

"We'll be having dinner about six o'clock," Sue said. "Would you like to join us? We'd love to have you."

It seemed to take a moment for Sue's offer to sink in. Tom shook his head. "No, I don't think so," he replied, "but I thank you for the invitation." He paused, as though thinking and his mouth puckered a little. "I don't want you to get the wrong impression," he said. "That fellow who writes for the newspaper wrote an article about me and called me a hermit. I don't know if you saw it. I didn't appreciate him writing an article about me one bit, I can tell you, or him calling me a hermit, either. What's that fellow's name?" Tom looked up toward the ceiling for a long moment as he tried to retrieve the writer's name. "John Frederick I think it is. He writes a column in the newspaper."

"We didn't see it," Sue replied. "I'm sorry it upset you. If you change your mind about coming down for dinner, come ahead. There'll be enough for one more."

"We're going into Kalispell in the morning," I said. "Would you like to ride along?"

Tom's expression changed again and I could see he was considering this new proposition. "Well, yes, thanks," he replied. "I believe I will. What time will you be leaving for town?"

Sue and I looked at one another. We hadn't thought about that. "About nine o'clock," I said.

"Pretty late," Tom replied. "I'll be down about eight thirty, if that's alright." He turned around, closed the door and returned to his table.

We saw Tom smile for the first time when he met Heather and Patrick the next morning. It seemed we were wrong about his attitude toward kids. He shook hands and seemed perfectly happy to sit in the back seat of our Oldsmobile wagon with them, three abreast. We started the long journey back to town a little before eight thirty since Tom had arrived at our cabin fifteen minutes early. "When's the last time you went to town?" I asked. Tom remained silent and I wondered if he'd heard what I'd said. "I believe it was three years ago," he replied.

I'm sure we all had the same reaction. "You haven't been to town in three years?" I exclaimed. "How do you get your groceries? How do you get supplies?"

"Oh, the mail lady brings them up," Tom said. "I get mail twice a week, on Tuesdays and Fridays, you know. Becky usually gets to my mailbox about noon and I always go down to meet her. If I need something, I give her a list and the money to buy it and she brings it and my change up to me next mail day.

This took a minute to for me to grasp. At length, I said, "Is there anything you'd like to do while we're in Kalispell?"

"I'd like to go to the bank and to the grocery store, if that's not too much trouble," Tom replied.

On our way down the road, Tom gave a running commentary about what we were seeing. "This is Wurtz Hill," he said, as we headed down a steep grade, followed shortly by a house and barn. The Wurtz family homesteaded the place, you know."

"Do they still live there?" Sue asked.

"Oh no," Tom replied. "They've been gone for a long time. It's owned by the Lawrence family now, I believe." A half-dozen miles down the road, Tom announced, "This is Ford Station." We crossed a creek that flowed into a large meadow on the left where several plain wooden buildings stood. "Forest Service logging station," Tom reported. "Loggers working the upper North Fork were required to stop here and have their loads inspected. I worked here for a number of years as a cook and as a scaler."

"What's a scaler?" I asked, thinking maybe it had something to do with tree bark.

"Well, the Forest Service needed to know how much timber the logging companies were taking out of the forest so they would know how much to charge them," Tom explained. "This is government land, you know. The scaler would count the number of logs on each truck and measure the butt-ends and the top ends in order to calculate the number of board-feet of timber the logger was hauling down to the mills in Columbia Falls. At the end of the month, the Forest supervisor down in Columbia Falls would send them a bill."

"Sounds complicated," I said.

"We used a book full of numbers and tables to do the calculations," Tom explained. "Only a few of us fellows were assigned as scalers, you know."

"How long did you work for the Forest Service?" Sue asked.

"I retired in 1963 after thirty years," Tom replied. "But it was always seasonal work. They would never keep me on year-round because they didn't want to give me a pension."

I could only shake my head. Thirty years working for the Forest Service and no pension!

And so we went, on into town, two and a half hours of Tom identifying homesteads and telling us a bit of history about the country. We took him to the bank, we did our grocery shopping and went to a hardware store. I rented a trailer at U-Haul to take the junk from our front yard to the dump. And Tom showed interest in everything. On the way out of town, he leaned forward and looked out the windshield. "Would you mind stopping at the ice cream store?" he asked. "There's a Baskin Robbins up ahead."

We were glad to stop and when we went inside, Tom took his time deciding what he'd have. He moved up and down the counter, evaluating each of the 23 tubs of Baskin Robbins flavors behind the glass. The young lady behind the counter smiled and waited patiently. At length he made his choice; "I'll have two scoops of vanilla," he announced. We tried to pay for him, but he would have none of it. He drew an old leather pouch out of this trousers, fished around until he'd found the right change, and paid for his double-dip cone. Over the years, we never took Tom to town without stopping at Baskin Robbins on the way back.

The morning after our return from town, we started the ugly business of loading the junk we'd removed from the cabin into the trailer. We soon discovered that there was more junk than space in the trailer, way more. When we could load nothing more into it, the pile was diminished but all manner of junk still lay scattered around. As we picked it up and piled it for future removal, we discovered still more junk hidden in the bushes. We dug that out, piled it and moved farther out from the cabin. The farther we went, the more junk we found. Here and there we discovered the repose of rusted tin cans, disintegrating car batteries, discarded tools and household items, even the frame and body parts of a 1928

Chevrolet! "It looks like you didn't take much of what you threw away to the dump," I said to Tom.

He stood, hands folded, watching us retrieve his stuff from the bushes, a disapproving scowl on his face. "Oh no," he replied. "Too far. None of us oldtimers took anything to the dump. We figured that if we just threw it out, the bushes would grow up around it and hide it. And we were right, you know."

Every time Sue and I went to town over the following ten years, we filled our vehicle – whatever we were driving – with junk for the dump.

One morning a few days later, a pickup truck drove up to our cabin and a young man with a good looking golden retriever got out. Sue and I went outside, hoping he was the builder Lynette had recommended. "I'm Ray Brown," he said. "Lynette mentioned that you might need some help with your cabin." Ray was a friendly, good looking young fellow with an infectious smile and enthusiastic energy. We shook hands. "This is Amos," he said, throwing a stick for his dog to retrieve. He began to walk around the cabin, poking here and there at the logs and inspecting the roof and broken windows.

"It's in bad shape," I said, stating the obvious. "Lynette said you would be a good person to talk to about fixing it up."

Amos brought the stick back that Ray had thrown and Ray threw it again. He stood up straight and put his hand to his chin, looking the cabin over. "There's not much worth fixing up," he replied. "You'd be better off letting me bulldoze this place and start fresh. I can build you a new cabin for less than it would cost to renovate this place." Amos was back, pestering Ray to throw the stick again.

Sue and I looked at one another. This was not what we'd expected. "I don't want a new cabin," Sue said. "I want to save this one. From the looks of it, it's been here a long time. It would be a shame to destroy it."

Ray was skeptical. "Look," he said, pointing to a bottom log that was resting on the ground, "it doesn't even have a foundation. These sill logs have rotted out. That's why the cabin isn't sitting straight. I'd have to raise up the whole thing, tear out the sill logs, put in a foundation and new sill logs. And the roof..." He pointed. "That has to come off. It can't be saved. I'm not sure what can be done about the front that's been torn out." He shook his head. "Basically, all you've got here is a pile of logs. You'd be better off letting me tear it down."

"How long have you been up here doing this kind of work?" I asked.

"I came out from Chicago a couple of years ago," he replied. "Lynette mentioned you used to work for an ad agency back there. I was a graphic artist at Leo Burnett."

What a small world, I thought. Leo Burnett was the largest advertising agency in Chicago, a primary competitor to the agency I'd worked for.

"I got tired of living in Chicago," Ray explained, "and thought I'd come out to Montana and get into construction. I've worked for a half dozen people up here, mostly on cabins. You can ask Lynette about the quality of my work."

"Do you think you could rebuild this if we decide to go that way?" I asked.

"Oh, I can do it," Ray replied. He went over to the cabin and picked at the logs. "These are large logs," he said, "and except for the sill logs, they're solid. They can be saved, so the basic structure can be rebuilt. I think you'd be better off with a new cabin, but if you decide you want to restore this one, I can do the work for you."

Sue and I looked at one another. "Give us a couple of days to think it over," I said.

"Oh, sure," he replied with a friendly smile. "Think it over. I'll come back day after tomorrow. You can let me know what you decide." Ray whistled for Amos who was rummaging around after some critter in the bushes. "Come on boy, let's go," he called.

Sue and I went back up to Tom's that afternoon to invite him down for dinner. We very much wanted to earn his trust and, if possible, win his friendship. "What are you having?" he asked.

"Don's going to grill steaks," Sue replied. "We'd really like you to come down."

"What time?" Tom asked. "My usual dinner hour is five o'clock."

"Be down at five," Sue said. "That suits us just fine." As we sat over dinner, Sue and I told Tom about our conversation with Ray.

"I don't know who he is," Tom said, "but I agree with him. This place isn't worth putting money into."

"How old is it?" I asked.

"This cabin was built in 1919 by Bill McAfee," Tom replied. "He was the fellow who homesteaded this place. In those days, the government would give you a quarter section of land if you plowed ten acres and could make a go of it for five years. McAfee built this cabin out of snags burned in the 1910 fire. Do you know about that fire?"

We didn't.

"Well," Tom continued, "that forest fire started all the way over in Washington State. It burned through western Washington and all the way through Idaho and northern Montana. It burned over this place and continued right over the mountains and out into the plains on the other side of Glacier Park. It's the biggest forest fire in the history of the country, you know. Well, McAfee used the larger snags from the fire to build this cabin. You can see the scars the fire made on the logs even now."

"This is part of the original homestead, then. It's an historic building," Sue said. "It's definitely worth saving. Do you have any pictures of how it looked back in McAfee's day?"

Tom shook his head. "No, not in McAfee's day. I do have a picture of how it looked when I bought it. I'll bring it down tomorrow if you like."

When Ray Brown returned, we showed him the black and white photo of the cabin Tom had taken years before. "We want it to look as much like it did originally as possible," Sue said.

Ray scrutinized the picture. "It's got to have a concrete foundation," he said. "I can match the roofline and probably save the original window frames, one of them at least. I've been thinking about the hole in the front of the cabin and have an idea that I think will work out pretty well. I'll put a good door and window in the space where the hole is and run cedar tongue-and-groove horizontally to match the log pattern. That way, it'll look pretty much the way it did before the hole was cut out. Most people won't notice the difference."

"It's got to have a hardwood floor and a new loft," I said.

"And a new ladder," Sue added. "Can you do all that?"

"Oh sure," Ray said, "if that's the way you want to go."

It was. "We'll need a new outhouse," I said.

"I can see that," Ray replied. "I can put one up for you, no problem."

"It has to be log," Sue said. "It has to match the cabin."

"That's going to cost you more," Ray replied.

"That's what we want," I said. "No frame outhouse on this old place."

"I'll probably build it in town over the winter and haul it up next spring, if that's OK. Sue and I shook hands with Ray and told him he was hired. He could begin work on renovating the cabin as soon as we left for home. I was as excited as Sue at the prospect of having a snug, comfortable cabin that had been a part of the property since if was first homesteaded. A piece of history would be preserved and it would be our Montana home.

We split the balance of our summer vacation days between our property and hiking forays into Glacier Park. Days that we stayed on our property, it was Sue's practice to climb the hill each morning and invite Tom down for dinner. He came most evenings. We could see in Tom's manner and the distance he kept between us that the unfortunate experiences he'd had with the previous owner had left a wound that had festered into a scab of protective distrust. Sue and I wondered what we might do to make amends, to heal the wounds. "You know," I said, "Tom has lived on this place for almost sixty years. No matter how long we own the property, it will always be thought of as Tom Reynolds' place.

Sue nodded. "That's true," she said.

"What if we named the place after him? We could call it 'Reynolds Ranch.'" Being an ad man, I liked the alliteration.

"What a great idea!" she exclaimed. "We could have a sign made and put it up by the road. I think that's entirely appropriate."

The next time we went to town we searched out a sign maker and had him make a large, two by three foot sign that declared "Reynolds Ranch." When we returned, Sue and I took the kids and the sign up to Tom's house. We kept what was written on the sign hidden as we approached. Tom saw us coming out the kitchen window and came to the door before we got there. "Tom," I said, "we'd like to name this place after you. You've been here so long, this place will always belong to you."

Patrick turned the sign around for Tom to see. "We thought we'd call it 'Reynolds Ranch' if that's OK," Sue said.

Tom's eyes lit up and it seemed to me that he tried to hide a smile. He wasn't successful. He rocked back on his heels for a moment, blinked a couple of times and put his hand to his chin. "Why, yes," he said, "that would be alright with me."

"Come on down to the road with us," I said. "We'll put up the sign."

"There's a large post down there that I hung a gate on years ago," Tom said. "We could put it on that. Just a minute, I'll get my hat." Everybody marched the half mile down from Tom's house to the North Fork Road. Patrick held the sign up to the post while Tom stood back to tell us when it was straight. I nailed the sign on while Sue snapped pictures of Tom, Patrick, Heather and me. The pictures showed Tom standing straight, hands folded by his waist, and a thin but proud smile on his face.

When in town, I'd bought a Husqvarna chain saw also. There were a number of dead trees near our cabin that I wanted to take down and several live trees that blocked our view of the mountains in the Park. But I had never cut down a tree and wasn't at all sure how to go about it. I sure didn't want to drop one on the cabin. Tom said he'd be happy to give me some instruction. Before he did, he mentioned that he liked his trees and didn't want them cut down. Sue and I assured him that we would not cut any trees without his approval. I asked about the dead trees and three that blocked our view. They were OK to take down, he said. Tom went to work. He showed me how to gas the saw, put bar oil in, adjust chain tension and start it. He showed me how to judge which way a tree is leaning, where it wanted to fall, and where to notch the tree to get it to fall where I wanted it to fall. We went over to one of the dead trees, he directed, I cut and the tree fell – just where I wanted it to. I felt confident. I got up early the next morning, eager to put

154

my newly acquired saw and woodsman's skill to work. I went to one of the trees we wanted to take down, judged how it was leaning, notched it and cut it. It fell – not where I'd expected but squarely on my new chain saw. Just then I looked around and saw Tom standing with his hands folded in front of him, an impish grin on his face. "Well," he said, "I see you're going to need another lesson."

One evening when dinner was finished, I said, "We're going to have to pull out and head home day after tomorrow."

Tom's sober expression didn't change but I sensed that this was news he'd been expecting but didn't want to hear. "Oh, you have to leave already," he said. "What time will you be leaving?"

"We'd like to get an early start. It's the better part of two days back to the Bay Area," I replied.

"You won't be back until next summer, I suppose," Tom observed.

"We'd like to come back in the spring if we can," Sue said. "We're anxious to see the cabin after Ray renovates it."

"I'll keep an eye on things, if you like," Tom said. "I don't want that fellow wasting your money. If you give me your address, I'll write you."

The morning before we left we were all sad to think about going home. Sue and I climbed the hill again to ask Tom to one last dinner. He saw us coming across the clearing and came to the door. "Will you come down to dinner?" Sue asked. "It's our last evening."

He shook his head. "No, thanks anyway." He closed the door and turned away.

Sue and I were surprised and disappointed. We thought we'd begun to earn Tom's approval.

We rose early the next morning. I was packing the car when Tom showed up. He was wearing his calf-high leather boots, trousers tucked in and a plaid coat. He didn't say much, nor did I. There wasn't much to say. When everyone was ready to get in the car, Heather and Patrick shook Tom's hand. Sue came up to him and embraced him. Tom looked surprised. She kissed him on the cheek and he smiled. I shook his hand. "Take care of yourself, Tom," I said. "Write and let us know how things are going. And let us know if you need anything."

"Oh, I don't need a thing," Tom replied.

I climbed into the driver's seat and started the car. As we drove down through the lodgepole toward the North Fork Road, everyone was looking back at Tom. He stood watching us, his hand raised in farewell.

Tom did write to us, every week. His hand was fine and readable, his observations cogent and his writing rather elegant. In his letters we saw not only his intellect but also a keen sense of humor. They invariably had a turn of phrase or some incongruous piece of common sense that made us chuckle. Tom included pictures Ray took as the cabin restoration proceeded. To our surprise, Tom was in most of them. One showed Tom sitting in the new loft Ray was building, his legs hanging down. There was one where Tom was holding one of Amos's sticks and another showing him standing by our new door that Ray had built. The building project and Ray's company, it seemed, had engaged Tom's interest and was making him happy.

In March, Tom sent a clipping from the Hungry Horse News, the local newspaper. It was a front page article with a color photo, no less. The headline read, "The Spiffiest Biffy on the North Fork." The color photo showed our new log outhouse in the back of Ray's pickup truck on the way up to Reynolds Ranch!

I wangled ten days away from my job during the kids' spring break in April and we headed north. We were all anxious to see for ourselves what Ray had done and spend time in our newly restored cabin. This time we took my uncle, Bob Sullivan, with us. Bob had been good to me when I was a kid growing up in an alcoholic family. He'd rescued me from bad situations several times. But over the years, we'd grown apart. The past fall, however, Bob's wife Margaret died suddenly of a heart attack and he came west from Iowa City where he lived, to be with us for a time.

Bob Sullivan was a remarkable man with a remarkable history. Though small of stature, Bob was strong as an ox and handsome as Clark Gable. He played football in high school and, before he could graduate, got thrown out of school for fighting. His reputation as a tough, hard living young man with few prospects got him hired by the Iowa mafia to run booze from Illinois to Iowa, which was dry at the time. The mob gave him a souped-up Chrysler with a leaded chassis for better handling and he regularly out-ran the Iowa Highway Patrol. Bob smuggled booze to speak-easies across eastern Iowa, from Davenport to Iowa City fifty miles away and all the towns in between. One time he was pursued by the Highway Patrol and it looked as though he would be caught. Bob stopped in the middle of a bridge, jumped out of his car and dumped his load of illicit liquor in the river moments before the cops arrived.

As time went on, Bob found himself being pressured by the mob to run their illegal gambling operation in the area. From time to time, he was forced to break the legs of bar owners who didn't pay their gambling collection fees, a crime Bob would regret to his dying day. The Iowa Highway Patrol finally got the goods on him and was about to bring him in. He only escaped jail by joining the army in 1942, shortly after Pearl Harbor. Trained as a radio operator in the 101st Airborne Division, Bob rode an unpowered plywood glider laden with fellow paratroopers down behind German lines in Normandy on D-Day. The glider crashed on landing, as most did, and Bob's radio broke loose from its moorings and landed on his leg. Despite a serious wound, Bob put the ninety pound radio on his back and went with his unit, relaying messages to and from other Allied units on the ground. He fought his way through France and was part of the liberation of Paris. Ultimately, he went all the way to Germany, collecting an impressive array of medals for his heroism. Bob mustered out of the army, married, got his GED high school diploma, and stayed out of trouble. When the Korean War broke out in 1950, he volunteered to go back into the service where he served as radio operator on huge ten-engine B-36 nuclear bombers.

We showed Bob pictures of Reynolds Ranch and he was anxious to go with us and see what adventures Montana wilderness might provide. It would be a good diversion from the loss he'd recently suffered.

When we arrived in the North Fork in early April, we found a lot of snow. The rounded mountains of the Whitefish Range to the west were blanketed in white. Deep snow remained in the forest along both sides of the road, though the road itself was clear except for water-filled potholes and mud. The ruts leading to our cabin were in the sun and mostly free of snow so we had no trouble driving in. Ray's truck was parked next to the cabin and when he saw us, he dropped what he was doing and waited for us to get out of the car. Amos came running and barking. "I see you made it OK," Ray said, a boyish grin on his face.

"This is my uncle Bob," I said as the two shook hands. I could see that Bob liked the looks of Ray.

"Well," Ray said, hands on hips, "what do you think?"

Once again, the appearance of the cabin that stood before us shocked me. I'm not sure what I expected, but the structure I saw behind Ray was even more wonderful than I had dared imagined. It had been completely transformed. The old logs stood straight and solid, resting on a concrete foundation. Sill logs had been replaced and new chinking filled cracks between the logs. The roof structure was completely new, topped with dark green aluminum roofing. Original multi-pane windows Bill McAfee had used on the west end of the cabin had been restored and on the south side, Ray had put in new crank-out units that matched. As I walked around it, I could scarcely believe how the hole in the front of the cabin had disappeared. Ray had been right; with a new door and window set in horizontal tongue and groove cedar siding, no one would ever guess it had ever been otherwise. The dilapidated cabin we'd bought had been reborn in the image of the structure Bill McAfee had built.

It's great!" I exclaimed. "It's hard to believe what you've done to this place, especially the front."

Ray beamed. "Come inside," he said.

The transformation on the inside was at least as remarkable as the outside. The dirt floor had been replaced with shining hardwood. A finely finished wooden staircase went up into the loft Ray had built with large, hand-peeled finished logs. Below, he'd put in a kitchen sink and counter and a three-burner cooktop, with an under-counter refrigerator. "Oh, this is really beautiful," Sue said. "I never would have believed you could have done all this."

"Hey, I'm glad you like it," Ray said. He attempted to appear casual but we could see how excited he was about our enthusiasm for the work he'd done over the winter.

I put my arm around Sue and the two of us stood there, soaking up the feeling of "coziness" and comfort and luxury our surroundings conveyed. "This is just terrific," she said.

"Come out and take a look at the spiffiest biffy on the North Fork," Ray said. As we went outside to inspect the log outhouse he was finishing, a rasping, buzzing noise caught our attention. It sounded like a high-speed engine of some sort and it was coming from the direction of Tom's house.

"What's that?" I exclaimed, somewhat alarmed.

"Oh, that's Tom," Ray replied. "I sold him my snowmobile. I bought a new one."

The buzzing noise grew and to our astonishment a snowmobile rocked down our road toward us. I had no idea that a snowmobile

159

could go that fast. We all instinctively stepped back toward the safety of the cabin. Had I not been so astounded, I might have laughed at the spectacle of 85 year-old Tom Reynolds on top of the machine, wearing a red motorcycle helmet. One second he was racing at breakneck speed, the next he was stopped still, fifteen feet in front of us.

"With Tom, it's either off or on," Ray chuckled. "I've tried to show him how to work the thing butTom gives it full-throttle all the time."

Tom slowly climbed off the snowmobile and removed his gloves and helmet. "Well," he said, "I'm glad you arrived safely." Sue gave Tom a hug and kiss, I shook his hand and introduced him to Bob Sullivan. I could see Tom liked Bob.

"We've been looking at the cabin," I said. "What do you think of it, Tom?"

Tom put a hand to his chin. "Pretty nice, I suppose," he replied. "But I don't think I would have spent all the money you've put into it."

That night we discovered one important feature that the renovated cabin lacked; heat. When Ray showed up for work the following morning, I took him aside, out of Sue's hearing. "It was a little frosty in the cabin last night. We need to get a stove. Sue would like to get a nice cook stove," I said.

"There are a couple of stove stores in town," Ray replied. "We could go in and get one. I'll haul it up, if you like."

"I don't want Sue to know what we're doing," I said. "I want it to be a surprise."

The next morning, Sue, the kids, Bob, Tom and I squeezed into our station wagon and headed for town where we met Ray. I sent Sue, Bob and the kids to the grocery store while I went with Ray to buy a cook stove. I found a beautiful nickel-plated black enamel stove that I thought Sue would love. It was small, just right to fit in a corner of our small cabin. Ray bought stovepipe, fittings and finished bricks to set it on and we loaded up his truck. He dropped me off at the grocery store, Sue none the wiser.

Shortly after we returned to the cabin, Ray drove up with the stove. We were all inside the cabin. "Close your eyes," I said to Sue. I led her outside to Ray's truck. "OK," I said, "you can look."

She could scarcely believe her eyes. "Oh my gost, It's a Sweet Heart Stove," she exclaimed with delight, seeing the red heart-shaped logo on the front. When did you have time to buy it? This is wonderful!" The stove proved to be a sweet heart. It cooked many a fine meal and kept us warm on many a cold night.

The week proved warm and sunny, so warm we put lawn chairs out on the three foot deep snow that surrounded the cabin. Heather and Sue sunbathed while I tried Ray's cross-country skis. Although I was an accomplished downhill alpine skier, I just couldn't seem to get the hang of the narrow, floppy, loose-fitting cross-country skis. I'd move forward ten feet and fall in a heap, get up, move forward and fall again. I decided I'd stick with downhill.

"We should try to find the corner markers," Bob said one morning. "The Forest Service should have marked the four corners of the property because your property is bordered by National Forest."

That sounded not only like a good idea but like an exciting adventure. So off we set through the two and three feet of wet, melting snow. Sue and the kids and I had proper snow boots but Bob had only high-topped cordovan dress boots with him. His pride and joy, he kept a perpetual military-style spit-shine on them. We slipped and slid through the forest and finally located the southeast corner marker. Using a compass, we climbed west until we located the southwest corner marker and then headed north. On the west property line, we encountered a two hundred foot ravine so steep we could only slide down the slope in snow and mud. The kids screamed and laughed while we grown-ups tried not to break our necks. Deep in the thick forest, we all kept our eyes open for bears, but we didn't see any. Crashing through the forest was hard work but exciting. Eventually, we located all four bronze medallions the Forest Service had set in concrete to mark the corners of our property. When we returned to the cabin, Sue and the kids and I agreed we'd had a great time, but Bob wasn't happy. His prize cordovan boots were covered in mud and soaked through. They never recovered. Bob bought another pair when he returned home to Iowa and vowed he'd never take them to Montana.

Tom came down for dinner every night. It was clear that he enjoyed our company and we his, even though we had to raise our voices when talking with him because of his growing deafness – which he attributed to the war. After dinner and conversation or a board game, Tom would get up, put on his hat and coat, grab the lantern he'd brought with him and head out into the night. I always asked him if I couldn't drive him up. His answer was always the same; "Oh, no, I like the exercise. It's what keeps me going, you know."

"Aren't you afraid of bears out there in the dark?" I asked one night.

Tom smiled. "They ain't et me yet!" he replied.

Like the previous summer, Tom came down to bid us farewell the morning we left for home. This time we were comforted, for he would not be alone. Ray would be with him, finishing work on our outhouse and preparing to build a small deck on the front of the cabin. In addition, we had commissioned him to start work on a log storage building I had designed to look like an alpine chalet. We'd call it 'The Bunkhouse.' He would start work on it as soon as he finished the cabin. "I'll look after Tom," Ray assured us. "He's good company."

The purchase of Reynolds Ranch marked another turning point in our lives. It shifted the focus of our love for Montana from Glacier National Park to the North Fork of the Flathead Valley. We would always return to hike the Park and there were many adventures yet to be had there. But our time would now be split, the North Fork claiming more and more of it as we discovered how much this remote corner of the world could enrich our lives.

CHAPTER 4

OUTRAGEOUS FORTUNE

When I think of the life of Tom Reynolds, I'm reminded of the words Will Shakespeare put in the mouth of one of his most memorable characters;

> *"To be or not to be, that is the question,*
> *Whether 'tis nobler to suffer*
> *The slings and arrows of outrageous fortune,*
> *Or to take arms against a sea of troubles,*
> *And by opposing, end them,*
> *To die, to sleep...perchance to dream."*

> *Hamlet*

Thomas Warburton Reynolds was born on October 14, 1896 To William Box Reynolds and Ada Sheffield Reynolds in Bournemouth, a resort city on the south coast of England. They lived at 1 Gunnor Terrace, an address Tom would remember to his dying day, though he left there at just six years of age, never to return. His father, William, was a professional musician, a flautist in the Bournemouth Symphony Orchestra. William was, apparently, able to provide a comfortable life for his family. Ada came from a wealthy background and, from Tom's comments, it would seem that she felt she married beneath her station. William and Ada bore 2 other children, William Jr. 2 years older than Tom, and Kathleen, 3 years younger.

William Senior was, according to Tom, a loving, devoted father. He apparently saw in his young son the considerable musical talent that would be displayed in Tom's adult life, for he introduced Tom to the clarinet when only 4 or five years old.

Unfortunately, William Reynolds was not in good health. He suffered from tuberculosis or, to use the old term, consumption. Penicillin had yet to be invented and in those days there was no cure. Very likely, the tuberculosis that dogged Tom his whole life was contracted from his father. Tom's tuberculosis affected his left leg and, in his later years, he could not sit long in one position without it hurting him. William Reynolds died in 1901.

Shortly following William's death, Ada Reynolds took each of her two sons to live with her two sisters, both of whom were well-off. Each sister took a boy. William, was 8 and Tom was 6. Ada kept Kathleen with her. Ada's whereabouts and activities during the time the boys lived with their aunts is unknown. However, Ada Reynolds was, by Tom's accounting, a beautiful woman. It appears likely that, coming from a wealthy background and having a husband who played in the Orchestra, Ada would have been attracted to the Symphony social circle like a moth to a flame. We can only speculate.

When Ada returned to her sisters a year later, they were furious with her for abandoning her sons and leaving them in their care.

Ada removed the boys from their aunts' homes and almost immediately put William and Tom in an orphanage. Two years later, Ada left for South America with an Irishman by the name of Dooley, taking Kathleen with them. She never returned.

Within the short span of two years, two little boys, Tom and William Reynolds, lost everything they had; a loving father, a beautiful mother, little sister, comfortable home, secure surroundings, bright future. The boys had, in effect, lost what is most important to little boys; their family. Tom never forgave his mother for abandoning him and his brother to an orphanage and he never stopped longing for what he'd lost as a young child.

Before the 1940's, no formal social services network for orphans existed in Britain and orphanages were generally ad hoc local institutions run by the Church of England or local businesses and charitable organizations that wished to do good. That said, orphanages in Britain generally reflected Victorian attitudes toward the poor and those who could not care for themselves. The prevailing thinking was that the underclass brought their problems on themselves through indigence or ignorance and should be punished. Consequently, life in orphanages in the early 20th Century was grim. Funding was inadequate, sanitation was poor, food scarce and beatings were common.

Perhaps that is one reason Ada Reynolds put her young sons in the Royal Military School in Chelsea, known until 1892 as the Royal Military Asylum. Established by the Duke of York in 1801, it was primarily an orphanage for children of British soldiers who were killed while in service or died after retirement. In addition, it admitted children of surviving widows who could not or would not care for their children. Apparently William Reynolds Sr. had served in the British Army, though no record of his service exists. One requirement for entry was the parent's agreement that the boys would stay in the orphanage until age 14, at which time they must either join the British Army or become an indentured apprentice to a civilian, at the discretion of the board supervising the institution. Over 80% of 14 year old boys chose to join the army. Clearly, Ada Reynolds never intended to take her sons back into her household.

Raising orphan boys was not an entirely altruistic endeavor on the part of the Duke of York, primary patron of the Royal Military School or of the British Army that supplied the staff to run it. A May 26, 1888 article in "The Graphic," a British newspaper, states "the Royal Military Asylum is intended primarily as a school to train boys for the army." Given the rather grim life of an enlisted man, the Army was forced to draw recruits from the poorest classes of society, many joining just to escape starvation. As a result, during the 19th Century, Army ranks consisted mostly of men who could neither read nor write, with little sense of the basic behavior society required of them. As late 19th Century technology began to transform the battlefield, The British Army knew it must have better men. The Royal Military School, run by the Corps of Army Schoolmasters, was there to supply teen-age recruits who could readily read, write and do sums. The cost to the Crown and the Duke of York was the cost of raising them.

Tom was tight-lipped about life in the orphanage. When asked what it was like, his reply was characteristically understated; "Pretty bad," he said, his eyes round and mouth puckered. "We were hungry most of the time." Tom said he could never read Dickens' Oliver Twist. The orphanage scene, in which Oliver was harshly punished for bringing forth his empty bowl and asking for more gruel, reminded Tom too much of his own experiences in his orphanage. "When I left that orphanage at age 14, I stood four feet seven inches tall and weighed 75 pounds," Tom said.

The 1888 article in "The Graphic" presents what the British Army described as life in the Royal Military Asylum. "The Asylum was run on military lines with military appointees in charge: commandant, adjutant, chaplain, quartermaster, and surgeon. In addition there was a sergeant major of instructions who, with his assistants, supervised the education of the boys.

"The children were woken by the beat of a drum, six o'clock in summer, seven o'clock in winter. They had two hours to clean their boots and shoes, wash their face and hands and generally put their dormitories to rights before breakfast at eight o'clock in the summer or nine o'clock in the winter. Breakfast consisted of milk pottage made of $1/6^{th}$ quart of milk and $1/10^{th}$ pound of oatmeal per child and $1/20^{th}$ of a quartern loaf. The school day started with prayers, read either by the chaplain or by the sergeant major of instructions. Lessons then followed with reading, writing and the first four rules of arithmetic so the children could cast accounts. Dinner was at one o'clock and allowed some variation. For example, on three days, the boys were given eight ounces of beef, roasted, stewed or boiled with twelve ounces of potatoes, $1/40^{th}$ of a quartern loaf and a half pint of beer. This was varied with boiled mutton, suet pudding or pea soup with milk substituted for beer. Lessons recommenced at half past two until five o'clock, followed by supper at seven o'clock in the summer and six o'clock in the winter. This meal consisted of cheese, bread and beer or bread and milk. There were periods of play fitted into the timetable although the boys were also drilled. Since moral education was considered crucially important, the chaplain taught the children their catechism and gave them religious instruction. The boys wore the uniform of the Asylum; red jacket, blue breeches, blue stockings and black cap."

Remembering that this description of life in the orphanage was given to a newspaper by those in charge of the Asylum, one may suppose that life for the young inmates was not always as described.

He indicated that he and his older brother William were close when they were boys. It seems likely the older brother was an important source of strength and comfort to Tom in the orphanage, and vice versa. That ended when, in 1908, William reached the age of 14 and was sent from the institution into the British Army. In 1909, at age 13, Tom began formal instruction on the clarinet which would, undoubtedly, have been a source of pleasure in a place with few pleasures.

On October 23, 1910, nine days after his 14th birthday, Tom followed his brother's path and entered the British Army. In one way, it can be said that Tom was fortunate. The Army Enlistment Act of 1870 reduced the enlistment term from 21 years and went to what was called the "Short Enlistment." Tom Reynolds would be required to serve in the Army for only 12 years.

Tom was assigned to Ravensdowne Barracks in Berwick-upon-Tweed, Northumberland, Scotland, headquarters of the King's Own Scottish Borderers, 25th Regiment of the Line.

This regiment had a long and storied existence. On the 18th of March, 1689, the Third Earl of Leven, David Leslie, was authorized by King William III to raise a regiment of 800 men on the northern border of England to defend Edinburgh against attack by rebels under James II. In the span of two hours, the Edinburgh Regiment of Foot was raised and armed and England was protected. In 1805, the name was changed and during the 200 years following the Regiment's inception, the King's Own Scottish Borderers participated in nearly every battle the British Army fought. Their bravery won an impressive array of honors, first among them in stature was the victory over the French at the battle of Minden on August 1st 1759 in the Seven Years War. The unparalleled heroism of the Regiment on that occasion marked it as "The Rose of Minden," making it one of the most respected, revered regiments in the British Army. Regimental soldiers wear a rose in their lapel every August 1st.

When he arrived in Berwick, Tom did not meet Regimental height and weight requirements and was put in the Regiment's school with other boys. Almost immediately, Tom sat for the British Army scholastic examination for a 3rd Class Education Certificate. The Army wanted to know what they had to work with. The Third Class Education Certificate "specified the standard for promotion to the rank of corporal". (This did not raise the recipient's rank to corporal, only qualified the holder for future promotion.) The Certificate "required the student to read aloud and to write from dictation passages from an easy narrative and to work examples in the four compound rules of arithmetic and reduction of money." On December 26, 1910, two months after arriving in Berwick and one day after Christmas, the Regimental schoolmaster presented Tom with his Third Class Education Certificate.

Tom spent 1911 and 1912 in the Regimental school. He said that the boys were forbidden to associate with girls but that some older boys sneaked into town from time to time and occasionally got caught. "They were drummed out of the Army," Tom said, his wide-eyed expression indicating the seriousness of their situation. "That was tantamount to a death sentence, you know." In the early 20th Century, retired soldiers and those "drummed out" often died in the streets of exposure and starvation. Tom grinned self-consciously as he said, "I stayed away from the girls, I can tell you."

He studied, was given basic military training and instruction on the clarinet. Along with the other boys, he drilled, cleaned equipment and his uniform and performed menial labor around the base. In late 1912, at the age of 16, Tom reached the Regimental physical requirements and became a soldier in the British Army, a Private. He was sent to join the 2nd Battalion of the Regiment stationed at Hollywood Barracks, eight miles outside Belfast, Ireland. Tom never liked the Irish, and must have been very skeptical of me, the Irishman from California who bought his property. His dislike of the Irish is understandable, considering that when he arrived at

Hollywood Barracks, the Easter Rising rebellion that threw Ireland into chaos was less than four years in the future.

Soldiers of the Regiment would have been conspicuous in their red tunics and white pipe clay belts, obvious targets for angry Irish mobs. However, the boys in the Regiment were not without their fun. Tom tells the story of going into Belfast by train on a Saturday for recreation and playing a prank on one of the locals. "We went into a novelty store," Tom said, "and we bought this and that. Some of the boys bought some stink bombs. If we weren't late, we could take the same train back to the barracks. In those days, English passenger trains had a corridor down the middle with doors to compartments on both sides. Well, on our way back, an Irishman – a fisherman I think he was, from one of the local villages – came into our compartment and closed the door. When this fellow wasn't looking, one of the boys dropped a stink bomb on the floor and put his foot on it. Pretty soon that Irish fellow's nose crinkled up. He looked around at us and said, 'Which one of you little bastards shit themselves?" Tom laughed every time he told this story that had happened seven decades earlier. The antics of these British soldiers remind us that Tom and his friends, conscripted to put their lives on the line for the King, were still just children.

The Regiment was posted to Dublin at the end of 1912 and billeted in Dublin Castle, a massive compound that housed headquarters of the occupying British government and the military. Like Belfast, Dublin was a hotbed of resentment against British occupation, with Irish leaders demanding home rule, independence and the removal of British troops. The Regiment was there to keep the peace and its troops were frequently sent into the streets to maintain order. Tom indicated that it could be a nerve-racking and even dangerous job.

Apparently, the Army saw potential in Private Tom Reynolds. During his time in Ireland, the Army continued his education. On February 5, 1913, he received his 2nd Class Education Certificate. The Army specified at the time that: "A Second Class Certificate, necessary for promotion to sergeant, entailed writing and dictation from a more difficult work, familiarity with all forms of regimental accounting, and facility with proportions and interest, fractions and averages."

On June 28, 1914, the world changed. Archduke Ferdinand of Austria was assassinated in Sarajevo by a Serb. One month later, August 1st, Germany declared war on Russia. Soon France and England joined Russia in an alliance that would contest what would become known as World War I. The King's Own Scottish Borderers, stationed in Dublin, were among the first British Regiments called to the Continent. As Tom and his comrades were packing their bags and getting ready to board a transport for the trip across the Channel, he received surprising new orders. He would not be going to France with his Regiment. His orders were to report to Kneller Hall, home of the Royal School of Music back in England. An official publication states that the Royal Military Asylum, from which Tom came, was an important source of pupils for the Royal School of Music. The Army apparently saw Tom, who had been studying the clarinet, as a soldier with both a keen intellect and musical talent, a boy with a disadvantaged past, perhaps, but a bright future.

These new orders undoubtedly saved Tom's life. In the first months of the war, two hundred thousand British soldiers were hastily assembled to stop three million German troops in their assault on France and Belgium. In the short span of three months, nearly every member of the Kings Own Scottish Borderers was killed or wounded.

Kneller Hall is located in Twickenham, fifteen miles southwest of central London. It had been the estate of Sir Geoffrey Kneller, court painter in the 17th Century. In 1857, at the urging of the Duke of Cambridge, head of the British Army at the time, the Crown bought it. It became the home of the Royal School of Music and headquarters of the British Army's Corps of Army Music. In the early 20th Century, the British Army had 29 regiments with bands. The purpose of the Royal School of Music was to provide standardized, high quality musical training for all band members and bandmasters.

Students (studying to be bandmasters) and Pupils (studying to be band members) were kept busy at Kneller Hall. Music instruction, general education studies and regimented physical activities began at 9 o'clock each morning and ended at 9 o'clock each evening, six days a week. Music studies included music theory, individual instrument instruction, playing together as a band and marching. Fine classical music by the best composers formed the basis of the Army's musical education. Tom said that he and other pupils were sent into London to attend professional orchestra performances and ballets as part of their training. Pupils generally spent between 18 months and two years at the Royal School of Music before passing the examination that gave them a certificate as a professional musician. This certificate was recognized both within the Army and by civilian professional orchestras. As a result, a Royal School of Music certificate was valuable and highly sought by young soldiers with musical ability because it conferred on them a profession. During his time at Kneller Hall, Tom studied the clarinet as he had at the Royal Military Asylum and was also required to learn the violin which he did not like much. "I wasn't very good at it. If I'd had to qualify on the violin, I'm afraid I wouldn't have graduated," he said.

Throughout 1914 and 1915, pupils at the Royal School of Music were spared from the carnage taking place in the muddy trench warfare that had spread across Belgium and France. By 1916, 660,000 British boys had been killed and twice that number wounded. With a population of just 46 million, nearly every household in Britain had lost someone. The nation was being bled white. In the summer of 1916, so many civilian musicians had been conscripted that London orchestras requested the Army to send students from the Royal School of Music to fill orchestra vacancies. Tom said he and other Kneller Hall pupils played numerous times at the Empire Theater, one of the larger venues in London.

By late 1916, the King had about run out of old men and young boys that he could throw into the insatiable maw of war. In order to provide desperately needed replacements, the Army dissolved non-combat units and sent their men to fight Germans. The Royal School of Music was closed for the duration. Musical instruments were replaced with Enfield rifles.

In November 1916, Tom, age 20, was sent to Belgium and ordered to report to First Army, I Corps, 5th Division, 13th Brigade, 2nd Battalion, King's own Scottish Borderers. One can only imagine the emotions that must have coursed through this young man whose life had yet to be lived. For the past two and a half years, Tom had undoubtedly read horrifying headlines and seen sickening pictures in London newspapers. No doubt he had scanned published casualty reports and searched for names of friends he'd left in Ireland, nearly all of whom would have been listed as dead or wounded. The prospect of descending into the hell of merciless trench warfare that had killed or wounded over two million Britons must have been terrifying. Still, he went. He was a soldier. There was no alternative.

Tom rejoined his regiment at a base near Ypres, France, a name made infamous because of the savage fighting and horrific casualties that took place there. There would have been few, if any, familiar faces, for the men of the Regiment were nearly all replacements. Unlike thousands of other soldiers who had been bogged down in the Ypres area for months in stalemate with the enemy, Tom did not stay long. His unit was soon given orders to move south. The KOSB was ordered to take part in a major new offensive near the French village of Arras.

For much of the war, the opposing armies on the Western Front were locked in stalemate because they were dug into a continuous line of protective trenches running from the Belgian coast to Switzerland. The British and French, with superior numbers, had long sought a breakthrough to fight a war of movement in the open country beyond the trenches. The battle of Arras was, in conjunction with a French campaign, designed to do just that.

The Battle of Arras was fought from April 9 to May 16, 1917. Vimy Ridge, held by the Germans since 1914, was a strategically important objective, for it was a high, narrow escarpment overlooking the Douai Plain. The British and Canadian commands determined that Vimy Ridge could be taken by the combination of an artillery barrage of unprecedented magnitude and tunneling. Four Canadian divisions and one British division totaling 170,000 troops were assembled in the spring of 1917 with the objective of taking Vimy Ridge. One thousand pieces of artillery were assembled by the British and the barrage began on March 20. It lasted 20 days, its intensity increasing to a non-stop crescendo the last week. The British and Canadians threw 1.6 million shells at the Germans. German artillery threw 1.4 million shells at the Canadians and British. A total of three million artillery shells were fired, making this the largest artillery bombardment in history. The assault by troops began on Monday, April 9 and, after more than 3,600 British and Canadian troops were killed, Vimy Ridge was taken three days later. Fighting continued in what is called the Battle of Arras until British and Allied commanders concluded on May 16th that they could not push forward beyond the ridge.

Tom's unit was one that participated in the battle of Vimy Ridge. He survived the bombardment and initial assault but, on May 15th, 1917, he was wounded on Vimy Ridge and taken prisoner by the Germans. He suffered a shoulder wound and was sent to a German field hospital. When he was able to travel, he was transported to a prison camp in Germany and made to work as a slave laborer in a steel mill.

When the war began, Britain had few troops to send to the Continent but they did have the Royal Navy. Two months after the declaration of war, the Royal Navy imposed a blockade on shipping to Germany, stopping ships in the North Sea headed for German ports and mining entryways to their harbors. The blockade was a war of attrition and did not affect the German war effort immediately. But with a serious reduction in agriculture production caused by the conscription of German farmers combined with the absence of a rationing system, the blockade became a leading contributor to the defeat of Germany. By the winter of 1916, staple foods such as grain, meat and dairy products were scarce throughout Germany. Even potatoes were in short supply and many Germans were forced to survive on the less nutritious turnip. German troops, well-fed at the beginning of the conflict, were reduced to rations of turnip soup in 1918. It is estimated that 800,000 German civilians died of starvation during the war. In times of starvation caused in part by the British blockade, prisoner of war camps holding British soldiers must have been at the very end of the food line.

Tom never talked much about the time he spent in the German prison camp, except to say, "A lot of the fellows in camp with me died, you know. We had nothing to eat." Tom's eyes got big and round and his lips puckered as they did when he wished to underscore the seriousness of a situation. "When I was repatriated in 1918, I stood six feet tall and weighed ninety pounds. My arms were nothing but sticks about this big around." He held up a hand and made a three inch diameter circle with his thumb and forefinger. "I spent three months in hospital recovering."

The end of the war caused demobilization of the British Army. Tens of thousands of military vehicles, artillery pieces and every form of equipment were sent back to England. Hundreds of thousands of soldiers exhausted by war were discharged from the Army and sent home. Tom expected that he, like them, would be discharged and could begin life as an ordinary civilian. While still in hospital, however, he was disabused of that idea. "You will not be discharged," he was told. "You still have four years to serve on your enlistment." Regimental records show that Private Thomas Warburton Reynolds, 2nd Battalion, Kings Own Scottish Borderers received the Victory Medal and British War Medal for his participation in the Great War.

Tom returned to Berwick-Upon-Tweed and Regimental Headquarters in early 1919 and when the Regiment came back from France in March, he was reassigned from the 2nd Battalion to the 1st Battalion.

With his Certificate of Musical Instruction from the Royal School of Music, Tom expected to join the Regimental Band. He went to the 1st Battalion Bandmaster and showed him the Certificate that qualified him as a Bandsman on the clarinet. The Bandmaster replied that he didn't need any clarinets. Undeterred, Tom asked what he did need. The Bandmaster said he could use a couple of oboe players. Tom said that he could learn to play the oboe but the Bandmaster dismissed that idea. He didn't have the time or resources to teach Tom the oboe. Tom told the Bandmaster that he could teach himself to play the oboe if the Bandmaster would lend him an instrument. The Bandmaster was skeptical but gave Tom an oboe and three months to learn to play it. Tom would have to demonstrate his proficiency within three months. Three months later, Tom passed his oboe audition and joined the 1st Battalion Band. He served the rest of his time in the Army as a Bandsman, a life separate from and in most ways better than the life of a common soldier of the "Lower Ranks," as enlisted men were called.

Tom came to have great respect and even affection for his Bandmaster. A picture of him hangs on the wall of our house that was once Tom's house. It shows a solid, chunky bearded man in full Scottish Highland regalia carrying a silver-headed four foot baton at a jaunty angle. He is wearing the Stewart Tartan kilts of the Kings Own Scottish Borderers Regiment, a sporran, a grand wide sash across his formidable torso, buckle shoes and knee-high socks. His picture suggests that he was a man of considerable character and importance.

The 1st Battalion was ordered to leave the British Isles again. It was to serve out the remainder of its tour in India that had been interrupted by the war. Tom went with the Regiment to Bombay, a major seaport on the west coast of the sub-continent. From there, he and the 1st Battalion travelled to Agra, in the northern state of Uttar Pradesh, about 125 miles southwest of New Delhi. The Battalion spent all of 1920 and most of 1921 there.

Agra, the 19th largest city in India was – and is – a major foreign tourist destination due to the nearby location of the Taj Mahal. Like Ireland, India in the early 20th Century chaffed under British occupation and clamored for home rule and independence. Like Ireland, it was ripe for civil unrest and revolution. The 1919 Rowlatt Act of Parliament was a response to what was considered seditious help Indians had given to the Germans during World War I. It allowed the British Army to imprison anyone in India without trial or conviction. This law led to widespread civil unrest and massive protests. In the Punjab, British troops fired on unarmed civilians in what was called the Jalianwala Bagh massacre, causing a nationwide uproar. The massacre led to Ghandi's Non-Cooperative Civil Disobedience Movement which began in 1920 and ultimately ended in Indian independence three decades later. The 1st Battalion's primary objectives in Agra would undoubtedly have been to keep the peace and protect British interests and foreign tourists from Indian insurrection.

While in India, Tom met – quite unexpectedly – his older brother William whom he had not seen since William left the orphanage in 1908, twelve years earlier. When Tom first entered the Army, he had requested information about his brother's whereabouts but had been unsuccessful in locating him. William, it appears, had been in the 1st Battalion KOSB for some time – probably since he joined the Army - but the 1st and 2nd Battalions never served together in the same place. It wasn't until Tom was reassigned to the 1st Battalion that they finally met.

Tom said very little about the one meeting he had with William, except to indicate that the meeting did not go well. William had changed. "He wasn't the same brother I knew before," Tom said. His tone suggested that Tom was sorely disappointed with the meeting. Tom and his brother did not establish a relationship and, after their meeting, William disappeared and was not heard from again.

In late 1921, Tom and the 1st Battalion was sent to Egypt to protect the strategically important Suez Canal. Egypt had become a British Protectorate at the beginning of the war. Like Ireland and India, it had become a hot spot of nationalism with crowds of Egyptians thirsting for independence, a threat not only to British rule but also to the Canal.

Within a year, the fight between Greece and Turkey called for Tom's unit to redeploy once more, this time to Turkey. Greece had been promised Turkish territory for their help in defeating the Germans and Turkey wanted it back. At the same time, nationalistic Turks were rebelling against the Ottoman Empire in a quest for Turkish independence. The KOSB was sent to Constantinople to, once again, protect British interests.

In 1923, 1st Battalion, Kings Own Scottish Borderers was finally ordered home. Tom and his unit arrived in the port of Gravesend, England in 1923, at which time they returned to Regimental Headquarters in Berwick-Upon-Tweed.

Having entered the Army on October 23, 1910, Tom should have completed his 12 year enlistment period on October 23, 1922. However, he was, at that time, posted overseas and the law allowed the Army to retain soldiers until one day before the 13th anniversary of their conscription. Tom received his discharge papers at Berwick-Upon-Tweed on October 8, 1923, twelve years, 350 days after he entered the Army. In a week he would be 27 years old.

Tom, now a civilian, was free for the first time to choose the course his life would take. He went immediately to London in the hope and expectation that his training in the Royal School of Music and the certificate it conferred on him would lead to a livelihood as a professional musician. His search for employment began on a promising note. On November 15, 1923, just five weeks out of the Army, he received his membership card for the London Orchestra Association followed very shortly by membership in the London Branch of the Musicians' Union. Tom bought an oboe and a tuxedo, both of which were necessary items for orchestra work. Tom said he played in the London Symphony as a "fill-in." It seems likely that he played in theater and other orchestras as well. However, the demobilization would have brought back many of the musicians that had earlier been sent to France and Tom was unable to secure a permanent position in a London orchestra.

The British Army in those days provided no pension for soldiers of the "Lower Ranks" who had been discharged and no social services network for the poor existed in Britain. Consequently, death on the streets from exposure and starvation was not uncommon among British veterans in the early 20th Century. Tom indicated that he was keenly aware of this danger. Always careful to save every penny he could, Tom would have had some savings to draw on when he left Berwick, but those savings could not have lasted very long in London.

In 1924, Tom decided to emigrate to Canada. I asked Tom one day why he chose to immigrate to Canada. (I thought it strange that he didn't come straight to the US, but didn't say so.) Tom looked at me in surprise. "Why," he said, "there are only two English-speaking countries in the Commonwealth, you know; Australia and Canada. I flipped a coin and it came up Canada. I certainly wouldn't have wanted to go to India or one of those other places." Tom's answer surprised me; it reminded me that he had been born and raised an Englishman and that it would not have occurred to him to immigrate to a country outside of the Commonwealth of Great Britain.

I never got the sense that Tom was sorry to leave England. It had, after all, not been particularly kind to him. In any event, his emigration was made necessary by lack of work and made easier by British Government incentives. Britain, at the time, was trying to deal with a shattered economy that needed to absorb two million demobilized men. Many more men were seeking jobs than there were jobs to be had. Commonwealth countries across the far-flung British Empire, on the other hand, were desperate for men, especially Englishmen, to populate and develop their large, essentially empty spaces. In a rare stroke of common sense, the British Government offered 50 pounds Sterling and free passage to any man willing to immigrate to another Commonwealth nation.

Tom arrived with thousands of other immigrants in Montreal. He hoped to find work as a musician in one of the larger Canadian cities in the east, but was unsuccessful. With savings running out, Tom set his sights on the West, where he'd heard there were jobs to be had. He packed up his oboe and tuxedo, went to the railway station in Toronto and told the stationmaster that he wanted to go as far as his money would take him. That turned out to be Moose Jaw, Saskatchewan. Nearly out of resources and no orchestra within 500 miles or more, Tom sought any work he could get. He was hired in late 1924 by a sheep rancher in southwestern Saskatchewan where he worked during the winter for meager pay. In the spring of 1925, Tom heard that sheep ranches in Montana paid better wages and he headed south. Tom crossed the border near the little town of Chinook, entering the United States for the first time in April, 1925.

He was hired by a rancher who owned a sheep ranch in the Sweet Grass Hills south of Chinook. There he met Billy Kruse. "Bill and I were both Old Country, you know," Tom said. "But I was an Englishman and he was a Dane." The two "Old Country" sheep herders hit it off.

Two months after they met, however, a Federal Marshall showed up at the sheep ranch and arrested Tom for illegal entry into the United States. In June 1925, he was taken to Havre and jailed. With the help of Billy Kruse, Tom posted bond. "It was $610," Tom said, "ten dollars for the fellow putting up the money, I suppose." It appears that Billy's role in springing Tom was locating a bondsman, someone whose services Billy may well have used before. Billy Kruse was, by all accounts, a hell-raiser, especially when he had too much liquor on board.

Once out of jail, Tom returned to the ranch where he was employed and worked there until his court date in Havre, two months later. In those proceedings, Tom was found guilty and deported back to Canada. "They asked me where I wanted to go," Tom said. "Well, I'd had enough of Saskatchewan, so I thought I'd try Alberta." On the way, the Marshall who was conducting him out of the country, told Tom that if he wanted to come into the US legally, he should report to a US consulate in Canada and apply for legal immigration.

When he arrived in Calgary he sought out the U. S. consulate. "I got an appointment with the Consul and told him I wanted to immigrate legally," Tom said. "He gave me a form to fill out and when I gave it back to him, he didn't look at it, just shoved it in his desk drawer without so much as a word. Well, I thought that was the end of it. I didn't expect I'd ever hear from him. But a year later I received a letter informing me that my quota had come up and that I had been granted permission to enter the United States. There was a quota for immigrants in those days, you know." Tom smiled and shook his head. "I was surprised that I ever heard from that fellow."

Tom said that after visiting the consulate that first time, "I got out of Calgary as quick as I could. I had $400 in savings and if I'd stayed there, I would have spent my savings in short order." Tom found work on a farm east of Calgary and was paid $15 a month.

In the summer of 1926, Tom returned to his old job on the Montana sheep ranch and resumed his friendship with Billy Kruse. "Billy was my pal," Tom said. "He was my sponsor to get into the country legally. You needed a sponsor in those days who would be responsible for you."

Tom and Billy worked on the sheep ranch south of Chinook for the following two years but, in the summer of 1928, the owner of the ranch told Tom and Billy that he could not keep them on. One of the periodic droughts that parched Montana was causing one ranch after another to fail. Owners were packing up what they had and leaving Montana. There's a well- known story about families on the Highline leaving for California in their Model T's; signs on the back of some cars read "Havre, Montana – You Can Have Her."

Billy Kruse had bought property in northwest Montana some years before and invited Tom to go with him to the North Fork. Tom said, "The Depression was settling in, you know, and we figured we could ride it out at Billy's place. We thought there would be plenty of game in the North Fork." Then he grinned and said, "Of course we were wrong."

Tom arrived in the North Fork for the first time in October, 1928. Sixty years later, Bob Barkley of Columbia Falls said, "I first met Tom in November of 1928, about the same month he got there with Bill Kruse. I was nine years old at the time. As a boy, I liked to visit Bill's place because he let me ride his horse. It was a big treat. But I could never figure the friendship between Tom and Bill – they were so very different. Bill was a happy-go-lucky fellow with a 'don't give a shit' attitude, a real bounder, very outgoing. Bill loved a good time. He was a real nice guy. Tom, on the other hand, was a hermit, a recluse, very reserved, very serious." Whatever the reason for the friendship between these two very different men, it was real.

Pictures show that Bill Kruse was a robust man of medium height. He often wore a white ten-gallon hat with a fancy rolled brim. A number of photos show Billy striking heroic poses with his chest puffed out, a bottle of liquor in his hand. One picture shows Tom and Billy standing outside Billy's cabin toasting one another, a collection of rifles leaning against the wall. Billy has a grand smile on his face while Tom's expression is sober. When Tom and Billy were wintering in Billy's cabin one year, a pack rat found its way inside. Billy was enjoying a drink when he saw that packrat running across a log. Billy grabbed his six-shooter and, in the confines of the cabin, began blasting away. Tom said he didn't hit the pack rat but he did put a bullet into the front of his Victrola. Billy's record player with the bullet hole in it is now in the possession of Larry Wilson.

If game was scarce on the North Fork, work was even more so. One reason Billy may have invited Tom to winter with him at his cabin in 1928 was the likelihood that Tom had several hundred dollars in savings stashed away. In any event, they got by in the North Fork wilderness on what they had until Billy could get hired on with the Forest Service.

In 1930, Billy got Tom hired, too. "There were two small crews – two man crews – working up on (Mount) Hefty," Tom said. "I was hired as the cook for these crews. Billy's job was to go up to Hefty each night and bring the men down for supper. One day Billy was up on the mountain, about to bring these men down and he spotted a doe." Tom said. "Well, he shot it. That was in June." Tom looked around and grinned. "Out of season," I observed.

Tom nodded, still grinning. "Yes. Well, Billy skinned it out and brought the carcass down. He cut off a hind quarter and gave it to Clyde, the postmaster. Clyde took it home and was cutting a nice steak off that hind quarter when the ranger came in. He looked at that hind quarter and said, 'Nice steak you've got there, Clyde. Where'd you get it?' 'Why, Bill Kruse gave it to me,' Clyde said." Tom laughed. "Billy was in trouble!" Tom's modest job as a cook for four men was the beginning of 30 years of seasonal employment with the Forest Service, ending only in 1961 when Tom "retired" at age 65.

Sometime around 1930, Tom bought 80 acres of land with a tiny cabin on it near Trail Creek. "The County had all these pieces of land that they took over because of delinquent taxes," Tom said. "Up here in the North Fork, they wanted a dollar an acre. I bought the 80 acres I later sold to Larry Wilson for 80 dollars." Tom moved out of Billy's place north of Trail Creek Road into the tiny cabin the original settler had built, leaving Billy to his own devices.

"Billy saw an advertisement in Heart & Hands Magazine," Tom said. "Well, this woman in New York had her picture in the magazine and said she was looking for employment. She was quite a looker and knew how to dress. So Billy wrote to her. He said he wanted a housekeeper. I don't think he wanted a housekeeper," Tom said, looking around at us with a grin. "I think he wanted a bed partner. Her name was Mary Powell but we all called her Madam Queen. I don't know what Billy wanted with a woman like that. Her husband had kicked her out for tomcatting around. When she got here, she had her nine year old daughter with her. Billy didn't know a thing about that when he brought her out. We called her daughter the Piss Ant. Well, they moved in with Billy to spend the winter, but I think she made Billy's life pretty bad. She was always nagging him to buy this or buy that and she wasn't too careful who she took up with. Usually it was whoever had the most money."

In the spring of 1931, Billy decided to return to the sheep ranch where he and Tom had worked. He planned to spend the summer and fall sheepherding, then return to the North Fork. He asked a neighbor, Ed Peterson who owned a homestead near Mud Lake, to look after Mary Powell while he was gone. Ed was happy to oblige. He sold 5 acres of his homestead to her, including a two story log house he'd built.

Billy didn't return until March, 1932 and when he did, he was furious to discover that Madam Queen had spent the winter with Ed Peterson. Kruse apparently went looking for Madam Queen at her place on Mud Lake but she was not there. She'd heard Billy was back, mad as hell and had fled to Ed's. When he arrived at Peterson's Kruse was liquored up as was often the case and there was an argument. Billy threatened to burn Powell's house down. The next morning, Ed Peterson took his rifle and went to Powell's house to see if Kruse had burned it. The house was still standing. When Kruse realized Peterson was outside, he left the house and confronted Peterson with a gun. Peterson shot Kruse with his rifle. Kruse staggered back inside Powell's house and died three days later from loss of blood. That's one version of the story.

The story printed in the newspaper indicated that the Flathead County Sheriff had been called to a cabin on the North Fork by locals who reported that Bill Kruse had been shot by a man named Ed Peterson. The Sheriff's investigation confirmed that Kruse had been shot and bled to death. Peterson claimed he had quarreled with Kruse over a woman and when he went to the woman's cabin to talk it over, Kruse pulled a gun on him. Peterson claimed he shot him in self defense. Neighbors indicated that Kruse was a "hot head" and probably had it coming. There were no witnesses to the shooting and the Sheriff concluded he would have to take Peterson at his word. The killing of Billy Kruse was listed as self defense and Ed Peterson was never charged.

Tom tells a different story. "After Billy brought Madam Queen out from New York, she took up with a fellow by the name of Ed Peterson. Peterson sold her five acres down there on Mud Lake and built her a cabin near his place," Tom said. "Billy was pretty mad about that. One night Billy went looking for Madam Queen. She left her cabin and went to Ed's because she thought Billy was going to beat her up. Billy stayed in her cabin, expecting her to come back. Well, that night she talked Ed into shooting Billy. Next morning, Ed went to Madam Queen's cabin where Billy was spending the night and knocked on the door. There was a pile of wood to the right of the door. Ed hid behind that pile of wood. Billy came to the door to see who was there and when he didn't see anybody, he went out around that woodpile and that's when Ed shot him. The bullet went in his left side by a lower rib and went up through his body and out through an upper rib on the right side. It went into Billy's arm and tore out a big chunk of flesh. Billy went back into the cabin and Ed took another shot at him through a window, but he missed. I found the slug in the wall myself. Well, Billy was bleeding pretty badly. Ed went away and told some local people that he'd shot Billy but that he wasn't dead. The locals wouldn't turn a hand to help Billy. They just let him lie there three days while he bled to death. Then they called the Sheriff. Peterson claimed he shot Billy in self defense but that was a lie. It was a foul murder." Tom could never tell this story without getting tears in his eyes.

"What happened to Madam Queen?" I asked.

"Oh, she went from one fellow to another," Tom replied. "She moved in with two brothers down near Polebridge." Tom grinned. "I don't know what went on in that cabin, but I can guess."

"You were never tempted to get together with Madam Queen, were you?" I asked.

"No," Tom laughed, "but she tried to put me together with her daughter when she was 16. She had a baby and gave it away. I wanted no part of that. One day I was walking down the road and a fellow with a wagon came along. I asked him if I could get a ride and he said 'sure, jump on up.' But then the Piss Ant jumped up on the seat next to the driver. I decided I wasn't going to get mixed up in any of that, and I walked along behind the wagon until the Piss Ant got off by Madam Queen's cabin. Then I got up in the seat by the driver. The last time I saw Madam Queen, she'd moved down country. I remember the Piss Ant had a drink in her hand

and I think she was trying to get some fellow to spend the night with her. I never saw them again."

The crash of 1929 and resulting Great Depression saw the election of Franklin Roosevelt in 1932. Thirty seven days after his inauguration in January 1933, he created the Civilian Conservation Corps to give employment to hundreds of thousands of men out of work. A large part of the CCC was administered by the U.S. Forest Service, planting millions of trees to reclaim land lost to the "dust bowl", constructing buildings and trails in National Forests and creating other new infrastructure.

To get work during the winter when there was no logging on the North Fork, Tom signed onto the CCC. In January of 1934, he was sent to California along with several thousand other Montanans. "You know," Tom said, "the government brought thousands of men from back East to work in Glacier Park. I never understood why they sent us fellows to California when we were right here." He worked in Inyo National Forest and Sequoia National Park in southeast California, around Mt. Whitney, the highest peak in the lower 48 states.

In 1931, before Tom left for California, Billy told him about a piece of property about five miles north of Tom's place that was for sale. It was a quarter section, 160 acres homesteaded by a man named Bill McAfee. Bob Barkley said, "McAfee was a ranger in Glacier Park, a real nice guy. He'd fought in World War I and was probably shell-shocked because he was always very nervous, his hands and arms shook all the time. In January 1926, McAfee was stationed in the Kishenehn Cabin in the Park, not far from the North Fork River, just across from Trail Creek. McAfee received a 'Dear John' letter from his sweetheart back in Texas where he was from, breaking off their engagement. McAfee called Park headquarters. In those days, telephone lines were run to all the back-country ranger cabins. He asked for leave so he could go back to Texas to work things out with this woman. His supervisor told him he couldn't go, they couldn't spare him. The next sound the supervisor heard over the phone was a gun shot. McAfee blew his brains out with a shotgun."

Bill McAfee's North Fork property went to his father in Abilene, Texas, who then put it up for sale. After Billy told him about it, Tom looked the property over and decided he'd write to McAfee's father and find out how much he wanted for it. McAfee wrote back, asking $100 for the 160 acres. Tom, ever the careful, thorough man, went down to the County court house in Kalispell to look over the deed. He discovered that two years back taxes were owing on the property, "ten dollars and something one year and twelve dollars and something the second." Tom offered McAfee $75 for the property and said he would pay the $23 in back taxes himself. McAfee insisted on $100 and, in January 1934, on his way to California, Tom bought the property. At sixty cents an acre, he knew it was a good deal.

Tom's plan when he returned from California was to move up to McAfee's cabin on the property he'd just bought. It was bigger than his. "Before I could move in, I had to do something to get the smell out of that stinking cabin," Tom said. "It hadn't been lived in since 1926 when McAfee killed himself and the mice and packrats had been making a home in it ever since. Well, I cleaned it out all right, but before I could move in, that packrat kept coming back and making a mess. I tried to shoot him but he was always too fast for me. I finally trapped him in his nest with a net. Then I beat the hell out of him. There wasn't much left of that packrat when I got through with him."

The North Fork, in those days, was a place with some pretty rough characters. Tom tells the story of Peg Leg and Alice. "Peg Leg and his woman weren't North Fork settlers, they were just drifters. They parked themselves in an empty cabin north of Trail Creek. One day Peg Leg was taking a Model T he'd borrowed back to his neighbor's and was mad about it. I met him on his way back. He said his neighbor wasn't home when he returned the Model T but there was beer percolating away in a crock inside the cabin. 'Well,' Peg Leg said, 'I pissed in that crock of beer. Don't tell them I pissed in it.' I didn't tell them," Tom said. "I was afraid to. I sat there and watched them enjoy that beer that Peg Leg had pissed in, but I didn't have any."

Peg Leg and Alice moved out of that cabin and into a vacant cabin on Trail Creek Road. Tom and his friend Shorty Waters went to visit them one afternoon. Shorty knocked on the door and when no one came, he opened it and they went inside. They saw Peg Leg lying on a bed in the bedroom, dead to the world, an empty jug of moonshine on the floor. He was wearing only an undershirt pulled up around his chest. Alice was on the bed with him with nothing on. Alice woke up and saw the two men. She took Peg Leg's limp penis in her hand and waggled it back and forth. "What do you think of this?" she asked. Alice got up and asked if they wanted coffee. Then she went to put wood in the stove, her backside to Tom and Shorty. "What the hell is that?" Shorty asked. "Oh," Alice replied, "you mean my ass?" Her buttocks were horribly disfigured by massive scar tissue. "Yes," Shorty said, "what happened to you?" "When I was a little girl, someone sat me on a red-hot stove," Alice replied. Tom said he didn't stay for coffee.

Some years later, Peg Leg pulled an armed robbery down near Bad Rock in the Flathead Valley and was sentenced to thirty years in the Montana State Penitentiary at Deer Lodge.

"The last time I saw Alice," Tom said, "was down near Polebridge. She was staying at a house someone owned and a fire broke out. The Forest Service went down to try to put it out and while we were standing there watching, the supervisor asked one of the men if he thought they would be able to get any money out of Alice to pay for fighting the fire. 'I doubt it,' the man replied. 'You might be able to take it out in trade.' 'What do you mean?' the supervisor asked. 'Oh, she's a madam, you know,' the fellow replied. After that, I never saw Alice again."

According to Tom, Shorty Waters and his wife Belle weren't the best neighbors either. A homestead about two miles south of Tom's place was owned by the Sheibs. "It was a nice cabin built out of large larch logs," Tom said. "Inside was a kitchen cabinet with drawers. Belle Waters took a fancy to that cabinet and over the winter nagged Shorty until he finally broke into that cabin and took the cabinet. I was walking down to the post office on Trail

Creek one day," Tom said, "when I came on Shorty and Belle in their Model T. Well, they had this cabinet in the back of the Model T. That cabinet was about six feet long and stuck out the back of their car. Shorty was sitting on it to keep it overbalanced so it wouldn't fall out. They asked me if I'd help them move that cabinet into their cabin. I told them I would. I didn't think a thing about it. I didn't realize I was becoming an accomplice. About six months later, I was coming down the road again and I thought I smelled smoke. Sure enough, there was smoke coming up through the trees about where the Sheib cabin sat. I went over to Shorty's place and said, 'I guess you touched off that cabin, didn't you Shorty?' Shorty said, 'Yes, I did. I'll show you how I did it.' Shorty said he'd trailed kerosene from one corner of that cabin to the other and touched it off. The owners lived in Whitefish and came up quite often during the summers. They usually had a lot of cars around their place so I guess they must have brought all their friends and relatives. Well, Shorty committed a crime, but it was a good thing that cabin went up in smoke. The cabin owners would put out salt to lure the deer in and when one came by to take a lick, they'd shoot it and can it and take the meat back to their family." Tom shook his head. "Bad business," he said.

Tom said that two years after Billy's death, he met Ed Peterson on the Road. Ed stopped him and asked to borrow $40. I was surprised. Tom hated the man who had killed his dear friend. "You didn't give him the money, did you?" I asked.

"Yes," Tom replied, "I loaned him $40."

"Why would you do that?" I asked.

"Well, he needed the money," Tom said. Tom's reply was a window into the close-knit, interdependent relationship that existed among the few people who populated the remote North Fork wilderness, a relationship that continues to this day among those hardy souls who live there.

Two years went by and Ed wasn't able to scrape together $40 to repay Tom. "Ed was logging at the time," Tom said, "and he asked me if I would settle up with him for a load of logs. I had been thinking about building me a proper house so I could get out of the settler's cabin. I told Ed that if he would bring the logs up to the bench where I'd thought to build my house, that would settle the account. That's what I built my house out of, $40 dollars worth of Ed Peterson's logs."

Some time around 1940, Tom bought his first car. Knowing Tom, he would have saved enough to buy the car with cash and still have money in the bank. The vehicle he bought was a 1928 Chevrolet pickup. Cars didn't last very long in those days, particularly given the rough Montana roads they drove over and long, snowy winters. We can assume, therefore, that Tom didn't pay much for this vehicle and that it was worth what he paid for it. The story he told of the time he purchased it is worth repeating. "I didn't know how to drive a car when I bought it," Tom said. "So the fellow who sold it to me showed me how to drive it. After about ten minutes of instruction, I set off for the North Fork. I got along alright until I came to a large tree that had fallen in the road. At that time, the North Fork Road was nothing more than two bare tracks with grass growing in the center, just wide enough for one car to pass between the trees. Well, I stopped and looked at that tree. I figured I could jump it if I got the car going fast enough. The front tires made it over alright, but the car high-centered on the trunk and got stuck. It took me two days working with an ax to chop that tree into pieces small enough for me to get it out from under."

Tom was, by nature, a generous person if it didn't cost him money. He allowed "the boys" working for the Forest Service at Ford Station to borrow his Chevy from time to time for their own use, but mostly Tom used it to get back and forth from his cabin to Ford. Tom was coming back to Ford Station late one evening in the pickup after having a few drinks. He missed the corner going into Ford and ran off the road. For some reason, nobody could get that Chevy to run again and Tom had it towed to Ralph Thayer's place on Trail Creek where it sat for several years. Finally Tom towed it back to his place where he dismantled it, throwing most of the cadaver in the weeds.

Tom was frugal. He straightened bent nails and saved them. He took worn-out machines apart to find out how they worked so he would know how to fix things and saved the parts, just in case.. So naturally, Tom never bought a new car or truck. Probably his best vehicle was a used 1948 Dodge truck that he bought when the Chevy gave out. He ran it until sometime in the late 60's when the engine began making terrible sounds and finally stopped running. Tom parked it next to his outhouse and let the weeds grow up around it. Years later, my uncle removed that truck with the intent of restoring it. To our surprise, three tires still held air. Mechanics doing the restoration cleaned out the gas tank, put in fresh gas, hooked up a battery and cranked it over. Despite having sat idle for at least 20 years, the engine fired up. It had a broken valve and made a terrible noise, but it ran. I'm surprised Tom didn't try to fix it.

Tom's last vehicle was an orange-red 1964 GMC pickup. He must have bought it cheap because the previous owner had rolled it. One side was smashed in and the whole truck leaned. When we knew Tom, he employed an unusual technique in starting that GMC. He'd raise the hood, take a whisky bottle with a cork in it that he kept nearby, pull out the cork and pour gasoline directly into the carburetor. Most times it started. That's when things got scary. The steering had six inches of play in it and the brakes hardly worked at all. The one time I rode in the truck, Tom was driving a load of firewood down the steep hill that led from his house. I was sitting on top of the wood in the back. As Tom raced down the hill pell-mell, sawing the wheel back and forth, attempting to keep the wheels in the slippery ruts, I was sure I was going to die. Somehow he avoided crashing into the ravine next to the road, but I never rode down that hill with him in the GMC again.

Dan Block, of Dillon, Montana, worked with Tom in the Forest Service. Tom was Dan's first partner. "I came up here in 1946 as a newlywed," Dan said. "My wife Jermayne was only 17 and a city girl. She was a little apprehensive. She was welcomed warmly by North Fork people, including Tom. Tom and I were supposed to share a tent in the tent camp but seeing that we were newlyweds, Tom gave the tent to us and he slept outside on the ground. He was always very considerate like that.

"When I first worked with Tom, he was an old guy, about 45 (he was 50) but when we were sawing timber on a cross-cut saw – him on one end and me on the other - Tom never asked for a break. I was 25 years younger than he was and I was embarrassed to ask for a break, so we worked all morning without stopping.

"One night my wife brought a cake up to Tom and me where we were working in the forest. She put it in a saddlebag on her horse. In those days, we didn't walk horses like they do today and she galloped most of the way up the mountain. When she got there, that twelve inch cake was squashed down to about three inches. We ate it anyway and it tasted pretty good.

"One other time she came up and tied her horse to an old broken-down hitch rail and the horse ran off. She was left with us, about eighteen miles from home and it was getting dark. She didn't want to stay the night in a tent camp with a new husband and an old bachelor. Tom said he'd drive her back in a Model T but it didn't have any lights, so he could only go part way before it got pitch black. Then she'd have to walk. Luckily, her parents saw the horse she'd been riding back in their corral and came looking for her."

One year Tom was working at the Big Creek Forest Service headquarters when he was sent to supervise two men who were to renovate a cabin on skids that was moved from location to location to house men working up in the mountains. It was winter and when Tom's crew got there, they couldn't get into the cabin because deep snow had pushed down the eaves, blocking the door. To make matters worse, a bear had broken out a window. Tom sent the men up on the roof to shovel off the snow while he put in a new window. Before they went to bed that night, the bear came back and pushed against the new window, putting muddy paw marks all over it. Tom said, "We've got to shoot that bear before he breaks out the window again." Tom took a large bone with a piece of meat on it and wired it to a rock near the cabin. Then he ran a wire from the bone into the skid cabin and attached it to the dishpan that he'd filled full of tin cans. He set the dishpan on the table. "The bear will try to take that bone in the night," Tom said, "and when he does, he'll pull the dishpan on the floor and wake us up." Sure enough, not long after the men went to bed, the dishpan went on the floor with a crash and clatter of tin cans. Tom jumped up and told one of the men to get his six-shooter. "I think it was a .38," Tom said. He opened the door and there was that bear trying to carry the bone away. When Tom flashed the light on him, he stood up and looked at them. He had a big white spot on his chest. "Go ahead and shoot," Tom said. The other fellow took aim and pulled the trigger. He missed and the bear ran off. Tom put the dishpan and tin cans back on the table and the men went to bed again. Pretty soon the dishpan and tin cans crashed to the floor. Tom grabbed his flashlight, shined it on the bear, the bear stood up and the fellow with the gun pulled the trigger. He missed again and the bear ran off. Once more the same routine was repeated with the same results. The next time the bear pulled the dishpan on the floor, Tom said, "You take the flashlight. I think I may be a better shot." The man gave Tom his revolver, Tom took careful aim and pulled the trigger. He missed and the bear ran off again. "I think your six-shooter shoots high," Tom said. "About this time we were all pretty tired because we hadn't gotten any sleep. The bear came back again to get his bone, pulled the dishpan on the floor, I shined the light on the bear and said, 'Now this time, take a fine aim on that bear and don't miss.' The fellow took a fine aim, pulled the trigger and down went the bear. 'About time,' I said, and went back to bed."

One time I asked Tom if his life had ever been threatened by a bear. "No," he said, "I was never threatened. But I didn't like bears. When black bears would come around the house, I'd gut shoot them and they'd run away to die somewhere." Why did you do that?" I asked. "Why didn't you just kill them with your hunting rifle?" Tom smiled. "Have you ever tried to dig a hole big enough to bury a bear?" he asked.

Bears did, occasionally, cause Tom trouble. One caused a lot of trouble during the time he was finishing his house. "I had bought a can of white shellac," Tom said, "and I had been working all day shellacking the logs in my living room so they would look nice. Well, I got tired sometime around supper time and I thought to get me some supper. I had just one top log left to do and I figured I could do that in the morning. So I put the lid on that can of shellac but I didn't put it on tight. In the middle of the night I heard a crash, bang. I figured it was a bear so I got out of bed and got my flashlight. Sure enough, a bear had broken into my kitchen through the back door. Well, I grabbed a broom and was going to chase that bear out but when I ran into the kitchen, I slipped and fell flat on my back. That bear had tipped over the can of shellac and it was all over the floor. The bear ran like hell but I spent the rest of the night trying to clean up that shellac. The shellac was all gone and I decided, the hell with it. I'll be damned if I'm buying any more shellac for that one log." The top log in our house – Tom's living room – remains unvarnished to this day.

Years later – in the late 1980's – another bear tried to break into his house. It was called the Geifer Bear because it first started causing trouble by breaking into cabins near Geifer Creek, down near the Middle Fork of the Flathead River. It came up the North Fork and famously broke into a reported 100 cabins. It apparently opened kitchen cabinets and ate everything it could find, but did little other damage. The Geifer Bear was hunted for several years without success. The old bear was cagey. "The Geifer Bear came up to my place a couple of times and put his muddy paws on the shutters I had on my windows, trying to get in," Tom reported. "So I went down and called this bear expert – Jonkel was his name. Doctor Jonkel came up to my place with his tape measure. He measured here and there and here and there." Tom grinned. "He never found that bear." The Geifer Bear was shot and killed a year later up in Canada.

Being hard of hearing, Tom worried about not being able to hear a bear should it attempt to break into his house during the night. To preclude that possibility, he constructed an alarm system that would go off if a bear entered his front porch and was about to break into his house. He piled empty two-gallon white gas cans high in front of his front door. If a bear tried to break in, it would knock down the cans and the noise would, Tom figured, wake him up!

At the age of 52, Tom did something quite unusual. In 1949, he went to Flathead County Court House and petitioned the court to change his legal name from Thomas Warburton Reynolds to Thomas Box Reynolds. This would not have been easy for him to do. It would have required multiple 180 mile round trips to town, probably involved an attorney and would have required his appearance before the court. I asked Tom why, in late middle age, he changed his name. He said only, "Box was my father's name. I wanted to take his name." I thought there was more to the story, but Tom was not forthcoming.

Tom had somehow located his sister Kathleen from whom he'd been separated since the age of six. They began a correspondence that lasted a number of years. Changing his middle name would have had no significance for anyone outside Tom's immediate family, so it is logical to think that the name change had something to do with Kathleen. The Warburton name is associated with a senior British Army officer who served in the mid-19th Century in India. It may be that Warburton came from Ada's side of the family. Lacking another explanation, it seems likely that, in changing his name, Tom meant to underscore his utter disdain for his mother Ada, the woman who put him in the orphanage, and register his love for his father.

Just before turning sixty years old, Tom did something even more unusual. In 1953, he travelled from the North Fork to Australia. In the four decades since they'd seen one another, Kathleen, had gone to Australia, married and raised a family. Tom had longed to be reunited with his lost family and he apparently decided to satisfy this longing by seeing Kathleen before age overtook him.

This could not have been an easy decision either. The trip to Australia would have been Tom's first time on an airplane. Only eight years after the end of World War II, trans-Pacific airline travel was anything but routine. The jet era had yet to arrive and long-distance overwater flights were made on slow, noisy four-engine piston aircraft. And not to be overlooked, this long trip would have been expensive. Never-the- less, the motivation to reunite with Kathleen was strong enough for Tom to buy a ticket and head for the airport.

He was reluctant to talk about his experience in Australia except to say that it didn't go well. He returned home early and vowed never to correspond with Kathleen again. For her part, she forbade her three children to be in contact with Tom. Clearly, Tom's hopes for reunion with his long-lost relatives were not realized. One nephew, Eric Pratt, did correspond with Tom despite his mother's injunction. However, much to Tom's disappointment, Pratt never paid a visit to him, even though he promised to do so and travelled to the United States several times.

From the few things Tom said and knowing his hatred for Ada, it seems likely that the blow-up had something to do with her. Tom said that Kathleen loved his mother deeply. I'm guessing that Kathleen brought Ada, in her declining years, to live with her in Australia. Tom would not have known that when he departed the North Fork. If he had, he would not have made the trip. Had Tom discovered his mother living with Kathleen when he arrived in Australia, he would have been furious with Kathleen for bringing Ada to live with her and for deceiving him. But this is conjecture. I cannot say with any certainty what caused the blow-up between Tom and his sister.

In 1954, Larry Wilson, a 16 year-old boy, approached Tom and asked him if he'd sell ten acres of the 80 Tom first bought. Larry's dad, Ross, had recently sold Kintla Ranch, a nearby dude ranch on the banks of the North Fork River that he'd operated since buying it in 1947. Larry liked working there and he enjoyed getting to know the guests, some of whom became life-long friends. Young Wilson was determined to stay in the North Fork, one way or another. Though he didn't know Tom well, Larry liked Tom's property because it was located near Kintla Ranch. Tom agreed to sell the boy 10 acres at $10 an acre and said he'd throw in an old Model T pickup if Larry would come up to his house and take a spare Model T engine he had off his hands. When Larry got to

Tom's house, he found the old engine sitting on a table in Tom's living room. Tom insisted that the sale of his land be done right. He met Larry at the offices of D. Gordon Rangelin, a distinguished attorney in Kalispell, and the deal was done. Larry became the owner of ten acres and a Model T pickup for $100, which he paid in cash. Later that year, Larry sold the pickup for $150, which paid for the ten acres and turned a $50 profit.

Several years later, Larry bought the remaining 70 acres, but the price had gone up; Tom wanted $50 an acre, $52 after legal expenses. As part of the deal, Tom reserved the right to cut firewood on Larry's property for five years. That was fine with Larry because much of the timber consisted of dead lodgepole pine which needed to be cut anyway. At the end of five years, Larry told Tom that he was welcome to continue cutting wood on his property, but Tom shook his head. "No, that wasn't the deal," he said. Larry knew that Tom had bought a 10-speed bicycle some time before, thinking he could ride the bike up his steep hill. He couldn't, so the bike sat unused. Larry offered to trade Tom one year of firewood cutting for that 10-speed. Tom accepted. For several years, Larry found something to trade so that Tom would feel justified in continuing to cut firewood on his property.

One day in 1958, Tom was cutting wood on that 70 acres when a station wagon pulling a travel trailer came up the road. Baird and Esther Chrisman from southern Illinois had bought the nearby Monahan homestead. They had their 3 kids and two dogs in the station wagon with them. When they saw Tom, they stopped and introduced themselves and told him they'd be staying in the trailer since the property had only the small cabin Monahan had built. They invited Tom to come down for coffee in the morning and told him they'd be going to town. Tom asked if he could ride along. He wanted to get his driver's license renewed. Baird said to come down around eight o'clock. Tom showed up a little before seven and when he didn't see anyone, sat down to wait. A half hour went by and when no one came out of the trailer, he went up and pounded on the door. Esther, wrapped in a bathrobe, opened the door and wondered what was going on. "I thought maybe

197

someone was sick in there," Tom said. "It's going on seven thirty, you know."

They had quite a car-full on the trip to town, with Baird, Esther, three kids, two dogs and Tom, who they'd just met, telling North Fork stories all the way down. "What will you do with the children this winter?" Tom asked. "There's no school up here, you know." "Oh, we'll be returning to Illinois before fall," Esther said. Tom was surprised. "You mean to say you won't be moving in permanently?" he asked. "No," Baird replied. "This is intended to be our summer place." Tom shook his head. "You must have paid an awful price for just a summer place."

When they pulled into Kalispell, Baird came to a stop under a hanging stop-and-go light when it turned red. Tom said, "Why are you stopping here?" Baird pointed up through the windshield at the stop-and-go light. "Red light," he replied. They went a little farther and Baird stopped again, this time for a stop light on a pole by the side of the road. Tom said, "Why are you stopping here?" Baird pointed to the light and said, "Red light." They went a little farther and Baird stopped for a stop sign. "Why are you stopping here?" Tom asked. Baird pointed and said, "Stop sign." Tom said, "Well by gol, the boys have been saying that every time I come to town I never stop but just drive right through. Now I know what they were talking about!" When they got back to the North Fork, Baird, a gracious, kindly man, said, "Stop in for coffee anytime, Tom." They were startled the next morning when they were awakened at seven AM by Tom pounding on the door. "You said to stop by for coffee," he said.

Over the years, the Chrismans and Tom became fast friends. Tom became very fond of Garnett, Baird's sister who bought the cabin on Mud Lake once owned by Madam Queen. Without doubt, Tom was attracted to Garnet and, in fact, petitioned the US Geologic Survey to change the name from Mud Lake to Garnett Lake. Tom was not only a fine musician, but also a talented artist. He filled sketch books with charcoal drawings of people pictured in magazines, some, like Richard Nixon and Leonid Brezhnev, famous characters. Many of his sketches are quite professional.

Some include Tom's written critiques of his own work or comments on the subjects he'd drawn. He also painted. One December, the Chrismans returned to the North Fork from Illinois to spend the Christmas holiday. Tom, who kept up a written correspondence with them and many other friends, knew they were coming. When Baird, Esther, their children, Granny Chrisman – Baird's mother – and Garnett were assembled in the cabin they'd had built by a man named Walt Hammer, Tom presented them with a Christmas gift. It was a painting. When he unveiled it to the family, Baird, Esther, Garnett and Granny gasped. Baird hustled the kids up to bed. The painting Tom had presented to them showed a full-breasted woman standing ankle-deep in a lake without a stitch of clothing on. Tom told me that it was a picture of Garnett, one he'd conjured up in his imagination. I always wondered about that. In any event, Baird thanked Tom and quickly turned the painting face to the wall.

Tom was always brutally honest. If you were afraid of an answer, you shouldn't ask Tom a question because he would tell you exactly what he thought. In some cases, feelings got hurt. Granny Chrisman was proud of her extraordinary baking ability, particularly her pies, particularly her cherry pie. One day Tom was dining with the Chrismans and after dinner, Granny brought out a fresh-baked cherry pie and proudly set it on the table. She served everyone and sat back for the usual accolades. When Tom finished his pie, he pushed back his plate but made no comment. Granny couldn't stand it. She knew that Tom, too, baked a good deal and wanted his approval. "How did you like the pie, Tom?" she asked. Tom looked surprised and said, "The crust was good but it's awful filling." Granny's face turned red, she jumped up and stormed out of the room. One will never know what Tom really meant; if he liked the pie and found it very filling or if, in fact, he thought the filling was awful.

1963 turned out to be an eventful year for Tom. He also met Paul and Maxine Maas that year. Paul, a gruff bear of a man with a no-nonsense crew cut, told me of their first meeting. "In those days, the U.S. Forest Service and the National Park Service were at odds with one another. Much antagonism existed between Forest

Service and Park Service men. Tom worked for the Forest Service. I was employed by the Park Service. I met Tom one day when he was hauling wood out of where he was cutting it on the piece he later sold to Larry Wilson. Now, I'd owned our place for seven years and it is adjacent to Tom's land. I introduced myself and Tom said, 'Oh yes, I've heard about you. You're a Park man, aren't you?' I looked him square in the eye and said, 'Yes I am. I know you're working for the Forest Service.' Tom said, 'Well, since we're neighbors, I guess we'll have to be friends.' I said, 'That's up to you. I've been here seven years and I've never met you. If you don't want to be friends, I don't give a damn.' Tom seemed nonplussed and we talked for another fifteen minutes. Finally, Tom said, 'You're a married man, aren't you?' I said, 'Yes, I am.' Tom said, 'Why don't you bring your wife up to see me next Sunday?' Maxine and I went up on Sunday. She was one of the first women to get into Tom's cabin up to that time, but she didn't get beyond his kitchen table right next to the back door. Tom offered us a bottle of beer he'd brewed and I'd heard Tom considered it an insult if somebody refused him. But Maxine said, 'I don't drink beer. It's against what I believe in.' The next time Maxine and I went up to visit Tom some time later, he said, 'Oh, you don't drink beer, do you?' He remembered."

Paul and Maxine lived near St. Louis most of the year. Paul was a school teacher who had summers off. Since the late 1940's he, Maxine and young daughter Karen had spent their summers in Montana, Paul working for the Park Service collecting garbage at various campgrounds. He'd pick up whatever campers discarded at Kintla, Bowman, Logging Lake and Apgar campgrounds and haul it to a garbage dump the Park Service maintained inside the Park. Paul said he'd always separate out the hotdogs and hamburger from the other garbage. When he pulled into the garbage dump, grizzly bears would come running. They knew the sound of his truck. After he dumped the garbage, he'd feed the hotdogs and hamburgers to the bears. He got to know them and gave each one a name. He often took Karen with him so she, too, could feed the bears. Paul and Maxine lived in Park housing until they bought their land. Their property bordered Tom's on the north and they kept a trailer just one mile from Tom's house.

Close neighbors in a vast wilderness, they exchanged visits frequently during the summer and, as the years went by, Tom and the Maas family became dear friends.

A dozen years after Tom retired from the Forest Service, he was discovered to have prostate cancer. At that time, John Senger was the US Customs officer stationed at the US-Canadian border crossing a mile north of Tom's place. John was a tall, dark, handsome young man with a quick smile and good heart. When he learned about Tom's ailment and impending surgery, he invited Tom to stay with him and his beautiful wife Wendy at their home near Kalispell during Tom's recuperation. The morning after Tom arrived at their home, John and Wendy were startled when Tom pounded on their bedroom door at six AM, shouting, "Are you all right in there?" It seems that Tom had been pacing back and forth for over an hour, wondering why they weren't up. Not hearing anything, he began to worry that something was wrong. Wendy got up and fixed breakfast for him; bacon eggs, toast and coffee. Tom took a sip of the coffee and pursed his lips after tasting it. Wendy could tell he was turning up his nose. "What kind of coffee is this?" he asked. "Hills Bros.," she replied. "I knew it wasn't Folgers," Tom said. "Folgers is what I use, you know." Wendy was furious. Here was a man she scarcely knew, staying in her home, waking her at six AM, eating a big breakfast she'd cooked and complaining about the brand of coffee. She said, "I'm not going out at six o'clock in the morning to get Folgers – or any other time. You'll drink Hills Bros. or nothing in my house!" After that, Tom gave Wendy no trouble. He ate everything without complaint.

Tom had little exposure to television until he stayed with John and Wendy in 1973 and he was fascinated by it. He liked the game shows and the news but he didn't like everything that was on TV. One Sunday afternoon, John and Wendy were watching an NFL football game. Though Tom had played on a Regimental football (soccer) team in India decades before, American football was completely different. "All these fellows would line up in a line facing each other and someone would grab the ball," Tom said. "He'd quick run around one end of that line. There would be two fellows from the other team waiting for him and they'd grab that fellow with the ball and – bang – they'd throw him down on the ground. Then they'd all line up again. The same fellow would grab the ball and run around the end of the line like he did before and there would be those same two fellows waiting for him. Bang, down he'd go again." Tom shook his head. "I don't know why the fellow with the ball didn't run the other way. It made no sense to me. I think American football is a silly game."

Tom returned to his home on the North Fork and, somewhat to his surprise, he recovered fully from his cancer. But shortly thereafter, he gave his property away, free and clear, to his nephew Eric Pratt in Australia. One day I asked Tom why he'd done that. "I'd kept up correspondence with my nephew and his wife Nini all these years after I went to Australia. Nini wrote to me and said that Eric had an opportunity to become a judge in Australia but that he couldn't afford to. She said that Eric couldn't make as much money as a judge as he could as a lawyer. "Well," Tom said, "I was about to turn 80 and I figured I wouldn't live very much longer. I wrote and told my nephew that I would deed my property over to him and that he could sell it. He could use the proceeds from the sale to become a judge. I would keep a life estate on the place so I could live out my life in my house." Tom grinned. "Of course I was wrong about how much longer I might live!" That conversation took place nearly fifteen years after Tom had given away his property.

Tom wrote to us often that first winter after we bought his property and our correspondence continued for many years. We were saddened when he wrote and told us that one of his parakeets had died. We wrote back and urged him to get another because we knew he loved his parakeets, but he didn't reply to this suggestion. When we returned the next summer, we were surprised to see his birdcage gone. We asked him about that. He said, "Well, I didn't want that surviving bird to be lonely, so I gave it away with the understanding that the new owner would get a mate for it. Besides, I didn't want that bird to suffer and die if I died in the winter." Tom knew the burden of loneliness and, despite that, had the capacity for love.

Beginning that second summer, we invited Tom down for dinner every evening we were there. For the first several years, he'd always ask what we were having and if he didn't think he'd like it, he would thank us but stay home. Later, he wouldn't ask, he'd just come.

One time Sue told him we planned to have chicken. Tom said, "No thank you. I had chicken one time at a neighbor's house and it was bloody. I don't like bloody chicken." Sue assured him that I would cook it thoroughly on the grill and there would be no blood. He came and enjoyed every bite. Tom loved mashed potatoes, so Sue had them often. There is no electricity in the North Fork, so she had to mash the potatoes by hand. At one of our first dinners, she asked Tom how he liked the mashed potatoes. "Pretty lumpy," he replied.

Tom came to love Sue dearly and, over time, he realized that his honest replies occasionally hurt her feelings. Having lived all his life in an orphanage or army barracks or by himself in a remote area populated by only a few people, most of whom were rough characters from another era, his lack of sensitivity was understandable. As the years went by, however, Tom learned. He never wanted to hurt anyone's feelings, particularly Sue's. He became much more sensitive and we could see that he would consider how his answers might be taken before he gave them.

We occasionally introduced Tom to new foods. Sue asked Tom down for dinner one day and told him we were having spaghetti. He hesitated but agreed to come. When we'd sat down to dinner, we passed around the salad, vegetables, fruit and bowl of spaghetti noodles. Tom took some of everything. Then Sue passed the spaghetti sauce to him. "What's this for?" he asked. "That's the spaghetti sauce," Sue said. "You put it on the noodles." Tom spooned the spaghetti sauce onto his noodles and cleaned his plate without a word. "How did you like the spaghetti?" Sue asked. "Pretty tasty," he replied. "I never liked spaghetti much but it tastes a lot better when you put that sauce on it."

One October afternoon, Sue and our daughter Debbi – now grown – flew into Spokane and rented a car to drive to Reynolds Ranch. On the way up the North Fork Road, they ran into a terrible thunderstorm. Rain dropped visibility to near zero, tornadic velocity winds blew trees down, hail pelted the car and the temperature dropped to near freezing. Sue, who was driving, stopped in the road until visibility improved. When they resumed their journey north, they came upon a tree that had been blown down across the road. There was no way around it. Sue was afraid that if she turned around to go back, they'd only be stopped again by a blow-down in back of them. Debbi got out of the car and, in the blowing rain, climbed a bank by the road, put her shoulder under the top of the tree and raised it just enough for the car to squeeze beneath it. When Sue had cleared the tree, Debbi ran down the bank toward the car, screaming "Don't leave me!" On their way north once more, neither Sue nor Debbi looked forward to arriving at a cold, shuttered cabin in the dark, opening it up and trying to build a fire in the stove. When they got there, they were surprised and relieved beyond measure to see Tom inside our cabin waiting for them. A fire was burning in the stove, the gas lights were on and the cabin was warm as toast. "With this weather, I thought you might have run into trouble," he said.

Many old people don't like trying new things. Not Tom. He was game for most anything. We took him on picnics, drives over Going to the Sun Road, climbed the trail to Hornet lookout and introduced him to board games like Monopoly and Trivial Pursuit. He liked all the games, but was particularly fond of Trivial Pursuit. He usually won! But he didn't care for some new experiences. One day we asked Tom if he'd ever floated the North Fork River. He hadn't. We asked him if he'd like to float with us in our rubber raft. He said he'd like to go. The next morning, we put our raft in our truck and assembled Tom and our kids for a day of fishing and floating. We were in swim trunks and water shoes. Tom wore his usual long-sleeved shirt, work pants and hip boots. We floated and fished and picnicked on the North Fork River and put out at the end of the day near Polebridge, 28 river miles south. Tom didn't say much afterwards. I asked him how he liked floating. "Pretty boring," he replied. That was his last trip down the river.

Tom employed unusual self-discipline. He drank beer but allowed himself only one at lunch. He enjoyed liquor – especially scotch – but drank only "two fingers" before dinner. And he maintained a strict regimen over how he spent his days. Monday was bread day. He spent all day making bread. He would mix dough from scratch and shape it into small buns. "Buns stay fresh longer than loaves," he said. He'd fill bread pans with his buns, light his wood cook stove and bring it up to just the right temperature, bake the buns, then, when golden brown, take them out and wrap them in wax paper.

Tuesday was mail day. The morning was for writing letters to the many friends he'd made in the Forest Service as well as summer North Fork neighbors who'd gone home. He wrote to his nephew in Australia and even old army buddies he'd left in Europe. He'd meet Becky, the mail lady, at his mailbox down on the road about noon, take his mail and whatever else she'd brought, then carry it up to his house in his backpack. He'd spend the afternoon reading mail.

Wednesday was wash day. He washed himself, the floors, the bedding, the lace curtains he kept at his windows, everything.

Thursday was for chores around the place; fixing what needed repair, cutting wood, hauling it to the woodshed, splitting wood, whatever. Friday was, again, mail day with the same routine as Tuesdays.

Saturdays and evenings were reserved for reading. Tom was an avid reader. He subscribed to nearly two dozen magazines and newspapers, ranging from Mother Jones' Earth Report to Newsweek to Popular Mechanics, Playboy and everything in between. Tom's house was piled high with books on every imaginable subject; music, art, history, philosophy, psychology, theology, climate, the paranormal and even the sexual practices of savages. One day I came up to find him reading theologian-philosopher Carl Jung's *Seven Sermons to the Dead*. "Kind of slow going," he said. "I can only read a few pages of Jung before I have to give it up for awhile." He owned dozens of "how to" and self-help books, but very few novels. "I don't like reading fiction," he said.

Talking with Tom was like talking to a college professor. His range and depth of knowledge was amazing. One evening we were all playing Trivial Pursuit. Tom teamed up with Patrick. A card came up that read; "What two famous people were born on April 26, 1564?" Tom answered immediately; "Shakespeare and Cervantes." The next card to come up read; "What is Mickey Mouse's wife's name?" Tom turned to Patrick and asked, "Who's Mickey Mouse?"

He was amazingly up to date on what was happening in the world. After the giant ad agency I was working for had become the victim of a hostile take-over by an English communications holding company, Tom said, "I understand your company was bought out by some English outfit." I was astounded. "How did you learn about that?" I asked. "Read about it in Newsweek," he replied. "I wondered how that might affect you."

Tom would save his Playboy magazines and when he'd collected several issues, he'd take them north across the border to Joe's place. Joe had a long Polish name that no one could remember or pronounce. Joe lived in the bush and that's what he was called; Joe Bush. There wasn't another private dwelling in British Columbia within 60 miles. He lived a quarter mile north of the border on leased Crown land where he had several hunting cabins and a large log lodge. A strong friendship developed between Tom and Joe, though they were remarkably different people. Joe drank too much and, in his younger days, must have been a hell-raiser. Even in his later years, he loved the ladies. North Fork women – Sue included – were careful not to visit Joe alone. Still, Joe had a heart as big as the outdoors and would give you the shirt off his back if you needed it.

Tom's Sundays were reserved for visiting friends. Every Sunday morning at eight o'clock, he would walk a mile down from his house to his good friend George Walters to have breakfast. George and his son Dave worked for the Montana Historical Society in Helena. Tom loved history and looked forward to his weekly talks with George and Dave. They became very close and when Emily, Dave's daughter was born, Tom became her godfather. We have a picture of Tom holding baby Emily, a wonderful smile lighting up his face. When Sunday breakfast with the Walters was over, Tom would often go up or down the road to visit other friends and neighbors. It's easy to understand why he was upset about being called a recluse in a newspaper article.

Tom did not like his weekly routine to be interrupted. Baird Chrisman told the story of delivering a load of firewood to Tom. "One day Allen (Baird's son) and I took a load of firewood up to Tom. I drove my truck around to the back of Tom's house and stopped by the woodshed. I saw Tom in his kitchen, but he didn't come out. I told Allen to begin unloading the wood while I went to get Tom. When I got to the door, I could see Tom bending over his stove, putting some bread in the oven. I knocked on the door and he looked up, surprised. He came to the door, opened it quickly and said, 'I'm not receiving guests today.' Then, just as quickly, he shut the door and went back to his bread baking. Allen and I unloaded the wood and put it in the woodshed for him."

"Tom never liked to admit that he could use help bringing in firewood for the winter," Baird told me. "He wouldn't accept charity, so Larry Wilson and several others of us always told Tom we had more firewood than we could use and that he'd be doing us a favor taking it off our hands." To the last, Tom cut down dead trees on his property with a chain saw, sawed them into 13 inch sections to fit his stove, hauled them out of the forest in an old army backpack, stacked them in his woodshed and split the wood as he needed it. By fall, he'd have his large woodshed completely filled and another pile of firewood just as big outside on the ground, covered with tarps. I always thought that was overkill, but Tom insisted he couldn't take the chance of running out of firewood for fear of freezing to death in the winter. I didn't understand how much firewood it took to heat his house until after Sue and I moved in and we stayed late one fall. Tom was right! He needed two woodsheds full of firewood.

Tom didn't have a well. He found a spring up in the forest a thousand feet west of where he built his house and used that as his water source. He dug out the spring and set a six foot diameter corrugated metal culvert vertically in it as a collecting tank. He put a wooden cover over it to "keep the bears out" and ran a 3/4 inch black plastic hose down from the tank, through the forest to a spot near his house. A continual flow of icy-cold spring water emptied into a metal bucket, the bottom of which had rusted out. He kept his vegetables and a couple of bottles of beer in the bucket to cool them. The water ran continually until something interrupted its flow. That was usually a bear. The sound of water running in the plastic hose drew their attention and they frequently bit into that water line. When the water stopped, Tom had to walk the thousand feet of water line until he found the break. That wasn't the only problem. Bears, it seemed, would tear the wooden cover off the settling tank as soon as Tom put it on and they enjoyed frolicking – or bathing – in the water. After we bought the property, Tom would ask Patrick – of whom he was inordinately fond – to go up with him and help clean out the tank. That meant Patrick jumping down into icy water and dredging out whatever was in the tank. Over the years, he brought out the skeletal remains of various critters that had fallen in, including a possum, a weasel and a fisher. Each year, Tom fell ill from time to time. We all told him it was bad water but he insisted his illness was influenza. Still, he told Sue to carry her own water when she came up for tea each afternoon. "I don't want you drinking my water," he said.

Larry Wilson remembers Tom carrying two buckets of water into his house every day, one in each hand. He wondered about that and asked Tom if he used two buckets every day. Tom said, "No, but I carry two buckets in because that balances the load. I throw the water I don't use out on the lawn to keep the grass green."

Years before we met him, Tom had dug a root cellar, lined it with rock and put a shed over it. Even on the hottest day, it was cool in there. It kept butter and eggs and other perishables perfectly well. He had no refrigeration, cook-top or gas lights in his house. When

I offered to pay to have these "conveniences" installed, Tom refused. "I'm afraid of propane," he said. "I won't have it run into the house. I nearly got burnt up in a propane fire one time, you know. Back in the 50's I was spending the night in a skid shack with another fellow in the middle of winter. Several feet of snow were on the ground and it was cold as hell. Well, this other fellow turned up the propane heater in the skid shack before we went to bed. I was awakened in the middle of the night when the shack caught fire. We had just enough time to grab our boots and get out before that skid shack went up in flames and took us with it. The men working around where we were had taken all the trucks down the mountain with them when they quit for the day, so we had nothing to drive. We had to walk down to Ford Station in our shirtsleeves because we didn't have time to get our coats on before getting out of that skid shack. It was snowing that night and when I knocked on the ranger's door down at Ford, we were half frozen. The ranger said, 'What the hell happened to you?' 'Propane fire,' I said." Tom shook his head. "I don't want any part of propane."

When we first bought his place, he would ride into town with us a week or so before we returned home in order to buy supplies that would last him the winter. Most of what he bought was canned goods – fruit, vegetables, stew, hash. He also bought baking supplies and liquor. He kept these staples in the spare bedroom in his house so he wouldn't have to get down into the root cellar when there was four feet of snow on the ground. He relied on Becky to bring meat, eggs and milk up from town on her regular mail route.

A couple of years after he turned 90, I told Tom that we'd be leaving in a week and asked if he'd like to go with us and buy his winter supplies. This time he surprised us. "No, I won't be buying any winter supplies this year," he said. Sue and I knew he didn't have enough food to get through the winter. We were worried and speculated on why he wasn't buying winter supplies. We assumed he must be short of money. We went to town without Tom but stopped in Sykes Grocery Store where he bought his supplies by the case. We bought the same goods in the same quantities we'd watched him buy previous years. When we returned from town, we drove up to Tom's house and presented his winter supplies to him. Before he could protest, Sue said, "This is your birthday present, Tom. That's all you're getting this year." Tom loved Sue and couldn't refuse. He just grinned. We bought his winter supplies for him every year thereafter. One year I screwed up my courage to broach a subject we'd stayed away from; money. "Are you running short of funds?" I asked.

Tom looked surprised. "Why no, he replied. I've got plenty of money. Why do you ask?"

"Well, you haven't been buying winter supplies," I replied. "We thought maybe you were short on money."

Tom sat back in his chair and laughed out loud. "Oh, that's what you thought! I don't buy winter supplies any more because if I die during the winter, those canned goods will freeze. I don't want to risk wasting food like that." We continued to buy Tom's winter supplies for him.

In Tom's 89th year, Sue discovered that he had never had a birthday party in his whole life. She arranged to have a party to celebrate his 90th birthday at the US Customs station at the border. She sent invitations to all Tom's friends in the North Fork and Flathead Valley. In early October, 1986, Sue, my uncle Bob and I returned to the North Fork from our home in Illinois, where we'd moved a few months earlier. That year, summer had been dry, the start of what would be another of Montana's long droughts. October was unusually hot, daytime temperatures in the low 90's. The forest was like a tinder-box. The morning of October 14, Tom's birthday, we were down at our cabin, working on preparations for his birthday party when a vehicle came racing up our lane. Forrest, a part-time Customs officer, jumped out of his truck and hurried toward our cabin. He looked angry. "What are you doing burning slash in these dry conditions?" he demanded. "Don't you know you could start a forest fire?"

"We aren't burning anything," I replied.

Forrest's eyes got big and round and he drew in breath. "I saw a big plume of smoke at the border. It looked like it was coming up from your place. I thought you were burning something. Where can we get a better look?" he said.

"Up on the bench," I replied, now fully alarmed myself. Forrest, Sue, Bob and I went as fast as we could up to the high bench where Sue and I first made the decision to buy the property. When we got there, we saw a large plume of smoke billowing high into the bright blue sky. Reddish color near the bottom indicated flame, though we couldn't see it. This was a hot fire. The plume looked like it was coming up right in back of Tom's house.

"I'll call it in to the Forest Service on our radio at the border," Forrest said, racing back to his truck. Sue, Bob and I took off running toward Tom's house. When we got there, Tom had no idea anything was wrong. Tall trees surrounding his house blocked his view of the smoke, as they had at our cabin. "Tom," I cried, "where's your shovel? I'll go in and see what I can do." I'd seen movies in which fire fighters used shovels to dig trenches and stop forest fires. Tom showed me to his shed and handed out two shovels. Bob took one and I the other. "Stay here," I yelled. "I don't want you to get hurt."

I headed south into the dense forest behind Tom's house, the direction I thought would take me to the fire. I crashed through bushes and over downed trees. Several hundred yards beyond the south boundary of our property, I stopped short and stared. A massive wall of fire hundreds of yards wide confronted me. The tops of pine and spruce trees fifty and seventy feet tall were "crowning," exploding with a "whoosh" into fierce, orange flame, one after another after another. Tree trunks, brush and downed trees in the interior of the fire were burning. The heat was intense, the roaring sound of the fire frightening. In an instant, I saw how stupid I had been to think that I could do anything to stop this raging beast. Holding the shovel in my hand, I felt small, helpless, foolish.

I turned and ran back toward Tom's house. In my flight, I became disoriented and was no longer sure which way to go. I started to panic. "Calm down," I told myself. I collected my wits and headed in the direction I thought was right, though the forest looked the same in every direction. Five minutes later I burst out of the forest onto the road in back of Tom's house. Tom was waiting for me but Sue and Bob weren't with him. "They went in to the fire," Tom said. "They thought they might be able to help you." I was suddenly fearful again. They might become lost and get trapped by the fire. I headed back into the forest. As I did, I met Sue and Bob coming out. "There's nothing we could do," Sue said.

Forrest returned from the border to say that he'd alerted the Forest Service by radio and that firefighters were on their way up from Columbia Falls. In what seemed a short time, a Forest Service truck roared up our road. Bruce McAtee, head of the Columbia Falls Hot Shot team of Forest Service firefighters got out and introduced himself. He had been driving north when he spotted the plume of smoke, all the way from Polebridge 20 miles away. "I could see it was a hot fire," he said. "I've called in my team of Hot Shots and they should be here in a couple of hours. I've also called for a fire retardant bomber and it will be here in a few minutes." Bruce looked at me. "Can you take me in to the fire?"

Bruce and I headed into the forest. Almost as soon as we got to the fire, the VHF radio he was carrying crackled with the voice of the fire retardant bomber pilot. He said he was five minutes out. I asked Bruce if it would be OK if I stayed with him to watch what happened. He thought for a moment and agreed. Bruce told the pilot to make his first drop on the north side of the fire where we stood in order to prevent the fire from moving toward Tom's house. As a pilot myself, I was interested and excited to watch. Moments later, a converted twin-engine P2V Neptune Navy patrol bomber with a bright red tail appeared above us, so low that I thought it might clip the trees. It was configured "dirty"; that is, the pilot had extended the flaps and landing gear to allow the plane to fly as slowly as possible. I could see the pilot in the cockpit looking down at us. Doors on the belly of the plane opened and a huge plume of red retardant dropped down onto a row of fiercely burning trees on the north edge of the fire. In an instant, a line of fire several hundred yards long was snuffed out. It was amazing. I could only admire the coordination between Bruce and the pilot, as well as the pilot's skill. Bruce and I made our way toward the west edge of the fire. It was tricky going. The liquid diatomaceous earth used as retardant made the ground and logs we were negotiating slippery. The plane made several more drops, this time on both the north and west boundaries of the fire, - and once on Tim and myself. Then it headed back to Kalispell for another load.

Bruce and I made our way around the perimeter of the fire. He estimated it to be about 23 acres and growing. We headed back to Tom's house and when we got there, we found Tom sitting on the back of a red fire truck, drinking a beer. He grinned. "I figured I might as well enjoy my birthday," he said. The Hot Shot crew – elite Forest Service firefighters – had just arrived. Bruce supervised the deployment of his "troops" and they headed into the forest to do battle with the raging fire. The crew on the fire truck went around Tom's house, looking the situation over. One of the men came to Tom and said, "Those two big spruce trees right next to your house should come down. If the fire comes this way, embers may set them on fire and there would be no way we could save your house."

Tom looked at the firefighter and said, "I won't allow those trees to be cut. I'll take my chances with the house. And I won't leave my property either. If the fire comes this way and burns the house, I'd just as soon go with it."

Fire crews kept arriving all afternoon and disappearing into the forest. The retardant bomber came and went. A helicopter buzzed overhead, drawing us to the beaver pond on the east edge of our property. Time and again, we watched the helicopter dip its bucket into the pond and race back to drop water on the fire.

At six o'clock, it was time for us to pick up Tom and head for the border for his 90th birthday party. There was nothing we could do with the fire. McAtee reported that his crews had punched in a fire line along the north edge of the fire and that he thought our property would be OK – unless the winds picked up. Tom was all dressed up, wearing his best red and black plaid wool shirt buttoned at the top, green Forest Service pants, knee-high leather boots and a brown fedora. He smiled self-consciously as he got in the car. "I don't think anyone will come to the party," he said. "Too far." Indeed, the US Customs office was at the very end of the long, bumpy North Fork Road. The gate into Canada closed and locked at 5 PM every day. However, a few vehicles were already there when we arrived. Tom seemed surprised and not a little pleased.

The place was an ideal venue for the party. Built by the Federal Government a few years before at the cost of several million dollars, the living area consisted of a large open area that included a full kitchen, dining area and living room. A robust wood stove stood in the center with comfortable furniture all around. A giant generator kept the lights on and everything running, including the indoor bathroom.

As soon as we sat Tom on the cushy sofa, people began arriving in droves, bringing dishes for the pot-luck supper and gifts for Tom. Everyone knew Tom liked a drink once in a while and soon he had enough Cutty Sark and Jack Daniels to open a saloon. Tom sat and grinned as one neighbor after another greeted him with birthday wishes. The place was soon filled to overflowing. Over 60 North Fork well-wishers came that night and everyone enjoyed themselves, none more than Tom. He'd never been the center of attention before and it seemed to us that, once he got a taste of celebrity, he enjoyed it. After dinner we got Tom to cut the birthday cake that Sue had baked and to say a few words. He'd had a couple of drinks and seemed glad to have the chance. In his reserved, polite, humble way, he thanked everyone for coming "all this way." He said he'd never expected to have a birthday party – certainly not one like this! Sue and Becky the mail lady each gave Tom a kiss for the photographers. The click of cameras recorded genuine happiness radiating from Tom's face.

The next day we learned that a burning tree had fallen on a woman firefighter and that her shoulder had been broken. She was evacuated to a hospital in Kalispell and would make a full recovery. Though McAtee's fire crews were making progress in containing the fire, it took the crews three weeks to finally put it out. The fire burned nearly 100 acres and came within 600 yards of our property. We were very grateful to the brave, hard-working men and women of the Forest Service who saved our place – especially Bruce McAtee. We learned some weeks later that hunters had built a campfire near a tree stump. The stump caught fire and smoldered, probably for a week or more, and then flared up, causing the forest to be set ablaze. The hunters responsible for the fire were never identified.

The day following Tom's party, Sue, Bob and I needed to return home. As usual, Tom walked down to our cabin to see us off. He was somber. Bob and I shook his hand. Sue and he embraced and she kissed him on the cheek. "We'll see you next summer," she said. Tom's eyes moistened. "Well, I hope so," he said. As we drove down our lane, we looked back as we always did. Tom stood alone in the middle of our lane, hand raised in farewell.

Tom truly loved the ladies, Sue foremost among them. But Becky, the mail lady who met him every Tuesday and Friday noon at his mailbox was not far behind. Then there was Diane, a vivacious blonde biologist studying the nascent wolf population, and Rosalind, a young, frizzy-haired biologist doing ground-breaking work on mapping old-growth timber. These three ladies, five and six decades younger than Tom, kept an eye on him. They watched over him, visiting him periodically, even in the dead of winter, and provided priceless companionship. They loved Tom and he loved them.

One year, Karen Feather, owner of the Northern Lights Saloon in Polebridge, arranged a late-fall, season-ending shindig for full-time North Fork residents who would soon be snowbound. It was called the Polebridge Prom. Since none of the local women had "prom dresses," a couple of ladies went into town and bought used ball gowns from Goodwill. The men scrounged what suit jackets and

215

sport coats they could find. To Tom's delight, Diane invited him to be her date to the prom. In his case, he didn't need to worry about what to wear. He still had the tuxedo he'd worn as an orchestra player in London. Seventy years later, it still fit. He had a wonderful time and we'll always cherish the picture of him in tuxedo with a white silk scarf around his neck, standing straight and tall with a grin on his face, age 91!

It took researching this book for me to understand why Tom never married. The greatest regret in his life was having his family snatched away from him as a boy. He longed to become part of a family again. That's what motivated him to make the long, costly journey to Australia. It's what motivated him to give his property away. Nothing, in my view, would have made Tom happier than to have cleaved to a wife, had children and been the head of his own household. So why didn't he marry? I asked him one day if there wasn't someone he'd fallen in love with. He smiled and said, "There was one gal down near Polebridge that I was pretty partial to years ago, but I felt I couldn't provide for her properly and she married another man."

The reason Tom didn't marry is simple; he had almost no opportunity. He spent his life among men; first in the orphanage and then in the army. After a brief stay in London, he removed himself, at age 29, to a sheep ranch in Saskatchewan. He spent the remainder of his life in sparsely populated rural areas where there were few single women, fewer yet with whom Tom would care to associate, much less marry. The one thing Tom wanted most in life was denied to him until near the end of his life, and then it came to him in an unexpected way. When we showed up in Tom's 85th year, my family became his family. Over time, he grew to love us as if we were his kin, and we him.

Tom's birthday party celebration at the Trail Creek Customs Station became an annual tradition. Each October, Sue, Bob and I returned to the North Fork to host his party. Two years after the first one, Tom presented a plaque on behalf of the North Fork Improvement Association to Becky, who lived in the Flathead Valley, making her an "Honorary North Forker." Everyone wanted her to know how much they appreciated her kindness and all the extra effort she expended in bringing mail and everything else people needed up the North Fork twice a week, rain or shine, summer or winter. The following year, the community gave Tom a plaque recognizing him as the North Fork resident who had resided there longer than any other. He loved it!

During the summer of 1992, we saw worrisome changes in Tom. Before, Tom had charged up that steep hill of his without so much as a deep breath, leaving us less fit tenderfoots puffing hard to keep up with him. This year, Tom had difficulty climbing the hill. His pace was slow and he stopped frequently to catch his breath. At dinner, we noticed that his breathing would occasionally become labored and we sometimes heard a rattle in his chest. Always thin, it seemed that he had lost weight over the winter and, for the first time he seemed frail. When he asked me to help him with something in his spare bedroom, I saw that he hadn't eaten half of the winter supplies we'd bought the previous summer. Sue and I worried. Tom swore he was feeling alright and refused our offer to take him to town to get a check-up. We invited him to come to Illinois with us to spend the winter – or at least a few of the worst winter months. "No thank, you," Tom replied. "This is my home."

When we returned in October to host his 96th birthday party, I was relieved to see that Tom seemed no worse. He showed the same grace and wit that he'd always had. We planned a special celebration. Sue bought a bouquet of big, brightly colored mylar balloons. On Tom's birthday, Bob Sullivan drove down to Kalispell to pick up a custom made sheet cake decorated with his name and "Happy 96th." Unfortunately, Bob drove too fast on the North Fork Road and the cake slid off the seat onto the floor. Sue was mad as hell and made Bob drive the 180 mile round trip back to Kalispell to pick up another cake. He arrived back at the Customs Station with a new cake – intact – just as the party began.

Despite six inches of snow on the ground and near white-out conditions that evening, the space around the Customs Station was filled with vehicles. Inside, it was shoulder-to-shoulder pandemonium. A boombox was blaring, people were talking, hooting and hollering and having a great time, none better than Tom. He kept a drink in his hand and a grin on his face as he chatted with old friends and watched all the goings-on. At one point, Sue brought the balloons over to the sofa where he sat. They fascinated him. He apparently had never seen mylar balloons. "How do they stay up?" he asked. Sue explained the helium-lighter –than-air routine but Tom didn't get it. Probably too much going on around him.

After supper Tom cut the cake and, as usual, was asked to say something. He got choked up and all he could say was, "I never thought this many people would come to a birthday party for me." Over one hundred friends and neighbors, some from a hundred miles away, braved the North Fork Road on a snowy night to celebrate Tom's 96th birthday with him.

That evening we talked with Becky and Diane and Rosalind and John Frederick. They, too, were worried about Tom. They said they would arrange for someone to look in on him every few days over the coming winter and keep us up to date on his condition.

Parting became more difficult every year. When we left to return home after the birthday party in 1992, both Sue and Tom cried. She kissed him on the cheek as she always did, and said, "We'll see you next summer, Tom." Choking back tears, Tom said, "No, I don't think so." There was nothing Sue could say, only cry and hold him. One of the hardest things I've ever done was shake Tom's hand, embrace him and drive away.

The winter of 1992 was a hard one in the North Fork. Snow started in October and by Thanksgiving, it lay two feet deep on the ground, temperatures during the nights sometimes falling below zero. Sue received a phone call from John Frederick one evening the first week in December. He said that Tom's team of friends had been looking in on him and that he was having another bout of flu. He was weak but getting around. He'd made it down to the mailbox the previous mail day. They would continue to look in on him. There was nothing we or they could do. He'd keep in touch.

218

On the night of December 15, 1992, I was in New York City and Sue was at our home in Lake Forest Illinois. When the phone rang in my Manhattan apartment and I heard the pain in Sue's tear-choked voice, I knew. Tom Reynolds was dead.

When Becky arrived at Tom's mailbox around noon that day, Tom was not there waiting for her as usual. She knew something was wrong. Without snowshoes, she waded a half mile through hip-deep snow up to the clearing where Tom's house sat. No smoke was coming from his chimney. Becky went in through the back door. The house was freezing. She looked across Tom's living room into his bedroom and saw him lying in bed, raised up on one arm, grasping an alarm clock that he kept by his bed. He was looking to see what time it was. He'd been waiting for her. A Bible lay open on his nightstand, turned to Psalm 23. Becky sat on his bed and cradled him in her arms. He was unable to speak. A half hour later, Tom Reynolds closed his eyes for the last time.

Despite never having come to visit Tom during his life, Tom's nephew Eric Pratt travelled from Australia to the North Fork almost immediately after Tom's death. He petitioned the court in Kalispell to have himself declared Tom's sole heir. Pratt telephoned Sue and myself and told us he was having Tom's body cremated and that he would be taking whatever possessions Tom had that were not physically attached to the house and property that we owned, as the law allowed. We attempted to tell Mr. Pratt what Tom had told us about his wishes relating to disposal of his assets and belongings. Pratt was not interested in what we had to say and told us that, as legal heir, he would make the decisions. He did agree to allow us to take possession of Tom's remains when we returned in the summer in order that his ashes might be buried on the property as Tom had wished.

We learned later that Tom had savings totaling $57,000. One account was owned jointly with Emily Walters. Emily was Tom's godchild and he had told us that it was his wish to give all his savings to Emily and her sister to pay for their college education. We were told that Pratt took for himself all of Tom's savings to which he was legally entitled. Emily told us later how disappointed she and her sister were that they did not receive the money for college that they had been promised.

While there, Pratt took Tom's oboe, accordion, watch and other possessions and disposed of them. We were told that he burned a number of Tom's books that he deemed inappropriate. Throughout his life, Tom was a prolific letter writer. For decades, he'd written dozens of friends each Tuesday and Friday. He saved nearly ever letter he'd received in reply and at his death, hundreds, perhaps thousands of letters were stored in cardboard boxes that he kept in his house. Eric Pratt, we were told, burned them all. Priceless history was lost. Pratt reportedly said there might have been personal correspondence that should not be seen. One can only wonder what Pratt was afraid of. No doubt Tom had saved letters he'd received from Kathleen, Pratt's mother. Was Pratt afraid that letters from Kathleen might be found that would embarrass or discredit his family? I suppose we will never know.

We received another call from Eric Pratt before he departed for Australia. He said that he had gone to Flathead County Court House and checked on our deed to the property. That surprised us. He said he found that we were the legal owners of the property and that "the deed was in order." We knew that. In May, 1993, five months after Tom's death, we received a letter from Mr. Pratt stating that he had "checked out with my lawyer the view I expressed to you as to your position in regard to the property and there seems to be no doubt as to its correctness." We thought it odd that Mr. Pratt (an attorney) would go to the trouble of examining the deed to our property and employ a second lawyer to examine it a second time. We wondered what Mr. Pratt's motivation might be. In the late 1970's, Pratt had sold the property Tom gave to him for about $550 per acre. Since we bought it from the speculator, we'd made substantial improvements. More important, basic land values across the North Fork had appreciated substantially. We wondered if Mr. Pratt's interest in the deed to our property had something to do with the fact that he'd sold the property in 1978 for much less than it was worth when he visited it in 1993.

An alternative explanation might relate to a concern Mr. Pratt may have had about the ethics of the land speculator from whom we'd bought the property. Tom maintained that the speculator had cheated him out of real estate commission he'd been promised and had attempted to log the property in violation of another promise. Mr. Pratt had financed the speculator's purchase of the property in 1978 and at the time we purchased the property in 1981, the speculator had not paid off the balance he owed to Pratt. The speculator, in turn, financed for us a portion of the purchase we made from him. Until we paid off our loan to the speculator, he continued to have a second-party interest in our property. If we defaulted on a payment, he could attempt to reclaim ownership. Likewise, until the speculator paid off Mr. Pratt, Pratt, maintained a third-party interest in our property. It's possible that Pratt's interest in our deed reflected his desire to prevent the land speculator from somehow regaining ownership of our property, however unlikely that possibility.

In any event, we thought Pratt's interest in our deed and the initiatives he took to examine its legality were unusual. Moreover, we didn't trust the speculator. We decided, therefore, to eliminate second and third-party interests entirely. Sue and I paid off what we owed to the land speculator in 1993, employing a good attorney to ensure that the speculator, in turn, used the monies he received from us to repay Pratt. These steps ensured that no one would have any financial or legal interest in our property except ourselves.

Several years before Tom's death we asked him about his wishes for a memorial service. He said he'd like done for him what had been done for Joe Bush when he died. They'd had a bagpiper down from Fernie B.C, poured beer on Joe's ashes as they were scattered around his property and enjoyed a potluck afterwards. Tom, however, didn't want his ashes to be scattered on the ground. He'd like them buried near his house.

Tom was always skeptical of religion, though the spiritual realm seemed to hold a fascination for him. He kept a number of religious and spiritual books on his shelf. A libertarian, Tom had little respect for denominational dogma or church protocol, however. I think he believed in a Higher Power, but maybe not God as traditional Christians conceive of Him. We thought it interesting that he had an open Bible on the night stand next to his bed the day he died. Maybe as the end approached, he reached out to the eternity that was about to overtake him. Or maybe Tom, a very private man, simply chose not to reveal his religious beliefs to anyone. In any event, he had made his wishes about his memorial clear: "I don't want any religious business at my memorial." We would honor his wishes in all respects.

During the spring of 1993, Sue and I planned Tom's memorial service for August of that year. We had acquired the names and addresses of his friends around the country and invited them, along with Montana friends and neighbors, to a memorial service at Reynolds Ranch. We asked those who could to bring a dish for the potluck we'd have afterward. With the help of Arlene, Joe Bush's daughter, we located the piper in Fernie who had played at Joe's service and hired him to come down to play at Tom's. We sketched out a memorial that would, we thought, honor Tom and his many friends.

When we arrived in Montana that June, we were greeted by three unpleasant surprises. At the funeral home, we were presented with a torn cardboard box holding Tom's ashes, some of which were spilling out. Eric Pratt had not purchased an urn. We bought one and told the undertaker we'd be back when he'd secured Tom's remains properly in the urn.

The condition of Tom's house was the second surprise. It looked as though vandals had ransacked the place. Paper boxes had been overturned, their contents simply dumped on the floor. Discarded papers, books, magazines, hardware, pots and pans and junk of every description littered the floor, in some places two feet deep. We had to wade through the refuse to move from room to room. It appeared as though Mr. Pratt may have been looking for something and simply dumped what he'd been looking through on the floor.

Before we could have a memorial service, we needed to get to work cleaning out the place.

Tom's outhouse was the third unpleasant surprise. It was full to the point of being unusable. There was no way we could have a memorial service without fixing the problem. We got hold of our friend Elmer Benson who was an accomplished backhoe operator. When Elmer looked in the outhouse, he said, "Well, Tom had to die. There isn't another shit left in his outhouse!" Elmer dug a new pit and moved the outhouse. He saved Tom's memorial service.

Tom's house felt remarkably different without him. He wasn't there as he always had been and despite all the junk, an emptiness haunted it. And oddly, the house felt like a refrigerator. It was permeated by an unnatural, bone-chilling cold that we couldn't explain. The July weather was warm and sunny. As I contemplated the mess and felt the cold, I thought to myself, there's no way I'll ever be comfortable living in this house.

A few days before the scheduled memorial service, I went up to Tom's house and dug a hole large enough to hold the urn containing his ashes and deep enough to protect them. As I dug through the rock-filled North Fork clay, tears flowed more or less continually into the hole. Digging Tom's grave was one of the saddest jobs I ever did.

The weather was glorious the day of the memorial service. Our plan was to start up the road from the mailbox at noon, the time Tom usually met Becky every Tuesday and Friday. Sue, following the Piper, would carry Tom's remains up the hill to his house. He'd made the trip hundreds of times. This would be his last. The Kids and I would follow behind Sue, with guests who wished to honor Tom's memory forming the balance of the procession.

That morning, Sue put on a nice dress. "Tom never liked me to wear pants or shorts," she said. Sue, - carrying the bronze urn with Tom's ashes - Heather, Patrick and I walked down to the mailbox about eleven thirty. The piper from Fernie had just arrived and was getting his bagpipe in order. He was dressed in full Scottish regalia, kilts, knee-socks, sash, bonnet, the works. To our surprise, he told us that his father had been a member of the King's Own Scottish Borderers, the very regiment in which Tom had served. The piper knew all of the regimental songs and would play them. No wonder Tom wanted this piper to play at his memorial. The piper would pipe Tom home to tunes he would have known by heart.

As noon approached, only a few cars were parked at our gate. We were disappointed. We'd hoped to see many more of Tom's friends and neighbors at his memorial service. We waited until ten after twelve and, when no one else showed up, we signaled the Piper to start up our lane. To the marching drone of pipes, our procession passed the McAfee cabin a quarter mile from the road and continued on toward the hill beneath Tom's house. The regimental tunes the bagpiper played were a soulful reminder of what we'd lost. Our hearts were heavy. Soon we would be laying Tom's ashes beneath the sod, the final, physical proof that he was gone. And only a few people cared enough to bid him farewell.

Half way up the hill, I glanced behind me. Then I turned and stared. I could scarcely believe my eyes. I called to Sue; "Take a look behind us." She turned around and gasped; the small procession that had started up with us from the mailbox had grown to a line of people stretching more than a hundred yards. "My gosh, there must be two hundred people here!" Sue exclaimed. Tears welled in her eyes. "They came after all! That's wonderful."

When we got to the top of the hill, we saw some of Tom's oldest neighbors puffing up that hill on foot. We'd arranged for cars to shuttle folks who weren't physically up to climbing the hill and walking the half mile to Tom's house, but no one rode. Everyone walked, even Paul and Maxine Maas who were up in years and not in the best health.

We'd set a table up in the clearing next to Tom's house. On it we'd placed a 12x14 inch framed picture of him that we'd taken the previous summer, in his 95th year. It was a classic. The close-up shows him seated in a chair with a coffee cup on his lap, one thumb curled inside to hold the spoon that protruded from the cup, as was his practice. A sparkle lit up his eyes, a mischievous smile crinkling his lips. He appeared happy, carefree, content, loving. It was the way we wished to remember him. Brightly colored Mylar balloons that Sue had tied to the table bobbed in the breeze. As the group of friends began assembling, Lynette Berg set a vase containing a huge bouquet of roses next to Tom's picture.

I began the service by reading a poem by the famous aviator, author and filmmaker, Ernest K. Gann:

"You are standing upon a shore…somewhere.
A ship before you spreads her white sails, and
Starts for the blue ocean.
She is a beautiful and strong ship and you watch her
Until she hangs like a speck of white cloud
Just where the sea and sky come down to mingle with each other.

Then someone at your side says,
"There…well, well. She's gone."

Gone where? From your sight-that's all
She is just as large in mast and spar
As when she left your shore,
Just as strong and able.
Her diminished size is in you,
Not in her, and while someone at your side
Is saying, "She's gone…"
There are other eyes watching her coming
And ready to take up the glad shout,
"Here she comes."

I choked up and had difficulty finishing. Sue and I told stories about Tom and spoke about the place he had carved in our hearts. We invited anyone who wished to remember him to step forward and say what was in their heart.

The first to step forward was Baird Chrisman. Baird was the epitome of a Montana rancher – though he farmed most of the year in Illinois. He was lean and weathered, a soft-spoken man of few words. When he spoke, people listened. Baird spoke from the wisdom of a life lived outdoors, a life well lived. He was a man to be relied upon, principled and unflinching when it came to right and wrong. His word was his bond. He cared about his friends and neighbors and there was nothing Baird would not do when someone needed a hand. Like fixing broken machines. He could fix anything. Baird didn't wear his heart on his sleeve. He was a private man who bore his joys and sorrows, fortunes and misfortunes with an easy grace. You could say he was a stoic, but that would understate Baird's depth of character and respect for those around him. So when he removed his well-worn cowboy hat and came forward, I was surprised. He bowed his head and began to speak of when he'd first met Tom four decades earlier and how, through the years, he'd come to think of Tom as a part of the Chrisman family. And then he did something I never could have imagined; Baird Chrisman cried.

One after another, Tom's friends and neighbors came out of the crowd to pay their tribute. People I never imagined would be comfortable speaking in public talked about their times with Tom and what he had come to mean to them. Many were the "Tom stories" that brought a laugh or a tear or both to his assembled admirers. When everyone had had their say, I picked up the urn and invited them to come to where Tom's ashes would be interred. With tears falling into the hole in the earth, I set the urn beneath the sod and shoveled dirt over it. We broke out a six-pack of Coors – Tom's favorite "store-bought beer" – and everyone – from grandfolks to kids – took turns watering his resting place just as he'd wished. As we did, the piper unexpectedly struck up "Amazing Grace." We didn't think Tom would mind. Sue released the Mylar balloons and they soared up into the sky – only to get stuck in the branches of a 50 foot high aspen. "Tom isn't ready to leave," Sue said.

As Tom had hoped, a pot-luck feast was enjoyed by everyone. I got the chance to talk with folks who knew Tom years before and wrote down what they said. Dan Block was one of those people. He said he and Jermayne, his wife of over 50 years, hardly ever argued but when they drove up from Columbia Falls, they had a terrible fight. "We laughed afterward and realized we were both just sore about losing Tom." Dan talked about Tom as though they were together just yesterday. I assumed they'd seen one another shortly before he died. "When was the last time you saw Tom?" I asked. Dan scratched his chin as he thought for a moment. "The last time I saw Tom Reynolds was when I left the Flathead in 1946," he replied.

A week later, the Mylar balloons were still stuck in the tree. Sue and I went up to where Tom's ashes were buried as we had every day since the memorial. This day we selected the spot where we would put the granite marker we had commissioned. It reads;

THOMAS BOX REYNOLDS
October 14, 1896 – December 15, 1992
Kings Own Scottish Borderers 1910-1923
North Forker 1928 – 1992
More Than A Friend – Always

As we were about to return to our cabin, a breeze came up and the aspen tree holding tight to the Mylar balloons suddenly released them. They soared high into the air. The last we saw of them they were mere specks in the sky, heading toward Glacier National Park. Oddly, the unnerving cold that penetrated Tom's house was gone. Tom was on the other shore.

CHAPTER 5

HIGH ANXIETY

The feeling of freedom and excitement and exhilaration we'd experienced over the years when hiking up skinny trails that snake across naked rock to high cirques and remote passes cannot be duplicated. There's just nothing like it. Though the North Fork had become our summertime home and we loved being there, we were determined not to abandon the thrill and awe and joy we'd felt in high backcountry of the Park.

One element in the thrill of the backcountry, the thrill that drew us back time and again, is danger - or at least the idea that one might encounter danger. There is always the possibility of falling from some high place or twisting an ankle miles from anywhere or being overtaken by one of Montana's monster storms. But there are also wild animals out there, animals that can not only kill you but eat you as well, belt buckle and all. It has happened. I always thought that if there were no grizzlies or mountain lions or black bears in Glacier's backcountry, some of the thrill would be gone and I wouldn't love it as much as I do. Of course the possibility of encountering real danger in Glacier Park is extremely low, so low, in fact, that we never really expected to come face to face with it. If we had, we probably wouldn't have gone.

Never the less, as the saying goes, if a monkey sits at a typewriter long enough, he'll eventually produce the works of Shakespeare. And if you clock enough miles in Glacier's backcountry, the odds of encountering a dangerous situation can go up, way up.

One of the most dangerous animals we ever encountered wasn't a bear or mountain lion. It was Ernie. Ernie was a horse used by Mule Shoe Outfitters to take dudes on trail rides at Many Glacier. One day, Heather and I decided to hike from Logan Pass to Granite Park Chalet and then north, over Swiftcurrent Pass and down to Swiftcurrent Lake, a good 16 miles. Sue would drive to the Swiftcurrent Hotel and pick us up at the end of the day.

She arrived at the Swiftcurrent Hotel just before a couple of wranglers were about to lead a string of horses carrying dudes up the steep trail to Swiftcurrent Pass and Granite Park Chalet. She thought that would be a marvelous way to spend the day and might even allow her to meet Heather and me on the trail. She bought a ticket but when she got to the corral, the wranglers didn't have a horse for her to ride. At the last minute, one wrangler remembered Ernie. He was a large sorrel used to take folks to Cracker Lake on a low, flat, easy trail. He had never been up to Swiftcurrent Pass. The wrangler asked Sue if she could ride. She could. In fact, Sue was an accomplished horse woman. Off they headed toward Red Rock Canyon where the trail begins its steep, three thousand vertical foot climb to Swiftcurrent Pass.

Hiking from Logan Pass, Heather and I made good time on the 7.8 mile trail to Granite Park and we still felt strong when we got there. We decided we would continue on and climb the eighteen hundred vertical foot trail up from Granite Park to the lookout on top of Swiftcurrent Mountain. The trail switchbacks steeply up through a desolate rock field that forms the east slope of Swiftcurrent Mountain. We were puffing hard when we reached the lookout, but the view from the top made us completely forget the effort we'd expended to get there. Far to the east lay our starting point, Logan Pass. To the east, four and a half thousand feet below, lay Swiftcurrent and Sherburne Lakes, looking for all the world like small ponds. Beyond, vast flat plains of the Blackfeet Reservation stretched to infinity. We sat on the steps of the abandoned lookout and drank in the spectacle afforded by being at the very top of the Park, feeling the exhilaration it afforded. Suddenly we spotted two golden eagles soaring in circles high above us. As we watched, we realized they weren't flying independently; they were somehow connected. The two eagles circled each other, coming close, then soaring down and away, then rising again and coming close again. To our amazement, they came together, body to body, breast to breast and grabbed each other's talons. The two birds, linked in embrace, drew in their wings and plummeted down through the air, falling hundreds of feet. Well below our perch on top of the mountain, they released their talons, spread their wings, caught the air and soared up again. Time and again, these lovers came together, clasping talons, falling, releasing, soaring, circling. We sat at the top of the world, looking up in awe at this spectacle. Had we not taken pictures of the birds locked together, I doubt anyone would have believed us when we described what we saw.

As we sat watching the eagles, neither Heather nor I could know the drama that was playing out on the rugged trail below us. The trail from the Swiftcurrent Hotel up to the Pass is, like the famous Grand Canyon trail, steep, narrow and exposed to sheer drops of as much as a thousand feet. It's no place for a person who is afraid of heights – or for a horse either, for that matter. The head wrangler had put Sue and Ernie in the middle of their string of eight horses. Never having taken Ernie up to Swiftcurrent Pass, he wasn't entirely sure how the horse would react. He figured putting horses that knew the trail in front and in back of Ernie might be helpful.

The ride went smoothly enough on the way up, but as they began their descent from Swiftcurrent Pass, Sue saw that Ernie was getting nervous. She guided him along, giving him encouragement and reassuring pats on the neck. Ernie grudgingly picked his way forward but when they came to a ledge with a thousand-foot drop-off, Ernie decided he'd had enough. He whinnied and threw his head up and down. He refused to go forward. When Sue got him going again, he stumbled on the rocky trail. She was able to guide Ernie down until they came to a sharp bend in the trail. At that point, it appeared that horse and rider were suspended in air, a thousand foot drop to the right of the trail, a thousand foot drop straight ahead where the trail made its turn. Ernie began to shake with fear. He stumbled badly and Sue was afraid they might fall off the ledge. He threw his head up and down again and his eyes grew wide and white. Suddenly Ernie reared up on his hind legs, precariously balanced on the three foot wide trail. Sue lunged forward and grabbed his neck. Somehow, she hung on. The wrangler at the head of the string looked back at Sue with a terrified expression but there was nothing he could do. Four horses and riders separated him from Ernie and the trail was just barely wide enough for one horse.

Shaking in terror, Ernie began to move, making straight for that thousand foot drop-off. It appeared certain that he would go over the edge, taking Sue with him. She gripped the reigns and pulled Ernie's head back with a steady hand. Inches from the precipice, she got him stopped. She squeezed Ernie with her knees, talking soothingly to him at the same time. "You can do this," she said. "Come on, pick up one foot at a time." Step by shaky step, Ernie inched around the steep bend in the trail, past the thousand foot drop-off. Sue coaxed and cajoled and urged Ernie forward, keeping a tight reign until she was able to ride him safely down out of danger.

Back at the corral behind the Swiftcurrent Hotel, the wrangler was still so shaken he could hardly speak. "My God," he said, "you did everything right. I didn't think you had a chance. You're a good horse woman. Thank God you kept your head and didn't freak out."

"I was too busy to be scared," she replied, "at least until we got off that ledge. Then I was shaking like a leaf. I want you to promise that you won't destroy Ernie. This was not his fault. He'd never been up that trail before. He's a perfectly good horse. Don't do anything to hurt him."

The wrangler nodded. "No Maam, we won't destroy Ernie. If there was a fault, it was mine. I'll know enough to keep him off the Swiftcurrent trail next time."

When Heather and I met Sue late that afternoon and learned what had happened, I was shocked and extremely grateful she was safe. I went to the corral to seek out the wrangler. I wanted to thank him for helping Sue. "I didn't do anything," he replied. "There was nothing I could do. Your wife saved the day. If she hadn't kept her head and known what to do, I don't think she would have made it."

"Had my mother not given me riding lessons when I was a girl," Sue countered, "I never would have known what to do. My father

231

– who was born on a farm – never liked horses and refused to give me riding lessons. But Mom did it anyway. She just didn't let him know about it. Thanks, Mom."

Animals aren't the only source of excitement in the Crown of the Continent. The weather can be equally challenging. When Patrick was 14, I decided that we would backpack from Lake McDonald on the west side of the Park, up over the Continental Divide to near St. Mary Lake on the east side. Our two-day route would take us about 21 miles. We would first climb thirty six hundred vertical feet to Sperry Campground. There we'd pitch our tent and spend the night. The following day we'd hike fourteen miles up over Lincoln Pass, past beautiful Lake Ellen Wilson, to a steep headwall leading up an additional one thousand feet to Gunsight Pass. From there, the trail traverses steep cliffs, descending 1,600 vertical feet to Gunsight Lake and, after an additional six miles through heavy forest, connects to Going to the Sun Road.

The weather that summer had been hot and dry. In fact, Montana was in drought. The climb would be hot, I knew, but once in the high country, we couldn't ask for better hiking conditions. We stopped at the ranger station in Apgar to pick up our backcountry permit that would allow us to camp at Sperry. I asked about the weather forecast. Hot and sunny for the next seven days, the ranger said.

We'd already packed our packs with the usual change of underwear, socks, t-shirt, warm sweatshirt and rain gear. With the weather the way it was, I figured all we'd need in the cool of the evening and morning would be a long-sleeve shirt. Rain gear and sweatshirts would add unnecessary pounds. I began rummaging through my pack to remove them. Patrick immediately objected. "I think we should take the rain gear just in case," he said.

"I don't want to pack rain gear when there won't be any rain," I replied and took out both his stuff and mine.

We started up the trailhead across the road from Lake McDonald Lodge early in the morning. The weather was as it had been all summer, hot and dry. Within 5 minutes, we stripped off our long sleeve shirts. Within 15 minutes, we were sweating on the steep 5.6 mile grind to Sperry Chalet.

Patrick and I arrived at Sperry in time for lunch, leaving us plenty of time to hike the additional mile up to the campground and spend the afternoon relaxing. We pitched our tent in a prime spot near a ridge with a great view of Lake McDonald and laid out our sleeping bags.

About six o'clock, the sun still high, we got out our backpack stove and freeze dried spaghetti dinners. While the water was heating, I glanced west toward the Whitefish Range in the distance. What I saw surprised me. A band of purplish clouds lay thick over the mountains. A frown swept through my mind. They weren't supposed to be there. It was unsettling. By the time the water on our stove was boiling, the clouds had turned almost black and were nearly upon us. While we waited the three minutes for our freeze-dried spaghetti to re-hydrate, the sun went out, the wind picked up and the temperature dropped. A spasm of dread tightened my stomach. Patrick dashed to the tent to get our shirts. As I stuck my fork into the foil bag that held my dinner, large raindrops began to pelt us. We grabbed our stove and dinners and retreated inside the tent. The pelting rain turned into a wind-blown torrent. We ate our dinner in the tent, something I'd never done in bear country, but going outside was out of the question. I found myself thinking this can't be happening. The rain surely must stop soon and the sun reappear at any moment, right? After all, the Park weather forecast said hot and clear as far as the eye can see.

But the storm continued unabated through the evening. We were captives in our tiny backpack tent. We could only listen to the wind howl and the rain pound the tent. We decided to go to sleep. There was nothing else to do. Besides, the sleeping bags felt good. It was getting cold and neither Patrick nor I had even a sweatshirt. I began to worry.

I woke sometime in the night and wondered what was happening. Something was falling on the tent, but it didn't sound like rain. I turned on my flashlight and opened the tent fly to have a look. I could scarcely believe my eyes. A blizzard raged outside with three to four inches of snow already on the ground. What's going on? I asked myself. This is August. The ranger said to expect hot and dry conditions for the next seven days. How can this be happening? What do we do now? I rolled over and tried to go back to sleep. Maybe the storm will blow out before morning, I told myself. If so, the snow on the ground wouldn't take long to melt under an August sun.

Wrong again. When Patrick and I woke in the morning, we found ourselves in near whiteout conditions. The tent was laden with about eight inches of the white, fluffy stuff, the wind howling ominously in nearby scrub sub-alpine fir. This was decidedly not good. The worry I'd slept with turned to fright. My heart began to pound. My God, I thought, Patrick and I are stuck here at 6.500 feet elevation in a raging blizzard, miles from our destination with only the shirts on our backs for protection. We had to make breakfast, pack up our gear, take down the wet tent and stuff it in my pack - in what looked like the middle of winter. I thought about Sue. She must know we're in trouble. If we fail to meet her when she's scheduled to pick us up, she'll be worried sick. It didn't occur to me that we'd be safe if we remained in our sleeping bags inside our tent until the storm blew out. My only thought was to get down out of the snow and wind as quickly as possible and reunite with Sue. "Come on, Patrick," I yelled, "let's get packed up so we can get out of here."

We began suffering as soon as we stepped outside. In seconds, wet snow soaked us to the skin. As we struggled to pack up, I considered the choices we had before us. If we continued on our planned route, we would need to hike fourteen miles, in the process climbing two thousand feet and crossing two eight thousand foot passes without rain gear or warm clothing. Retracing our steps and returning to Lake McDonald Lodge was by far the easier way to go. The trail was just half the distance of our planned route and it would be downhill all the way. Once we headed down, the snow would probably turn to rain. This was the logical choice but my mind rebelled. Sue and Bob were planning to pick us up at the trailhead near St. Mary Lake on the other side of the Continental Divide, forty miles east of Lake McDonald. I worried that we wouldn't be able to get in touch with them if we changed our plans and went back down to Lake McDonald. Sue would be worried to death if we didn't show up as scheduled. Then, too, I was pulled by an illogical but intense impulse, an impulse that had driven me all my life; I just couldn't give up and abandon my goal. I made the decision to push ahead to Gunsight Pass.

We shouldered our wet packs and headed up toward Lincoln Pass. The wind blew directly in our faces and the snow stuck to our shirts and eyelashes. The exertion of the climb warmed us some and I figured we'd be OK. At the Pass, however, the wind increased and the trail leveled out and began to descend. As we edged along above Lake Ellen Wilson, exertion no longer warmed us. The wind drove snow across the open slopes above the lake and into our faces. It pounded through my thin, wet shirt directly into my body. My hands grew numb from the cold and halfway around Ellen Wilson I lost feeling in my arms. My mind slowed and its workings shrank down to a single thought; keep going, keep going.

Two miles beyond Lincoln Pass we reached the foot of the headwall leading up to Gunsight Pass. In the lee of the cliffs we were about to climb, the wind slowed some but the snow continued. We needed to be careful on the steep, slippery trail lest we fall. I wasn't sure that either Patrick or I could get back on our feet if we did.

The strenuous exertion of climbing the thousand feet to the pass with loaded packs caused our pulse to speed up and our hearts to pump more blood through our bodies. Though I couldn't feel my hands or arms, I sensed my body temperature rise. Miserable as we were, I was confident we'd make it. We could take shelter in a crude hiker's hut at the top of the pass. I'd start our backpack stove and make some hot cocoa. We'd ride out the storm. We'd be fine.

When we climbed beyond the windbreak afforded by the headwall and reached the crest of the pass, the wind was so strong it nearly knocked us off our feet. It blasted snow horizontally and snatched breath from my lungs. Patrick turned his back to it and faced me, immobile. I spun him around and pushed him toward the hiker's hut a few yards away. We struggled against the wind to the metal door. I pulled it open, pushed Patrick inside, followed him in and pushed the door closed against the wind. I was surprised to see a half-dozen hikers, all in heavy down parkas, seated on a stone bench. They looked up in surprise when we came in, but no one acknowledged our arrival or made a move to help us.

Suddenly my hands and arms began to shake. I had difficulty helping Patrick take off his backpack. My entire body started shaking and I had even more difficulty removing my own pack. I tried to open it to get our stove but the shaking became so severe that my hands simply refused to work. I thought that I was about to go into convulsion. Somehow my numbed mind began working again. We were experiencing hypothermia. I realized that the tremors wracking my body began only after we entered the hut. I sensed that the stones, of which the hut was constructed, were sucking the heat right out of our bodies. The ice-cold stones, I realized, were the problem. We had to get out of that hut or we would die.

Shaking uncontrollably, I somehow picked up Patrick's pack and put it on him. Struggling with approaching convulsion, I managed to get my own pack on also. I opened the door to the hut and found the raging wind still ripping snow horizontally over the pass. I grabbed Patrick by the shoulder and shoved him toward the door. The expression on his face indicated that he did not understand the logic of being thrown out of the hut into a raging blizzard in just shirtsleeves, but neither of us could speak. Going out into the blizzard seemed like madness, but it was better, I knew, than dying of hypothermia in the frigid hut.

I pushed Patrick forward. We leaned our bodies against the wind-driven snow to reach the trail that would take us down to Gunsight Lake. The trail immediately began a steep descent across a vertical wall. Within a half mile, the wind dropped and the snow turned to rain. To my immense relief, my body stopped shaking and I found myself merely cold and wet. We faced a ten mile slog through drenching rain but, unlike snow, rain was survivable. We hiked the remaining ten miles to the trailhead in under four hours.

When we climbed the rise to Going To The Sun Road, we were met by the most beautiful sight I'd ever seen. Sue and Bob were there waiting for us. "When I got up this morning and saw the weather, I knew you'd be in trouble," she said.

Patrick and I stripped off our sodden clothes right there by the side of the road and put on warm wool clothing Sue had brought. Nothing ever felt so wonderful! We climbed into the car, dry for the first time all day. Sue had the heat turned up full blast and, while the car may have felt sweltering to her and Bob, it was like heaven to Patrick and me. Sue gave us hot soup and sandwiches that she had prepared. What a marvelous gift. This was our first meal of the day. Patrick and I luxuriated in the warmth, the food and just being dry. No one who has experienced a situation like the one we'd survived that day can fail to appreciate how wonderful these simple pleasures can be.

Although I'd made the wrong decision in not heading back down to Lake McDonald from Sperry Campground or staying put in our tent and sleeping bags, somehow we'd survived. Call it toughness, physical strength or just dumb luck, we'd made it. Patrick had been right, of course, about carrying rain gear. Never again would I venture into the back country without warm rain gear, regardless of the forecast. Never again would I leave the safety of a dry tent and warm sleeping bag if weather overtook us in the future. I'd learned that weather can be as dangerous as any grizzly bear.

****

Even last week's weather can prove dangerous in the high country. One year Heather and I planned a 36 mile hike from Many Glacier to Waterton Lake and Canada. Our route took us through the

Ptarmigan Tunnel, a 50 yard long hole carved through the very top of the Continental Divide. The thin arête above Elizabeth Lake is so steep that the engineers who constructed the tunnel in the '30's could find no other route from one side to the other.

The first evening we camped at the foot of Elizabeth Lake and did some fishing. To my chagrin, Heather pulled one trout after another from the lake while I whipped up the water with my lure to no effect whatever. She never let me forget that one.

The next morning we hiked north, past Dawn Mist Falls and down to the Belly River. Though the weather was great, the previous week had seen a lot of rain and the river ran high. We clung to a wire that was stretched across the outlet of Cosley Lake to ford the fast-running water that reached up to our chests. It took all our strength to keep our packs above our heads and out of the water as we negotiated the slippery stones on the river bottom.

On the north side of the river, the trail turns west past Cosley and Glenn's lakes. The second night we pitched our tent at one of just two campsites on the shore of Mokowanis Lake. This small, round lake lies in the shadow of Mount Cleveland, the highest peak in Glacier. Surrounded by dense forest of alpine fir and large platforms of moss-covered stone, Mokowanis is one of the most remote and beautiful backcountry campgrounds in the Park.

We saw that the soil in a meadow not far from our tent had been torn up by grizzlies digging camas root. We thought about that as the sun went down, not another human within ten miles. What a feeling, that contemplation of dangerous possibility! When we stepped out onto the trail the next morning, we hadn't gone 50 yards when a full-grown cow moose the size of a Clydesdale bolted out of the forest and ran across our trail, not ten feet in front of Heather. It was a close call. Had we been five seconds earlier, she might have been trampled.

A mile beyond, the trail starts up two thousand vertical feet to 6,908 foot Stoney Indian Pass, one of the most remote in the Park. The lower reaches of the long, steep trail run through huckleberry bushes that grew higher than our heads. That year the bushes were loaded with berries and the possibility of bears crossed our mind. When we reached a switchback near the top of the berry field, sure enough, we spotted a grizzly a hundred yards above us. We hesitated to head higher and watched the animal for several minutes. The bear was in the bushes a good 50 yards to the south of the trail and it was busily stripping berries from branches and stuffing them in its mouth. So long as we didn't challenge if for the huckleberries, I knew we'd be alright. We headed up, past beautiful Paiota Falls which drops a thousand feet from near the top of Stoney Indian Pass.

When we reached the bench just above the Falls and just below the Pass, we were confronted with an unexpected problem; Paiota Creek. In previous hikes to Stoney Indian, crossing the creek had posed no problem. Park trail crews had thoughtfully placed flat, square stepping stones ten inches thick across the creek which usually ran only a few inches deep. Hopping from stone to stone was no problem. We'd never gotten our feet wet. This time, however, the rains of the previous week had raised the creek level nearly two feet. The tops of the stepping stones were submerged beneath rapidly running whitewater in the creek. Ten yards to our right, the rushing waters disappeared over the thousand-foot precipice that formed Paiota Falls. We were in a scary situation. To get to the other side of the twenty-foot wide creek, we would have to step into the ankle-deep water that flowed over these submerged stones and risk the possibility of being swept off our feet and over the precipice. Heather and I looked at one another. "What do we do now?" she asked.

That was a good question. If we turned back, we faced a 25 mile hike out. Sue, who was to meet us in Waterton Lakes, would be a hundred miles away. If we tried to cross the creek, we risked our lives. I considered the options.

I looked carefully at the clear, cold water rushing over the submerged stepping stones; six to eight inches deep, I judged. We were carrying heavy packs and that should reduce the risk of being swept off our feet unless we slipped on the stones. If we planted our feet squarely on each stepping stone and moved quickly, I judged we could make it. I looked at Heather. "Jump from one stone to the next," I said. "Make sure your foot lands squarely on each stone and move fast." Without waiting for her reply, I jumped as fast as I could from stepping stone to stepping stone, immersing my feet up to my boot tops in the icy, rushing waters. In ten seconds, I was across. Heather followed without a word. Seconds later she stood next to me. "Good Job," I said. "You did everything just right."

"You took off so fast that I didn't have time to tell you I couldn't do it," she said.

"I know," I replied with a grin.

✱✱✱✱✱✱✱✱✱✱✱✱✱

While mountain weather can be dangerous, it's bears most people worry about. One year I joined a group of four other men on a hike to Lake Isabel. The fishing there was reported to be the best in the Park. Part of the reason is that Isabel is hard for fishermen to get to. It is square in the middle of the southern section of Glacier Park, twelve miles west of Two Medicine Lake and sixteen miles east of US Route 2, the western boundary of the Park. To get there requires hiking up 1,600 vertical feet over the Continental Divide at Two Medicine Pass, down 600 feet to Park Creek, then back up 900 feet to Lake Isabel. With heavy packs, it's a full day and then some. The climb up past Cobalt Lake and over Two Medicine Pass was hot and tiring. As we headed up Park Creek, we encountered numerous blow-downs across the trail. The trail crew hadn't been there for a long time. When we arrived in late afternoon, everyone was hot and tired from the twelve mile trek. A couple of fellows looking exhausted.

From the looks of the campsite, it was clear that we were the first humans to visit the lake that year. While most of us began setting up our backpack tents and rolling out sleeping bags, one fellow took his fishing gear down to the shore and cast a lure out into the lake. He immediately yelled; "I got one!" He reeled in a fat sixteen-inch brown trout.

Everyone dropped what they were doing, grabbed a fishing pole and ran to the water. I was excited. I threw my line out and – bang!- immediately hooked a fish, a big one. Everyone was catching fish as fast as they could cast a line out and in less than five minutes we had more trout on our stringers than we could eat. From then on it was catch and release. No one could believe what was happening. It was virtually impossible to cast a line out without catching a fish. The water was frothing with fish going after our lures. After fifteen minutes of reeling one fish in after another, the thrill was gone. I hooked my lure to my pole and moved back to the campsite. One by one, my fellow hikers hooked their lures on their poles and left the lake shore. When you know you'll catch a fish every time you throw out your line, fishing isn't much fun!

Lake Isabel is a round, relatively small lake nestled high in some of the most rugged peaks in the Park. It lies in a tight cirque, surrounded almost entirely by naked walls of stone that rise straight up. While we were cooking our trout dinners over our camp stoves, someone noticed something moving in this confined area, on the opposite side of the lake. We all jumped up to see what it was. A large grizzly was slowly making its way across stones directly across from us. It was moving to our right, circling the lake, the only path open to it and we were squarely in the bear's path. I felt my heart jump into my throat. The bear disappeared behind some bushes on the water's edge, then reemerged, closer to us. We all looked to one another, no one wanting to admit the obvious; everyone was frightened. "What do we do?" someone asked. I looked around for a tree to climb, but the trees nearby were small, poor specimens, none good climbing candidates. Besides, my body was exhausted. I was too tired to climb a tree, even if I could find one. It seemed we all felt the same. We had no good options. "I guess we'll just have to let him eat us," someone replied.

241

We could hear the bear moving through the brush to our right, not more than fifty feet away. All I could think of was the smell of fresh-cooked trout being sent out from our frying pans. When the bear moved out of the brush, we got a good look at it. It was s big, muscular fellow with a thick tawny coat. The massive power embodied in this wild animal caused my heart to pound and my stomach tighten. What would I do if he came our way? I didn't know.

The bear kept moving straight ahead, no longer following the shoreline which would have led him to our campsite but farther back, among the scraggly fir. The bear, it seemed, wanted to keep distance between him and us. I sensed that it had chosen to ignore us despite the aroma of our dinners. It moved deliberately, resolutely ahead, not altering its pace or path or even indicating it was aware of our presence. It went beyond our camp site and disappeared down the trail we'd used to get to the lake. A sigh of relief went up from our little group, followed by titters of self-conscious laughter. Everybody had been afraid, everybody was relieved and nobody wanted to admit it. The insane clamoring of fish for our lures was forgotten. The bear was all anybody could talk about that evening. Fear and relief had been replaced by excitement over the rare experience we'd had, a close encounter with the Park's top predator.

After dinner, someone invented a game that brought us back to the lakeshore. The idea was to throw out a lure and reel it in so fast that fish couldn't catch it. Whoever brought his lure in without a fish on the line was the winner. It took the group ten minutes of casting out and reeling in to get a winner. The fish, it seemed, just wouldn't be denied.

Although we'd planned to spend two days fishing Lake Isabel, we left the next morning. The fishing was just too good to be much fun, sort of like golf in hell where every stroke results in a hole-in-one. After packing up early in the morning, we headed down Park Creek for the grueling eighteen mile hike to the Izaak Walton Ranger Station on the western boundary of the Park where we would meet our rides back home. Though the trail was mostly downhill, we encountered trees down across the trail nearly the whole way which made a long hike that much more difficult. The Glacier Park trail crews, it seemed, hadn't had time to clear this little-used trail.

When we emerged at Highway US 2, we were all tired but happy. We'd climbed the Continental Divide to reach one of the most remote lakes in the Park. The route had taken us completely across the southern section of Glacier Park, through some of the most remarkably beautiful mountain scenery in the United States. We'd experienced fishing that was truly unbelievable and come up close against one of nature's most magnificent predators. It was an experience that few, very few people would ever have.

****

August 18, 1989, a Friday, is a day I will never forget. A few months prior to our summer vacation, Patrick, 19, had recently recovered from twelve-hour surgery at Mayo Clinic in Rochester, Minnesota. What was then an experimental procedure relieved him of a serious, long-term illness and restored him to health. A few days before we were to return to our home in Chicago, Patrick and I decided to hike the Highline trail as we often did at the end of a vacation. Our route was a familiar one; from Logan Pass to Granite Park Chalet and down to Sun Road via the steep, 4 mile-long Loop Trail.

The weather was as good as it gets in the Park. Rugged mountain tops still dotted with late-summer patches of snow stood out vividly in the clear air and bright sunshine. Perhaps a hundred other hikers crowded the popular trail, taking advantage of the Highline's fantastic views. Patrick and I were strong hikers and we blew past vacationers of every description; families with little kids, little old ladies in tennis shoes and one man from Tennessee who labored under a giant video camera he carried on his shoulder.

We covered the 7.8 miles between Logan Pass and Granite Park Chalet far faster than we'd planned and arrived before noon. We were wired for speed that day and ate our lunches quickly. "If we hike down now, we would still have time to go to the fair," I suggested. The Northwest Montana Fair was taking place in Kalispell sixty miles away.

"Sounds good," Patrick replied. "We can meet Mom at the Loop by 2 o'clock."

We shouldered our day packs and started down. Granite Park and the Loop Trail are notorious because of their history of human encounters with grizzly bears. The campground just below the Chalet became famous in 1964 when a grizzly killed a woman there, one of two fatal attacks on the same night, attacks popularized in a best-selling book, The Night of the Grizzly. But as Patrick and I raced down the trail that August day, hoping to beat our previous best time, the thought of encountering a bear was the last thing on our minds. We passed more hikers, some laboring up the trail, a few heading down. We said a quick 'hello' to one young couple who were hiking down nearly as fast as we were.

After a traverse of nearly two miles across an open mountainside, the trail switchbacked to the east and entered a dense forest of new-growth Douglas fir. The trees were small and close together, crowding the trail on both sides. As we continued racing down, we came to a place where the trail turned to the right. The trees blocked our view ahead. Suddenly I sensed that large animals – my mind said horses – were racing up the trail towards us. I didn't hear anything or see anything but I definitely sensed what was happening. It could only have been a sixth sense. An instant later, three bears burst around the bend into view. They were racing towards us like fighter jets in formation. I remember my mind saying in my head, "I never knew bears ran in packs!"

Patrick, who was a few steps ahead, turned toward me, his eyes wide with fear. He ran past me, starting back up the trail. In an instant, the bears rushed past me, apparently seeing only Patrick. In another instant they would be on him. I only had time to yell, "Patrick, get in the tree."

At the sound of my voice, the three grizzlies put on the brakes, sending up a cloud of dust. I recognized them as a sow grizzly and her two second-year cubs, nearly as large as their mother. They whirled around and came for me as Patrick leapt into a tree at the edge of the trail. My mind began working in slow motion and my vision went black and white. I remember thinking, "This can't be happening. This can't be real." But it was real. It was happening. At that moment, I was more terrified than I ever thought I could be.

In a second, the bears surrounded me, biting and bumping and jostling me, trying to bring me down. I was startled at how angry the mother bear was; she was absolutely furious. She wanted to kill me. All I could do was try to fight them off, try to save my life. I found myself engulfed in bears, buffeted this way and that, dust and debris flying in the air, all in slow motion and black and white. I heard a voice in my mind say, "This is like being in the middle of the biggest dog fight I've ever seen!"

I struggled to move through the melee toward a tree with the hope of climbing to safety. I felt like I was in stuck in molasses, moving slowly, in slow motion as the bears tried to kill me. I became furious with myself for not being able to move more quickly. Why must I move so slowly? I wondered. I remember flailing at the bears and hitting one on the nose.

To my surprise, I found myself standing at the foot of a small tree at the edge of the trail. The branches of the tree were hardly thicker than a pencil and close together. It would have been hard to climb without having to deal with bears. But somehow I managed to get my left foot on a low branch and, holding onto branches above my head, began inching myself up. The bears seemed to back off a little. I found another foothold and leveraged myself higher. When my feet were about four feet off the ground, mother bear jumped up at me and grabbed my left calf with her mouth. She bit down. I knew she had me this time. My calf was firmly clamped in the bear's jaws. I looked down at her head which was attached to my leg. We were face to face, eye to eye, inches apart. I will never forget how big her head was or how she looked. She was a handsome animal. Her eyes were yellow and some kind of white pollen – like bear grass only not bear grass – was on the top of her head.

Suddenly the bear began shaking me like a terrier shakes a squirrel. My body bounced back and forth against the hard branches of the tree. In a few seconds, the bear stopped shaking me and began to pull me down. When I looked down into her face, I saw her two yearling cubs at the base of the tree looking up at me, one on her left, one on her right. My mind said, "If you go on the ground, you will die." I clung to the small branches above my head that I was holding onto but as the bear pulled, the branches bent and my hands began slipping off. My mind said, "You're going on the ground. You are going to die."

Then something most unexpected happened. I heard a different voice in my mind. It said, "It's OK. It will be alright." In that instant, my terror left me and a calmness, a peacefulness I had never known came over me. I knew then that it would be alright. I don't remember letting out a cry, but Patrick – who was watching in his own terror – said I did. He said the sound was like a final cry of someone who was dying. In that moment, the mother bear released her grip on my leg.

I tried to move up a little higher in the tree without much success. The sow came up twice more, attempting to get hold of me again, but failed. Then she went back down on all fours and circled the base of the tree I was in, scratching up dirt and "woofing". I could see she was still furious. The next thing I knew, she was on the other side of the trail with her two cubs. It looked almost like they were having a family conference; "Should we try to get him again or let him go? Should we let him go or try to get him again?" An instant later the sow shot off the trail, cubs close behind. She raced straight up the mountainside, through the brush, and disappeared.

Patrick called to me from his position in the tree he'd jumped into. "I'll get help," he cried as he started down.

The story of Jerry DeSanto flashed through my mind. Jerry was a well known Park ranger and accomplished naturalist who encountered a big grizzly at the head of Kintla Lake, one of the most remote spots in the Park. Seeing that the bear was aggressive, Jerry climbed a tree. The bear disappeared into the forest. Jerry stayed in the tree for two hours to make sure the bear was gone. When he got down, the bear charged him from the brush and brought him down. A fellow ranger at the foot of the lake nine miles away got a feeling that something was wrong and that he needed to look for Jerry. It was a premonition. He took the speedboat at the ranger station and raced to the head of the lake. He found Jerry bleeding from a severed femoral artery, one of the largest in the body. He immediately put a tourniquet on Jerry's leg and called in a medevac helicopter. Had he not arrived when he did, Jerry would have bled to death. I wondered where our three bears were and worried that they might return.

"Stay in the tree," I shouted.

Patrick stayed where he was for about 60 seconds, then jumped down and raced back up the trail. A few minutes later he returned with the couple we'd encountered on the way down. I looked down at the trio from my perch in the tree and realized they could be in danger. When I got out of the tree, the young woman wanted to look at the wounds in my leg but I refused. "We need to move down the trail right away," I said. "There's an open area ahead and if the bears return, we'll be able to see them in time to climb a tree."

Patrick and the young man put their arms around my waist and we hiked down about two hundred yards to the open place I had remembered. They put me on the ground and the lady quickly wrapped the bandana she'd been wearing around my calf, just below the knee. The bleeding from my main wound slowed to a trickle. It turned out that the young woman was a veterinarian from Colorado Springs. She knew just what to do.

As she tended to my leg, we could hear motorcycles rounding the Loop on Going to the Sun Road. We were within a quarter mile of the road. With no other alternative, I said, "I think I can hike out if you give me a hand." I put my arms around the shoulders of Patrick and the young man from Colorado and we headed for the Loop.

When we came near the road, a crowd of excited tourists gathered around, asking what happened. When they learned about the bear attack, a number of them started up the trail, hoping to see the bear. "Don't go up there!" I shouted. "Close this trail. The bears are still out there somewhere."

I asked Patrick and the young man to set me down when we reached the side of the road. At that moment, Sue spotted us from the small parking lot at the Loop. We had arranged to meet her there. She put her hand to her mouth as she stood looking at me. "How big was she?" she asked. Sue knew what had happened. She was shocked and alarmed at my wounds but she could see I was alive and that they were probably not life-threatening. "Get him to the car," she said.

As the guys were helping me into the back seat of our Suburban, a Red Bus full of tourists rounded the bend, heading up toward Logan Pass. Sue flagged down the driver and told him to radio Park Headquarters and send an ambulance up. Not waiting for help that she knew must be long in coming, she put Patrick in the back seat with me, started the car and headed down.

The scene Patrick and I created in the back seat was bizarre. I found myself laughing almost hysterically, thinking, "My God, I'm alive, I'm alive." It was a shock. I did not expect to be alive. Right next to me Patrick was crying hysterically, suffering terribly from the ordeal of watching bears trying to tear his father apart.

As we passed the turnoff to Packers' Roost, two Park squad cars, red lights flashing, sirens wailing, blasted up the road towards us, headed for the Loop. We saw that the rangers were carrying rifles. Sue honked the horn and tried to wave the rangers down. "We're here, we're here!" she shouted. The squad cars raced by us, never realizing that we were the victims.

248

Help was not available to us until we'd travelled the 25 miles to the Park entry station in West Glacier near Park Headquarters. Sue stopped our car in the middle of the wide asphalt just inside the entry station. A ranger carrying a large bag appeared immediately. Somehow he knew who we were and what had happened. He helped me out and laid me on the asphalt. "I'm Gary Moses," he said. "I'm the ranger in charge of bear attacks." He quickly assessed my wounds and before I knew what was happening, pulled a giant syringe from his bag. It was a foot long and two inches in diameter. "This is antiseptic," he explained as he shot my leg wound full of the stuff. "What happened?" he asked.

"We were attacked by a sow grizzly and her two yearling cubs on the Loop Trail," I answered. "Don't hurt her. She was only protecting her cubs."

Gary looked hard into my eyes. "Are you sure?" he asked. "She was protecting cubs?"

"I'm sure," I replied. "Don't hurt those bears."

Moses turned away and picked up a two-way radio. "Cancel the kill order on the Sullivan bears," he said.

A reply from the radio said, "We've got the sow in our sights. Are you sure?"

"Cancel the kill," Gary repeated. He turned back to me. "Why do you think the grizzly let go of you," he asked?

My reply just popped out. I didn't have to think about it. "It wasn't my time to die," I said. Now, decades later, I still can't think of a better answer.

Moses administered emergency first aid and suggested it would be faster to drive to the hospital than wait for an ambulance. Lights flashing, we followed his patrol car to North Valley Hospital in Whitefish. Dr. Bill Miller was waiting for us when we got there.

He'd attended a number of bear attacks in past years. He saw how traumatized Patrick and Sue were and said they could come into the operating room to be with me while he treated my wounds.

He cut off my jeans and found that mother bear's canine teeth had punched holes in my calf all the way to the bone. The bone, he said, was visible in the largest wound. Sedated but conscious, I felt and heard the crunching of his instruments cutting away loose flesh. It was creepy. Dr. Miller put a drain in the largest wound, sewed me up, bandaged my calf and stepped back. "Where else are you hurt?" he asked.

"Nowhere," I replied. "Just my leg."

Dr. Miller pointed to my chest. "What happened here?" he asked. I looked down and found that my T-shirt was stiff with blood. "Let's take a look," he said. He cut off my shirt and pointed at my chest. "How did this happen?"

I looked down at my chest and saw several long cuts across it. "I guess the branches caused this when the bear was shaking me," I replied.

Dr. Miller laughed. "It looks like that tree had five big claws on it!" In fact, the bear had whacked me on the chest and broke three of my ribs. I don't remember that happening but Patrick did. "The bear hit you in the chest when you were trying to get to the tree," he said.

It was then that I realized I had not felt any pain in my ribs. In fact, I hadn't felt any pain at all, not until we left the operating room. Then the pain hit me. It was substantial and lasted far longer than I imagined. I learned later that it is common for victims of bear attacks not to feel pain during and immediately after the attack. Nobody knows exactly why, but doctors speculate it is due to the amount of adrenaline that the body pumps out during an attack.

When I was released from the hospital and we returned home to Reynolds' Ranch, Tom Reynolds could scarcely believe what had happened. All he could say was, "Well I be go to hell!"

Shortly after the attack, we returned home to Illinois and I began to worry. I was afraid that I would be afraid of bears. I was afraid I would be afraid to hike in the backcountry and sleep on the ground. I would never know until I again ventured onto a trail in Glacier National Park. It wasn't until November that Sue and I returned to Montana. It was time for the drain in my leg to be removed and we wanted Dr. Miller to do it.

Following that procedure, we drove into the Park and up to the Loop parking lot. I needed to see how I would feel walking into the forest where I'd met the bears. The Park was deserted. Tourists had returned home to work and school. The shops and hotels were shuttered. We walked up the Loop Trail to where the attack had taken place and sat down on a log directly under the tree I had tried to climb. I was apprehensive. We sat quietly in the late-fall afternoon sun, listening to the little sounds of the forest. Suddenly we heard an animal moving in the brush a few yards up the trail. My heart leapt into my throat. Moments later a beautiful doe stepped serenely out of the brush and onto the trail. She looked at us and we looked at her. In that instant, I knew I would be alright. I knew I would not be afraid. I'd be sleeping on the ground far from civilization next summer. I was once again one with the wild.

CHAPTER 6

WILD KINGDOM

For the few hardy souls who choose to live in the mostly empty lands of the North Fork, absence of the nuisance of a crowded civilization combined with a rich variety of wildlife provide ample recompense for living miles from a supermarket, light line or telephone. No other place in lower North America retains the full complement of predators that were present when Meriwether Lewis came near two hundred years ago. This rare habitat is home to grizzly and black bears, mountain lion, wolf, coyote, fox, badger and lynx. It is the last sanctuary of the wolverine. Deer, elk, moose, bighorn sheep, mountain goats and a dwindling population of Dolly Varden and West Slope Cutthroat Trout make their homes here.

Two hundred years ago grizzly bears roamed most of what is now the western United States, from St. Louis to San Francisco, Albuquerque to Fort Benton. Biologists estimate that, at one time, three million of the big bears populated this region. Today their habitat has shrunk to small portions of just three states - Montana, Wyoming and Idaho. The majority of grizzlies are located in mountainous western Montana, primarily in the ecosystems of Glacier and Yellowstone Parks. A biological study done in the early 2,000's showed the North Fork to have the highest density of grizzly bears of five discrete regions in and around Glacier/Waterton Parks. Even so, grizzlies remain rare; it is estimated that only about 375 grizzlies populate the one million acres of Glacier Park. Black bears, on the other hand, are much more numerous and researchers tell us their population in Montana is holding steady despite shrinking habitat.

Being surrounded by forest in Glacier Park to the east, Crown Land in British Columbia to the north and Flathead National Forest to the west and south, we see bears pretty regularly at Reynolds Ranch. It's not unusual to see one along the road on our property or in the meadow below Tom's house, the place we now occupy. But like Tom, we've never felt threatened by bears. They are generally shy creatures and, unless you come upon a sow with cubs, they'll almost always run away when they see a human. I occasionally have to replace boards on the shed where I store the garbage until we haul it to the dump and sometimes their presence will cause us to stay inside, but mostly they are just fun to watch.

Not long after Ray Brown had renovated our McAfee cabin, Sue got up just before sunrise and went outside to savor the peace and beauty that can only be found in this special place. She walked north, to a slight rise next to the cabin and there came face to face with a bear: a grizzly bear. She stopped short, only a few yards from the surprised bear. The bear stood up on hind legs and looked at Sue. We were new to the North Fork and she did not fully appreciate the potential danger of this meeting. She very much wanted to drink in the beauty of this magnificent creature with her eyes, so she lingered. The bear, however, dropped down on four feet and began to move its head back and forth in a swaying motion. Sue sensed danger and somehow did everything correctly. She didn't panic and run. She kept facing the bear and said in a calm, soothing voice, "Good morning, Mr. Bear. I'm going to turn and walk away and I won't hurt you." The bear cocked his head as though trying to understand what she was saying. She turned and walked slowly back to the cabin. When she came near the door, she ducked inside and called for me to get up and grab the camera. In my skivvies, I eagerly followed Sue to where she'd had her wonderful encounter, but Mr. Bear was not there. That taught me not to lay too long in bed.

One evening we came back from a day of hiking in the Park and found a sow (female) black bear sitting on our porch. We enjoyed watching her until someone had to go to the bathroom. I decided it was time for the bear to leave. I got out and yelled at the bear. The bear seemed interested but didn't move. I got back into the car and honked the horn. The bear still didn't move. As the kids' desire to visit the outhouse grew more urgent, I grabbed a broom that we'd left outside and shooed the bear off the porch. I wouldn't have tried this technique had the bear been a grizzly!

While we North Forkers love to watch bears, bears sometimes find it fun to watch people. Not long after we moved into Tom's house, we spotted a griz behind a bush just beyond our front yard. The bear suddenly popped up behind the bush, standing on hind legs. He was looking at us. After a few moments, he dropped back down and ran behind another bush. He stood up again and peered at the house as he had before. The bear made nearly a complete circle around the house, hiding behind one bush after another, then popping up to look. It seemed he was curious about us two-legged creatures.

We found that bears can be playful but, at the same time, troublesome. Early one morning when we were living in the McAfee cabin, Sue got up to go to the outhouse. She came back in as quickly as she'd left. "A bear has bitten a hole in our tire!" she cried. I thought she must be mistaken. I got out of bed and went outside. A loud hiss from the direction of our car greeted my ears. What I heard was the air going out of a front tire. Tooth marks in the rubber indicated that Sue had been correct. A bear had sunk his teeth into our tire. Tom affirmed that bears like to chew soft things. The previous winter he'd gotten his snowmobile stuck at the bottom of his hill and left it there overnight. In the morning the seat was ripped off and chewed to bits. Not learning from Tom's experience, I left my motorcycle out one night only to find in the morning that a bear had bitten the seat off. It cost me over a hundred dollars to get a new one and I never left my bike out overnight again.

In 1985, Sue and I had Ray Brown build a new log cabin for my Uncle Bob who had learned to love the North Fork as we had, for perhaps different reasons. Bob loved a good time and in those days, the Trail Creek Customs Station at the US Border one mile north of our place was open. A hundred yards on the other side stood the Canadian Customs Office. On average, six cars crossed the border during a summer day, leaving the customs officers with plenty of time on their hands. Ron Fontana or Bill McSeveny or whoever was stationed in Canada would regularly walk the hundred yards down to visit John Senger or Joe Lang, US Customs officials. And vice versa. There was almost always a cribbage or poker game going on. After the border closed at 5PM, the good times would start. The North Fork was hip-deep in young biologists and researchers studying bears or wolves or ungulates or trees or what-not. Most were graduate students, many were young women. Guys and gals would congregate at either the US or Canadian Customs office after hours and party.

Bob Sullivan spent almost as much time at the border as the customs officers. He loved the card games, the story-telling (no one could top Ron Fontana) and whatever they were drinking. One night around two AM, Sue and I were awakened in our McAfee cabin to loud rock music. We jumped out of bed and ran to the window. It was Bob coming home. The windows in his brand new Ford Explorer were rolled down and he had the stereo cranked up. The sounds of the Rolling Stones followed Bob's car up to his house and stopped. Sue and I laughed and shook our heads and went back to sleep. The next morning we saw Bob hoofing it down through the meadow to our house. We thought that odd. Bob never walked when he could drive. He was puffing when he came in our door. "Damned bear tore the seat out of my car!" he announced. Sue and Bob and I jumped in our truck and raced up to his house. Sure enough, the leather driver's seat from Bob's Explorer sat outside the car, in tatters. The door to the car was open and the inside was a mess. "I forgot to roll the windows up last night," Bob explained. Indeed.

We learned later that Marca, one of the gals who regularly partied at the border, had experienced a similar problem a few days before. A bear had broken into the trunk of her Honda through the back seat. She had left her garbage in the trunk overnight, thinking to take it to the dump in town in the morning. The bear, we figured, was looking for garbage in Bob's car. Bob said he had a heck of a time explaining the situation to his insurance agent back in Iowa. He never left the windows in his car rolled down over night and Marca never left garbage in her trunk again.

One summer a smallish sub-adult black bear was frequenting our cabin and making a nuisance of itself. He would show up every morning about daybreak and nose around the cabin, apparently hoping to find food. He was not afraid of us and we decided it was time for the bear to move on. When in town, I put a call in to Dave Weedum, the Montana Fish Wildlife and Parks expert whose job it was to deal with problem bears. Dave hauled a small bear trap up behind his pickup one day and put it fifty feet from our cabin. He baited it with dead chickens, road kill and other disgusting stuff, checked the mechanism that sprung the trap door and told us to call him when the bear was trapped. The next morning we looked out our window, waiting for the bear to show up as he had every morning for the past two weeks. The bear didn't appear. The second morning we got up expecting the bear, but he didn't show. This went on for two more days. No black bear. We figured that bear was smart enough to know he should stay away to avoid being trapped. We decided to go to town the next day and tell Dave to take his trap away.

The next morning we looked outside. This time, we saw a bear coming up our lane from the direction of the North Fork Road. But it wasn't our black bear. It was a very large grizzly bear, a bear way too big, I thought, for Dave's trap. Still in my underwear, I ran out the door to the trap, thinking to spring the door so the grizzly couldn't get stuck inside. I pulled on the mechanism. To my surprise, it wouldn't budge. The big grizzly kept coming toward the trap. I put more muscle against the lever. No luck. I got up on top of the round trap thinking I could exert more leverage on the mechanism that way. It still wouldn't budge. By this time the grizzly was not more than twenty feet away, heading straight for me, and I'm sitting in my underwear over a rotting chicken dinner.

Sue opened the cabin door and yelled at me to get inside, quick. I jumped off the trap and could see there was no way I could reach the cabin before the bear reached me. I ran to our car which was parked nearby, hoping the door was unlocked. It was. The grizzly reached the trap about the same time I got inside the car. He proceeded to stick his front half into the trap and gobble down the dinner that Dave had so kindly left for him. When dinner was finished, he backed out of the trap and ambled back down our road the way he came. The trap door never did spring. Sue and I decided we didn't want a bear trap on our place – especially one that didn't work - and called Dave to remove it. Bear traps, we decided, only attract bears. The black bear hadn't returned, we realized, because of the presence of the big grizzly. Grizzlies sometimes eat black bears!

Wolves are another story. Before Columbus made his great discovery, the grey timber wolf – along with two subspecies – was found throughout North America. Beginning about 1880, the United States government, at the behest of ranchers, put a bounty on the hide of the grey timber wolf with the intent of exterminating them. That policy succeeded. By about 1930, no wolves existed in Montana or indeed, anywhere in the lower 48 states, save for a small population in northern Minnesota. Tom Reynolds, however, told us that he'd seen the occasional wolf on his property from the time he moved there in the early 1930's. They were, no doubt, wandering pack members from British Columbia where extermination efforts had not proven entirely successful. In the late 1970's, more and more reports of wolf sightings in the North Fork were made. The wolf, it seemed, was migrating down from Canada, reintroducing itself into Montana. The University of Montana launched a wolf study project that continued for three decades. Tom's property, one mile south of the B.C. border, was directly in the path of the migrating wolves and soon after we bought it, we met these rare and elusive wanderers.

One morning before daybreak, a sound shattered the silence that surrounded our little cabin. Sue and I awoke instantly and sat straight up in bed. The fur on the back of our Siamese cat bristled. Long plaintive howls in several different keys blended together into the amazing sounds produced by a wolf pack. The source of the sound seemed very near. Sue and I and the cat jumped out of bed and raced to a window. In our yard, not more than thirty feet from our cabin, we saw a pack of five full-grown wolves, muzzles raised to a crescent moon, howling, howling. The sound was at once blood curdling and wonderful. It was the sound of the wild, the sound of nature, the sound of the past. The howling, yelping, gabbling sounds of the pack lasted perhaps five minutes before the wolves sniffed and whirled and ran off down our road, bushy tails waving like happy flags.

Wolves, especially in those days, are exceedingly rare. It is probable that, at the time, this was the only pack in the North Fork on either side of the river. We understood what a rare privilege we'd been given and would always remember these magnificent animals and the sounds they made. Over the years, we've seen the occasional wolf on the North Fork Road or in the Park or somewhere on our property. One day I was about to do some brush thinning when I almost stepped on a brown female wolf. She was on one side of a tree, I on the other. When we met, we were both startled and she quickly ran off. Another day, perhaps fifteen years after Sue and I had moved into Tom's house, we heard an ungodly noise down the hill, in the direction of the new cabin we'd had Ray Brown build for Bob. The cabin was empty. Sue and I knew we were listening to a large pack of wolves. We walked as quickly as we could down to Bob's cabin and, when we got there, found a pack of perhaps twelve wolves running around Bob's front yard, howling and talking and gabbling. I'd never seen so many wolves in one place. When they saw us, they raced off into the forest.

Having lived in wolf country now for three decades, I would make two observations, both of which run counter to prevailing Montana wisdom. First, forty years after their return, wolves continue to be extremely rare. Even in the North Fork where populations are acknowledged to be highest in the nation, we're lucky to see one wolf all summer. At last count, only three packs of five to seven wolves each inhabit the entire North Fork drainage which covers perhaps a million acres. Second, wolves are harmless to humans. Even in packs as large as the one we saw by Bob's cabin, wolves run at the sight of a human. That's why seeing a wolf continues to be so wonderfully exciting to Sue and me and the practice of hunting them again, so distressing.

While North Fork conversations usually center on bears or wolves, the predator making the greatest impact on North Fork wildlife population may be the mountain lion. They are rarely seen, but they're there. One late afternoon, Sue and I were sitting in our front yard enjoying our view of the Livingston Range when the quiet was suddenly shattered by a horrible sound out back of our place, in thick timber. It was not a sound that anyone wants to hear and Sue ran inside to escape it. It was the scream of a big cat followed by an agonized cry of an ungulate – a deer or moose. It was a cry of terror and pain and desperation, a death cry. The next morning I went into the forest in the direction of the sound to look for the remains of a kill, but I found nothing. I asked Larry Wilson, who has lived most of his life in the North Fork, about that. He said it wasn't unusual not to locate a kill. Mountain lions generally pull their kills deeper into the woods or sometimes into a tree, leaving little or nothing behind.

Some years later, an old cow moose came to the little pond in front of our house. She seemed about to collapse. Her back carried a large open wound, probably caused by a big cat trying to bring her down. She drank long from our pond and slowly made her way through our meadow. We saw her again several days later. We were happy, for she looked stronger, though the wound hadn't healed. We did not see this moose again.

Though we'd heard their sounds and seen the work of mountain lions, it took 20 years before I actually saw one. They are elusive critters. The lion was walking down the North Fork Road, a couple miles south of our place. I was astounded by the size of the mountain lion; imagine a house cat six feet long, not including its tail! Equally impressive is the tail. The lion's tail was fully as long as its body and looked to be four inches thick.

Mountain lion sightings came fast and furious after that. The following year I saw three. Sue and I were driving north, just above Polebridge one bright, summer day. Thick, twenty-foot high lodgepole – first growth from the 1988 Red Bench fire – crowd both sides of the road. As we came around a bend, I slowed and then stopped. A doe was standing in the middle of the road. Oddly, she didn't run at our approach but seemed fixated on something. Suddenly a mountain lion leapt out of the trees, not three feet from the side of our truck. It bounded once in the road right in front of our truck and in the next instant was on the other side. The lion was so close that, in one frozen moment, we could see the whiskers on its muzzle, muscles rippling under its tawny skin, large, thick pads of its feet and extended claws. What a magnificent sight! As our eyes followed the lion, we saw that the doe had vanished into the trees. We wondered if it got away. After we arrived home, Heather, driving our Jeep five minutes behind us, jumped out, excited. She reported seeing a mountain lion crossing the road just north of Polebridge. It was headed the opposite direction from where we'd seen it. The doe had obviously escaped.

That same year, I rode my motorcycle down from our house to the North Fork Road, intending to go north to visit the McDonough's, our nearest neighbor. As I rounded the first turn and started down a hill, a large mountain lion jumped up onto the road from a ravine on my left. I stopped and watched a very big cat walk casually across the road in front of me. He seemed in no hurry. Like big cats we've seen in the circus, he leapt with powerful grace up a cut bank on the right and disappeared into the trees. I thought about that cat up there above me and decided to turn around and go back home. It didn't seem wise to ride my motorcycle beneath the cut bank at that moment. A visit to my neighbors, Gary and Karen, could wait another day.

Two weeks later, our daughter Heather was sleeping on the screened porch at the cabin we'd built for Bob. She was awakened in the night by a licking sound. She assumed it was a moose licking the salt in her front yard. The licking sound continued and she was unable to go back to sleep. She took a flashlight and went outside with the intent of chasing the moose off. But when she shined her light toward the salt, two glowing eyes of a big mountain lion stared back at her from not more than twenty feet away. She beat a hasty retreat to the cabin and decided to move inside for the night. The next morning I reminded her that it isn't wise to try chasing a moose off either.

Bears and wolves and mountain lions share the vast wilderness around Glacier Park with a carnivore that may be even more amazing, the wolverine. The wolverine's strength, stamina and toughness are legendary. There are reports of wolverines fighting off grizzly bears, though the bears often outweigh them ten to one. The first American study of the wolverine was done in 2009 in Glacier Park and the North Fork. Radio collar data in the study indicated that one wolverine traversed 50 miles of mountainous country, going from one side of Glacier Park to the other in a single day. What made that trip so remarkable was that it took place during winter and the route the wolverine chose was a straight line, going up over the Continental Divide and back down again without regard to the steepness or difficulty of the terrain. The study found that only about 50 wolverines inhabit the million and a half acres of Glacier Park and the North Fork. Wolverines are the rarest of the rare.

We were, therefore, fortunate in the extreme to see a wolverine on our property some years ago. Sue and I headed out just before sunrise to take a hike in Glacier Park. As we got to the North Fork Road and turned south, I stopped our truck. An animal of some sort was walking up the middle of the road towards us. In the dim light, we couldn't at first make out what kind of critter it was, but we could see it was unusual. The creature was about two feet high and two feet wide. It marched resolutely toward our truck, in a straight line. As it got to within fifty feet, we could see it was a wolverine. It's wide, flat body, short legs, pointed snout and striped head were unmistakable. The wolverine marched right up to our truck, gave one brief glance up at us, and continued on straight ahead, changing its course only enough to clear our truck by perhaps twelve inches.

Over the years we've seen many of the wolverine's cousin species. One day I was riding my motorcycle on the North Fork Road just south of the McDonough's. As I reached the north edge of our property, a badger jumped out of the forest into the road and nearly ran into my bike. The badger and I were both startled. The badger took off running in the direction I was heading. He ran along at 20 miles an hour, not more than two feet from my bike. Neither he nor I seemed to know what to do. The two of us continued on in

261

formation for perhaps a hundred yards. Then the badger finally made a decision; he disappeared back into the forest!

One year, a family of pine martins, a small species of the weasel/badger/wolverine family, made their home in back of our woodshed. Five babies were born. We saw the adults only occasionally, but what a treat it was. Unfortunately, the martins apparently like to chew soft materials. They chewed completely through my garden hose in several places. We were careful not to bother them, but one morning mama martin decided to move her offspring. Carrying each baby in her mouth, she took her family across our driveway to a new home somewhere in the forest.

Unlike much of the North Fork, the land we bought has few lodgepole pine, a species that generally favors dry soil. Our property is covered in spruce, fir and aspen which prefer more moist soil. Like few places in the North Fork, about half of the trees on our property are deciduous. The reason for the difference is the land itself. The forest to the west of our house is wet and marshy with numerous springs. Beaver lodges anchor both ends of reed-filled ponds on the east edge of our property. Thick clumps of willows grow in meadows and open areas in between, rich browse for moose. Two or three mornings each week we wake to find these startlingly large creatures, animals much bigger than a horse, standing in our front yard. Cows, some with a calf, generally show up about sunrise and spend a half hour or forty minutes alternately licking our salt and drinking from the pond. Wary creatures, they watch the house, listening, always alert to danger. Young bulls with their freshly sprouted spike antlers come too, sometimes showing up in the company of a powerful adult bull with a six-foot spread. We never tire of watching them.

In addition to ubiquitous deer that come to the pond every day – and occasionally frolic about in the grass in our front yard – elk, too, sometimes find their way to the pond, especially in the fall. One night Sue got up to find a whole herd of elk in the front yard. She called me to the window. The scene was ethereal. These regal animals were bathed in the cold blue light of a full moon. Clouds of illuminated breath wrapped them in a ghostly fog. We watched them for a long while, until the herd dissolved into forest shadows.

CHAPTER 7

SAVING HEAVEN

The three million acres of boreal forest encompassing Glacier and Waterton Lakes Parks and the lands drained in Canada and U.S. by the North Fork of the Flathead River are very different from every other place in the lower United States. Located in the northwest corner of Montana and southern Province of Alberta, the Crown of the Continent, as it is known, remains a wild landscape. It is a land of towering mountains, sparkling lakes, plunging waterfalls and a handful of dwindling glaciers yet to be melted by a warming world.

This is a rare and special place, a land not yet overtaken by man's seemingly irresistible determination to replace the world as it was in the beginning with something more, something better, something grand. This land is devoid of pavement and shopping malls, airports and skyscrapers, smart phones and trophy homes. This small patch of America remains a quiet, peaceful, unhurried place, isolated from the thousand daily distractions imposed by 21st Century civilization. In many ways, it is a place that time has forgotten. To paraphrase Thomas Blakiston, a 19th Century Canadian explorer – it is a land that remains as it was when it left the hand of its Creator.

From the human perspective, these are essentially empty lands. Perhaps five hundred people live year-round in these 5,000 square miles. Bears outnumber humans. Summer vacation brings tourists, of course, but it's a truism that the number of people varies inversely with the number of feet one moves from a paved road. It is possible to walk a full day in the back country of the Crown of the Continent without meeting another human being.

This empty place is a wild landscape wrapped in a wild climate. The temperature can change from sweltering heat to freezing cold in an hour. A bright, sunny day can turn into a blizzard when hidden clouds move over a ridge. I've seen wind speed exceed

100 miles an hour, so strong it is impossible to stand. An easily managed stream crossing can become a life-threatening torrent following an afternoon thunderstorm. Comprised of soaring mountains, icy lakes, racing rivers, and emptiness, this landscape can be a thin-edge balance of gain and pain, excitement and tedium, peace and terror, freedom and isolation. Those who venture into this special place tend, I believe, toward characteristics that were more common a century ago than today; self reliance, toughness, courage, and perhaps most important, a thirst for freedom and adventure.

Nearly all Crown of the Continent land is public land, owned by provincial, state or federal governments. Save for a few small in-holdings in Glacier Park, the exception is a strip of land along the western side of the North Fork Flathead River where Reynolds' Ranch is located. There, in the North Fork, a handful of intrepid 19th and early 20th Century settlers staked homestead claims in what is now Flathead National Forest. Even here, one of the very few areas in the Crown of the Continent where there is privately owned land, 97% of the land is still owned by the Federal or state government. Only 3% of North Fork land is in private hands.

We were surprised to discover that some people who had lived for decades in the North Fork - either full time or seasonally - had never visited Glacier Park right next door. Tom Reynolds was one of those people. Some others may have been to the Park once or twice but hadn't been back in years. These people – as well as many new landowners – were there because of the North Fork. Glacier National Park was irrelevant.

A few were there because of the circumstances of their lives – inherited land, troubles elsewhere, or simply the ability to live cheaply. Some came to escape the burdens of our high-speed civilization. Most stayed in the North Fork, I believe, primarily because of the unique values it provides – remoteness, beauty, wildlife, tranquility, history, friendships, adventures and an amazingly rich social life for a community strung out along fifty miles of dirt road. Most people, I believe, see the North Fork as an opportunity to live a simpler life closer to the natural world. In the late decades of the 20th Century and early years of the 21st, that opportunity has attracted new landowners and visitors from every region of the country and every walk of life.

Yet our 1981 decision to buy land in the North Fork had absolutely nothing to do with the North Fork. In truth, we didn't even know there was such a thing as "The North Fork." Our decision to buy what became Reynolds' Ranch related solely to the property itself and its proximity to Glacier National Park. We had no idea that the "North Fork" would, in time, become dear to us, more dear even than the Park.

The more time we spent in the North Fork, the more we discovered things that make it special. We began to meet people outside of Tom Reynolds' immediate group of friends, people on Trail Creek and Whale Creek and Moose Creek and in the tiny hamlet of Polebridge 20 miles to the south. As the years passed, these people became friends, dear friends, our dearest friends. We discovered amazing trails in the Whitefish Range, some just behind our property. These hiking trails might not be quite as spectacular as some in Glacier Park but none-the-less, trails that take you to places that cause amazement and make your spirits to soar. We learned about Sondreson Hall, halfway between our place and Polebridge and became members of the North Fork Improvement Association that owns it. We picnicked at the "bubble-ups" where gushing springs rush out of the ground, turning a dry creek bed into Trail Creek, white water from bank to bank. We stood amazed at the magnificent views of Glacier Park and Flathead Valley afforded at Hornet and Cyclone and Thoma, Forest Service lookouts atop the Whitefish Range. We floated and fished the North Fork River, enjoyed community picnics and square dances at the Hall. We learned the stories of early settlers of the North Fork, people of amazing toughness, ingenuity and character. We listened to endless silence, experienced the darkness of night unbroken by a single light bulb, marveled at the Milky Way. Most importantly, the simple life afforded by the North Fork taught us to live in the moment, to experience "now," reality. Yesterday and tomorrow seem less necessary when living simply, close to the earth, self-reliant, independent.

The more time we spent in the North Fork, the more resistant we became to changes in the North Fork. Sue and I had lived in some of the great cities of America – Chicago, San Francisco, New York City. We travelled to other great cities throughout the world . We were familiar with the countless attractions and benefits big cities can provide and we enjoyed them. But we were also all too familiar with the pressures and difficulties of living in an urban environment. We saw, moreover, that year by year, towns and cities were spreading to every corner of our country and indeed, the world. Places to which one could escape "civilization" seemed destined to disappear. The North Fork was the exception; a tiny island refuge from the beehive lifestyle of urban America. We didn't want to lose it.

Change in the natural landscape, we knew, proceeds, like time, in one direction only. That direction is from less human activity to more human activity. As Aldo Leopold, a Forest Service official in the 1930's said, once wilderness is gone, it is gone forever. Wilderness can never be re-created. Change, we knew, inevitably meant more people, more development, more services, more traffic, more of the world outside and less of everything we'd come to cherish in the North Fork.

When we first came to the North Fork in 1981, it never occurred to us that the remote sea of trees in which our property was immersed could ever change. There were few signs of human habitation outside of Polebridge - which could not really be considered more than a curiosity, a cluster of a few cabins and a store. The land seemed empty, a natural landscape lacking agents of change. The Park, we knew, would never change. So, like the Park, the land next door that ran from the North Fork River to the summits of the Whitefish Range and beyond could never change, could it?

Our first suspicion that unwanted change might be coming occurred in 1982, the first summer we spent more than just a few days there. That suspicion was sparked by eighteen wheel logging trucks racing up and down the North Fork Road in great clouds of dust, seemingly every 15 minutes. Tom advised us to buy a citizen band radio for our car and listen to the channel that loggers used to avoid being run into or forced off the road by Peterbilts loaded with ten tons of freshly cut logs. Loggers, he said, were mindful of the rule that time is money, so loggers drove the road as fast as possible.

Heavily loaded logging trucks racing down steep grades on the North Fork road could not easily be stopped. Consequently, loggers had posted mile marker signs on trees all along the 56 mile route from Columbia Falls where the lumber mills were located to the Canadian border. By listening to a CB, motorists could anticipate where logging trucks were and pull off the road should they be close to their location. When a logger called out "mile 46, loaded," it meant a logging truck was headed south, down the mountain, at mile marker 46 with a load of logs; get out of the way! With steep embankments edging much of the road and vehicles being forced off from time to time by racing logging trucks, it was wise to keep the CB volume turned up.

Considering that thousands of North Fork acres were blanketed in dense forest, the supply of trees seemed almost infinite. But under the constant stream of trucks hauling trees down to the mills in Columbia Falls, couldn't that supply of trees, sooner or later, run out?

We asked Tom, who had spent 30 years in the Forest Service working with loggers about this. "Oh, I don't think they'll run out of trees," he said, "but I don't like what they're doing. They're clear-cutting up Whale Creek and Moose Creek, you know. You can't see it from the road, but that's where most of the logs are coming from. I don't approve of clear-cutting," he said, his most disapproving pucker on his lips. "I've seen what's left and it's all a mess. That's why I stopped them from logging this place."

We'd read about the controversy over clear-cutting in the press since the early 1970's and, like many city people, we thought it was probably wrong. But until now, it hadn't been an issue that touched our lives. After all, we lived in the city and our only contact with forests were those in Glacier Park. There was, of course, no logging to worry about there. But now the issue took on some importance. "What can be done about it?" we asked.

"Oh, there's nothing anyone can do," Tom replied. "The government tells the Forest Service supervisors down in Columbia Falls how many board feet of timber it expects them to harvest each year and the supervisors always try to beat their quota. That's the way they're judged, you know, by the number of board feet." Tom's sour expression left little doubt about how he felt.

One day he offered to take us up to Hornet lookout. We hiked up to enjoy the view of Glacier Park to the east, which is truly spectacular, but were alarmed by what we saw to the west and south. The vast sea of dark green trees that covered the North Fork Valley and flanks of the mountains in the Whitefish Range were marred by light colored patches of denuded land. This was the first time we'd seen a clear-cut and it came as a shock. These patches consisted of churned up bare ground strewn with a tangle of tree tops and small logs the loggers didn't want. Not a tree was left standing. The scene reminded me of pictures I'd seen of shattered trees and bare earth on battlefields in World War I. Nothing lived in these no-man's lands. It was obvious that clear-cutting, like war, destroyed both forest and wildlife habitat.

One day a young woman with shocks of long, dark wiry hair that flew out in every direction stopped by to visit Tom. Rosalind Yanishevsky was one of Tom's friends. A biologist, Rosalind owned five acres of land up Whale Creek. Her land was in the midst of old growth timber, huge old trees on land that had never been logged. Rosalind, too, was worried about clear-cutting but her greatest concern was for the preservation of old growth forests. There weren't many areas in the North Fork that hadn't been logged in the past hundred years. No one knew how much old growth remained, but the Forest Service had it all slated for harvest. Rosalind told us she was embarking on a ground-breaking study to map old growth timber in the North Fork and determine how much was left in an effort to save it from the loggers' saws.

We also met Diane Boyd, another of Tom's friends. Diane was a graduate student biologist studying the small population of wolves that had re-introduced themselves into the North Fork from British Columbia. She was worried about the impact of large scale clear-cutting on wildlife habitat. She worried not only about its direct effect on wolves but also on ungulates – deer, elk, moose – upon which wolves and other North Fork predators depend.

One day when we were buying goodies at the Polebridge Mercantile, we met a fellow who was definitely not among Tom Reynolds' circle of friends. John Frederick was the author of the newspaper article describing Tom as a hermit, thereby earning him Tom's undying enmity. John had, a few years earlier, moved to the North Fork from Ohio. When we met him, he was the proprietor of the North Fork Hostel, one of only three commercial enterprises in town. (The other two being the Merc and the Northern Lights Saloon.) John looked out of place in western Montana. His appearance projected the image of the avowed environmentalist he was – round wire rim glasses, beads, an un-minded thatch of sandy-colored hair and, worst of all, sandals.

John told us he was worried about logging as well as several other issues that he believed threatened the pristine North Fork environment. He'd founded the North Fork Preservation Association, the goal of which was to advocate for the protection and preservation of what he described as the rare, pristine, undeveloped ecosystem in which we lived. We took him up on his suggestion that we join. We were now members of both the North Fork Preservation Association and North Fork Improvement Association. We didn't realize that, at the time, these two organizations were often at cross purposes. If we had, we would have joined them anyway.

John Frederick was both an idealist and a realist. Though he ardently opposed clear-cutting and large scale logging in the North Fork, he concurred with Tom Reynolds' assessment of the situation: Forest Service officials and employees were engrained in a culture of working side-by-side with loggers to facilitate the efficient removal of timber from the forest. "They take their orders," John said, finger pointing skyward, "from on high. Their orders come from bosses at the regional headquarters in Denver – who take their orders from Washington. Nobody around here can do a thing to influence them one way or the other."

Cecily McNeil, a co-founder of the North Fork Compact, has owned property near Moose Creek since 1959. She has been an ardent advocate for conservation and recollects an incident that reflects the resource extraction philosophy of the US Forest Service in years just prior to our arrival. "I remember a Forest Service 'Show Me' trip in the 1970's to boast about the clear cuts on Moose Creek Road. The man who conducted it could not comprehend our lack of enthusiasm for a Stalingrad landscape in our area."

To understand the culture of the Forest Service at the time and the hold it had on those who ran it – from top to bottom – requires an understanding of the men who played leading roles in its development. President Teddy Roosevelt was the first national leader to recognize that, though vast, America's natural resources were finite. During the 18th and 19th Centuries, settlers and industrialists used vast quantities of America's timber, iron ore, coal and other natural resources to turn a few small Colonies clustered along the Atlantic seaboard into a great and powerful nation that spanned the North American continent. Indeed, it was America's vast natural resources that made this unparalleled expansion possible. But Roosevelt saw that the unfettered consumption of America's resources could not go on forever. Sooner or later, America would run out of forests and iron and minerals and agricultural land. An avid adventurer and big game hunter, Roosevelt believed that measures needed to be adopted to ensure that the natural resources America would need in the future would always be there. He argued for a systematic, scientific management of America's natural resources, especially the nation's forests. People of power and influence listened and the first conservation movement was begun.

As President, TR created the United States Forest Service in 1905 and installed a 34 year old friend named Gifford Pinchot as its first

Chief. Pinchot, who came from an East Coast family of great wealth, had always been interested in forestry. After graduating from Yale, he rejected an opportunity to run his family's business and went, instead, to Europe to study forest science where man had been successfully managing the balance between forest conservation and economic development for hundreds of years. By 1900, Pinchot had the reputation of being a leading expert in forestry and forest management.

Pinchot recognized that America's vast forest lands represented one of the nation's most valuable assets. His goal was "producing from the forest whatever it can yield for the service of man." As Chief of the USFS, Pinchot turned public land policy from dispersing public lands into private hands to one of maintaining them as part of the federal government. His aim was the most economically efficient use of natural resources, waste his enemy. He introduced scientific methods to forestry and turned it into a professional discipline. He reformed forest management to ensure the conservation and renewal of forests so that an adequate supply of timber would always be available for the nation's use. Roosevelt and Pinchot had envisioned that public timber should be sold only to small, family run outfits, not big syndicates which, they feared, could abuse the public's trust and ravage the nation's forests. Two of Pinchot's consistent themes were "Working forests for working people" and "Small scale logging at the edge, conservation at the core."

Pinchot was, I believe, more pragmatist than idealist and as a result, he attracted controversy and enemies on both sides of the conservation issue. John Muir, the famous California conservationist and founder of the Sierra Club ended his friendship with Pinchot when the latter backed the damming of the Hetch Hetchy River north of Yosemite to provide much needed water to the city of San Francisco. Pinchot, on the other hand, publicly and vehemently criticized the policies of Richard Ballinger who had been appointed by President Taft as Secretary of the Interior. Pinchot was convinced by Ballinger's reversal of Roosevelt's policies that he was determined to destroy the conservation movement. This split the Republican Party and embittered Taft who fired Pinchot in 1910.

Pinchot was succeeded by Henry S. Graves, founder of Yale School of Forestry and a close associate of Pinchot whose policies he continued to promote. He served from 1910 to 1920 when he was succeeded by Bill Greeley.

Greeley had graduated at the top of Yale's first Forestry School class and was hand-picked by Pinchot as USFS forester for Division 1, 41 million acres of national forest in four western states. A deeply religious man, Greeley saw the great wildfire of 1910 that swept through forests he managed in Washington, Idaho and Montana as the work of Satan. As Chief, Greeley completely redirected the focus of the Forest Service. Its overriding mission - the raison d^etre of the USFS - became fire fighting. The USFS became the fire department of the national forests, protecting trees from burning so the timber industry could cut them down later at government expense. Pinchot was appalled. The fox was in the hen house. Greeley left the Forest Service in 1928 to become a lobbyist for the timber industry.

On a trip with Henry Graves to National Forests in Montana and Idaho in 1937, Pinchot could scarcely believe what he encountered. Greeley's legacy was modern chain saws and networks of forest roads that facilitated large-scale clear-cuts. This, Pinchot saw, had become the norm in western National Forests. Entire mountainsides, mountain after mountain, were denuded of trees. Big timber syndicates controlled the forest resources that Pinchot and Roosevelt had intended to protect. It "tore my heart out," Pinchot said

Greeley set the mission and established the culture that Forest Service officials, managers and workers grew up in and spent entire careers working toward during the 1920's, 30's, 40's, 50's, 60's and 70's. It is not surprising that Cecily McNeil's Forest Service guide did not appreciate her reaction to the clear-cuts he so proudly displayed to her.

A large, hide-bound government bureaucracy like the Forest Service generally follows Newton's First Law of Motion; "Every object in a state of uniform motion tends to remain in that motion unless an external force is applied to it." In 1982, powerful external forces were building to cause the massive USFS to change course, if ever so slowly.

It all began two decades earlier with something written by a biologist who worried about the effects of misusing pesticides. Rachel Carson's 1962 Pulitzer Prize winning book 'Silent Spring' raised the public's consciousness of the importance and fragility of nature. She challenged practices of agricultural scientists and the government and called for a change in the way humankind views the natural world. The book broke onto the world scene like a bombshell and sparked debate and research that continues to this day. 'Silent Spring' had as profound an effect on America's – and indeed the world's – view of man's relationship with the earth as any book written in modern times.

The media and academia began questioning government and industry policies and conduct as they affect the environment, sparking wide-scale debates about man's responsibilities toward the natural world. The work and philosophy of Aldo Leopold was rediscovered and began to take hold in scientific and academic circles. Leopold worked for the Forest Service in the 1920's and wrote the first comprehensive management plan for the Grand Canyon. He wrote the first Forest Service game and fish handbook and by the 1930's was acknowledged to be America's foremost expert on wildlife management. Leopold believed that man's ethical relationship to the land was progressing in a direction that increasingly leads to decisions based on expediency, self interest and conquest. Leopold rejected the utilitarianism of conservation preached by Roosevelt and Pinchot and called for conservation of America's forests and wildlife with the simple aim of preserving them for future generations. Leopold believed there should be some places safe from the influences of modern civilization. He said, "Of what avail are 40 freedoms without a blank spot on the map?" While working for the Forest Service, Leopold proposed the first National Wilderness and, in 1935, founded the Wilderness Society.

Dramatic events in the 1960's and '70's engaged the public's interest. Pictures of planet earth sent back from the moon by Apollo astronauts in the late '60's were vivid evidence of man's dependence on this island refuge in the airless void of space and suggested its corollary; it is in man's own self interest to protect it. Meanwhile scientists were discovering that industrial pollutants released into the air were causing acid rain to fall in the Adirondacks and other parts of the East, killing millions of trees and threatening entire forests. In 1969 the Cuyahoga River, laced with pollutants, caught fire. Birth defects and sky-high cancer rates among people living on land that was once an industrial canal in New York State were found, in 1976, to have been caused by extreme concentrations of carcinogens and other deadly chemicals buried by a chemical manufacturing plant in the 1920's. Love Canal, as it was called, was one of the most appalling environmental disasters in America.

A consensus began to build that something needed to be done. Public pressure mounted for legislation that would reverse what many saw as government indifference to commercial activities that were degrading and in some cases destroying the elements of nature on which Americans' well-being depend – clean air and water - as well as unspoiled places and natural environs that enrich human life. In the decade between the mid-1960's and mid-1970's, legislation was enacted that would define government policy toward the environment and cause sweeping changes in industrial practices.

The Wilderness Act of 1964, signed into law by President Johnson, defined wilderness: "Wilderness, in contrast to those areas where man and his works dominate the landscape, is hereby recognized as an area where the earth and community of man are untrammeled by man, where man is a visitor himself and does not remain." Wilderness designation banned motorized devices and man-made facilities. The legislation initially set aside 9 million acres of public land as Wilderness. Wilderness Areas have since expanded to 107 million acres, or 4.8% of the United States.

The National Environment Policy Act of 1969 established, for the first time, government policy regarding the environment. Enacted by the 93rd Congress and signed into law by President Nixon, the bill declared national environmental goals and policy, established enforcement actions and created the Council on Environmental Quality in the Executive Branch. NEPA established the legal requirement that environmental issues be considered equally when compared to other issues in the decision process when federal approval of a project is required and/or federal monies are employed. Environmental Assessments or Environmental Impact Studies were made requirements for any such project.

The Endangered Species Act of 1973, also signed into law under the Nixon Administration, was designed to "protect imperiled species from extinction as a consequence of economic growth and development un-tempered by adequate concern and conservation – and to protect the ecosystem upon which they depend." U. S. Fish and Wildlife and the National Oceanic and Atmospheric Administration were given responsibility for enforcement of the provisions of this law which would come to have a significant impact on the North Fork of the Flathead Valley. The act required designation of threatened and endangered species, protection of which would fall under this law. Bull Trout were listed as endangered and grizzly bears were determined to be threatened. For a time, grey wolves that had re-introduced themselves into the North Fork, were also listed as endangered.

The legislation described above had some influence on Forest Service policies and practices but it took The National Forest Management Act of 1976, enacted after strident national debate over clear-cutting, to set into law a new mission for the USFS. This legislation was the force that caused the Forest Service to change the mission and policies it had pursued for decades. It required the USFS to conduct planning to ensure a diversity of plants and animals within National Forests. It was intended to protect forests from damaging and excessive logging practices.

Congress instructed the USFS to develop regulations that limit the size of clear-cuts, protect streams, restrict annual rates of cutting, ensure prompt reforestation and protect imperiled species.

In combination with these other legislative initiatives, The National Forest Management Act changed the Forest Service in fundamental ways – eventually. But change came at a glacial pace. Generations of Forest Service managers and workers had been schooled in, worked toward and evaluated by the culture established by Bill Greeley – a culture of facilitating the harvest of as much timber as possible with the least possible effort. That in-grained culture resisted what many long-time Forest Service managers and employees saw as a betrayal of everything the Forest Service stood for. Finally faced with increasing Congressional criticism and a blizzard of litigation by powerful environmental organizations, the head of the US Forest Service issued the 1989 Chief's New Perspective Initiative. It aimed to place timber management in line with other forest values including biodiversity, water quality and recreation and required forest service management plans that worked toward these goals. The combination of environmental legislation and new Forest Service regulations increased the complexity of managing National Forests enormously. Following these laws and regulations required professionals trained in a multitude of disciplines not previously available. New disciplines based not only in forestry but also biology, chemistry, and other sciences, even archeology were needed. Retirement, attrition and the need for these new professionals led to the recruitment of a new cadre of professionals, causing, in time, a complete turnover in Forest Service personnel. Unlike their predecessors, these new managers fully understood and embraced the direction the Forest Service had taken.

All this had a major impact on the North Fork. Selective cutting began to replace clear-cuts. By the mid 1980's, fewer logging roads were being cut into the forest, plans to harvest old growth were abandoned and the number of logging trucks racing up and down the North Fork Road declined. CB radios could eventually be thrown into the dump bin and, over time, most of the mile marker signs that had been nailed to trees disappeared.

But factors other than government environmental legislation were at work, too. Increases in lumber imports and reduced demand for forest products by the construction industry caused lumber prices to fall. Over time, a weak market for forest products combined with the new USFS marching orders ended large scale logging in the North Fork. The forests were saved.

Not everyone in the North Fork agreed that the environmental legislation enacted over the years by Congress was a good thing, though most approved of the end of clear-cutting in their back yards.

Indeed, there were downsides to the end of large scale North Fork logging. Loggers who had worked their whole lives in the forest and knew nothing else lost their jobs. In town, idle Peterbilts appeared in vacant lots with "For Sale" signs in their windows. Lumber mills and wood processing plants in Flathead Valley cut back on the number of shifts they ran and the number of workers they employed. Most plants, in the end, shut down. Families suffered and local businesses that depended on people who made their living in the logging industry were hurt. The Flathead County unemployment rate rose to become one of the highest in Montana. County revenues shrank and local governments had to increase taxes and cut back services. Before the Forest Service changed their policies, logging had been the largest industry in Flathead Country. By the turn of the 21st Century, tourism was number one.

Although these problems were not caused solely by changes in Forest Service regulations, environmentalists were blamed. Resentment against "tree-huggers" grew. Yellow signs reading, "This Business Supports the Logging Industry" began appearing in windows of stores and restaurants as defiant protests to what some saw as a cruel philosophy that favored the welfare of trees and grizzly bears over the lives of people.

Differences between those opposing changes in the way things had been and those supporting them were not based on economics only; they reflected a deep-seated political and philosophical divide as well, a divide reflecting the opposing paradigms that Greeley and Pinchot set down decades before.

On one side were people who believed the National Forests belonged to the public and not the government. Closing down logging in National Forests was, they felt, deeply wrong. Providing jobs and supporting livelihoods in the harvest of renewable timber and realizing whatever economic gain that National Forests might provide was the right of the people. When the Forest Service began closing logging roads in accordance with USFWS research that indicated a correlation between grizzly bear sustainability and road density, people who used these roads for hunting or snowmobiling or other forms of recreation felt they were being locked out of their own land by a government agency that had no right to do so. The public had the right to use the forests as they saw fit. Increasing rules and regulations governing what people could and could not do on Forest Service land caused some people to believe their traditional American freedoms were being taken away by an over-reaching government.

The environmental crowd, of course, saw things differently. Those favoring environmental protection considered loggers and their ilk as unenlightened, backwoods folks who simply did not understand the importance of preserving small remnants of the earth that hadn't yet been ruined by them. They ardently believed that the rights of the individual must be subordinate to the greater good of society. If it were otherwise, the individual, acting only in self interest, would disregard the greater good and reap rewards that come at the expense of society. They saw, correctly, that environmental legislation had given the Forest Service the responsibility of protecting public lands that the timber industry had been destroying. They embraced the work of hundreds of researchers and scientists who, over the years, ventured into North Fork forests to conduct dozens of studies which seemed usually to prove that the heavy hand of man could be a danger to the North Fork ecosystem. Scientific proof was on their side.

Consequently, they took the position that the presence and activities of man within this ecosystem must be limited and regulated for the greater good by the only power that could do so, the Federal Government.

The battle lines were drawn. On one side, the individual rights side, were, it is fair to say, mainly people who had lived and worked in Montana and the North Fork most of their lives. The environmentalists, on the other hand, were primarily newcomers, most of whom had come from big cities.

The "native Montanans" questioned how people who had no experience living in the North Fork could presume to tell those who had been there for decades or even generations how the North Fork should be managed. Moreover, what right did newcomers have to tell them what to do? They believed fears that the North Fork could be ruined were unrealistic. They pointed to the fact that logging, mining and recreation had been going on in the North Fork for a century without destroying it – or even changing it much. Besides, some kinds of development in an area devoid of services or public infrastructure would be good, they reasoned.

Those who had recently arrived in the North Fork believed that many people who had lived there all their lives simply did not appreciate how truly rare and special the North Fork was, nor had they experienced the problems of living in a crowded, overdeveloped, urbanized society. Moreover, they felt that people who had lived in the woods simply could not understand modern society's insatiable appetite for development of whatever was left undeveloped, an appetite that had devoured virtually every other unprotected spot in America. It was naïve, they believed, to think that the North Fork could resist change without government protection and pointed to development of the Swan Valley as an example.

These philosophical divisions had an effect on the North Fork community. They sometimes caused personal animosities to develop between North Forkers, resulting occasionally in a sharp exchange of words, usually at North Fork Improvement

Association monthly meetings. But generally, people got along. The sparseness of North Fork population and degree of difficulty encountered in living there tends to draw people together. That said, in attempting to follow the complex matrix of new federal laws and Forest Service regulations, chief ranger Jimmy De Herrera and other managers in the Glacier View District heard plenty of complaints by North Forkers – from both sides of the issue. Those people opposing new rules objected to restrictions on use and access the Forest Service was putting into place, while environmental groups complained it wasn't doing enough to protect the ecosystem.

But logging was not the only issue threatening the North Fork in the latter decades of the 20th Century. Subdivision of private land and potential residential and commercial development were also problematic. The North Fork is special, one of the few remaining un-crowded places in the lower 48 States. It is a place of thick pine forests, pure water, clear, dark night skies, magnificent vistas and abundant wildlife. Lacking electricity or phones, the North Fork feels like it's been left behind by the modern world. It is a sanctuary, a place of quiet and solitude. In the late 1960's, a group of North Fork landowners found they had a common concern about the potential loss of these values through subdivision of private land. They were concerned that excessive subdivision might lead to the kind of ex-urban sprawl that was becoming common around national parks in the US.

The County placed no restrictions on the use or subdivision of private property in the North Fork at that time. Anyone could do anything they wanted with their land. There was nothing to prevent the owner of 160 acres from cutting it up into one acre parcels – or smaller – and selling them to people who could put up whatever they wanted. Because of the County's traditional indifference to land planning, these far-sighted landowners knew they could expect no help in the form of regulation and if something was to be done to limit subdivision, it would have to be done on a voluntary landowner-by-landowner basis. In 1971, informal discussions between Helen and Orville Foreman, Cecily and Ed McNeil, Tom Reynolds, Larry Wilson and others

281

progressed to a formal planning meeting at the Foreman's log home north of Trail Creek, to which all landowners were invited.

After much discussion and not a little wrangling, the group developed a plan they believed could reduce the danger of excessive subdivision and thereby maintain the unique values of the North Fork. They asked Orville Foreman, an attorney, to create the legal framework that would enable landowners to voluntarily limit subdivision of their own property in perpetuity. That framework became the North Fork Compact. In 1973, the Compact was signed by those who wished to join and was recorded at the Flathead County Courthouse as a land covenant that limited subdivision of property owned by Compact members to parcels to 5 acres or larger in perpetuity. The Covenant goes with the land whenever the land changes ownership.

Though allowing subdivision in parcels as small as 5 acres sounds like a modest accomplishment today, this was a ground-breaking initiative in 1973. The North Fork Compact was one of the first land-planning organizations in Montana. The only reward these landowners sought or got was the knowledge that their land would never be cut up into parcels smaller than 5 acres, no matter who might own it in the future. Originally there were 34 Compact signatories covering about 2,500 acres or 15% of private land in the North Fork. In 2005, the Compact charter was amended by members, further limiting subdivision to a minimum of 20 acres.

Most landowners did not join the Compact, leaving the bulk of private North Fork land vulnerable to unlimited subdivision and development. Commercial real estate brokers marketed the North Fork as a "natural paradise right next to Glacier Park." Speculators like the one who sold Tom Reynolds' property to us bought and sold land with the expectation that values would rise. As the founders of the Compact had envisioned, private land in the North Fork was progressively cut up into a greater number of smaller parcels. In the ten year period between 1987 and 1997, for example, the number of lots increased 25%, from 570 to 714 lots. Average acreage dropped from 30 acres to 21. Even without additional subdivision, that left the possibility of 714 dwellings at a time when only about 400 existed.

By the mid-1980's, people up and down the road were discussing the future of the North Fork. Many people recognized that the lack of County regulatory restrictions on subdivision was problematic, but others disagreed. People who supported "property rights" resisted any thought of the government – or anybody else – telling them what they could and could not do with their own land. Developers and landowners contemplating commercial profit in the North Fork were, of course, opposed to any restrictions.

Serious discussion about subdivision and its potential impact on the North Fork began within the North Fork Improvement Association, North Fork Compact and North Fork Preservation Association. In the summer of 1986, representatives developed the North Fork Neighborhood Plan as a part of the County Master Plan. It emphasized the importance of preserving the rare, intrinsic values of the area but, lacking any regulatory protection, acknowledged that preservation depended solely upon voluntary restraint. In 1987, County Commissioners created the North Fork Land Use Advisory Committee to act as liaison between landowners, the County Planning Board and the Commissioners in plotting the forward course of North Fork land use. The NFLUAC was composed of representatives from the NFIA, NFPA and Compact. A mechanism was now in place that could, for the first time, provide some official direction to North Fork land planning.

Public meetings were called to solicit landowner input on the need for County zoning to regulate subdivision in the North Fork. Consensus was hard to come by. North Forkers tend to be independent-minded folks who, some joke, can't agree on the time of day.

However, a consensus was beginning to build. A survey was sent to all North Fork landowners in 1990 and only 5% of respondents believed that voluntary limitations on subdivision were adequate to protect the North Fork. A majority believed that County zoning in the North Fork was needed. Over the ensuing five years, many

283

public meetings were held on the subject of subdivision zoning and every landowner was encouraged to participate. Information and assistance in crafting a plan for the North Fork was sought from the Flathead County Planning Department which willingly complied. Planning Department professionals made presentations at public meetings in the North Fork about the process to be followed and gave invaluable help to North Fork planners. More meetings to solicit public input were conducted and every effort was made to ensure landowners were aware and involved. Progress was reported at regular NFIA and NFPA meetings.

Under the leadership of NFLUAC committee members, a zoning proposal to limit subdivision of privately held North Fork land to parcels no smaller than 20 acres was presented to landowners for their consideration. In January 1997, a second survey covering all elements of the zoning proposal was sent to all landowners. The results of the survey indicated that, after 15 years of planning and discussion, the majority of North Fork landowners were finally in agreement that the community had a zoning proposal that should be presented to the County for consideration and approval. The zoning proposal would be subject to evaluation by the County Planning Board prior to submission to the County Commissioners. A meeting with the Planning Board was scheduled for August, 1997.

Officials from the County Planning Office who assisted in the development of the zoning proposal warned Land Use Advisory Committee members not to expect a warm reception by the Planning Board. Their warning, it turned out, represented vast understatement. When the North Fork community met to present and discuss its zoning recommendations to the County Planning Board, it encountered closed minds, derision and hostility.

To the surprise of North Fork landowners who were not conversant with Flathead County politics, they found that the County Planning Board consisted mainly of men and women who made their livelihoods either directly or indirectly through commercial and residential development, including a couple of building contractors.

The meeting forum allowed for a presentation of the elements of the North Fork proposal – which ostensibly Board Members had read – followed by comments from the public expressing support or opposition. Most North Fork landowners who spoke supported the zoning proposal. A smaller number of people expressed their opposition, some of whom were people nobody from the North Fork recognized.

Opening statements by the Chairman and Planning Board members consisted of lectures on "property rights." They made it clear that our proposal was going nowhere. It was dead on arrival. Based on the Board members' statements and misstatements, it appeared some had not read the zoning proposal document or listened to arguments presented on its behalf. Demonstrated facts used to support the proposal were contradicted as untrue. Logic employed by proponents was ridiculed. Results of the survey that showed the majority of North Fork landowners supported the zoning proposal seemed irrelevant. The County Planning Board summarily rejected the NFLUAC zoning proposal as poorly thought out, inconsistent with County planning guidelines, and unworthy of consideration. It would not, they said, go forward to the County Commissioners.

After the meeting, the consensus among North Fork residents was that the statements Board members made were contradictory, inaccurate and downright wrong. They felt that Board members were disrespectful of the citizens they were supposedly appointed to serve. Many participants felt they had been treated as ignorant, naughty children who should not be wasting the Board's time. It seemed clear to nearly everyone that the Flathead County Planning Board was ideologically driven, opposed in principle to any limitation on land subdivision or – for that matter- any impediment to economic development in the North Fork.

"What do we do now?" was the common question heard that night. In addition to being independent-minded, North Forkers tend to be stubborn. Supporters agreed they weren't going away quietly. The Committee met again with the Flathead County Planning

Department and got to work rewriting the proposal, hoping to make it more palatable to the Planning Board without watering down its provisions.

The following summer, a second meeting with the Country Planning Board was scheduled to be held in Kalispell, 70 miles distant from Polebridge and 90 miles from our place on the upper North Fork. Close to 100 of our neighbors made the 150 mile round trip to attend the meeting which was scheduled to be held in a County building at 8:00 PM. The meeting room was packed when three Board members came in and took their seats. They talked among themselves for a few minutes. Then one Board member looked out at the audience and announced that, because of the absence of the other Planning Board members, they didn't have a quorum and the meeting was cancelled. We citizens of the North Fork – one who was suffering terminal cancer – had made the trip for naught.

Following several angry letters to the editor in the Hungry Horse News – the local newspaper – the Planning Board generously offered to hold the make-up meeting in Columbia Falls, only 50 miles from Polebridge. That meeting went no better than the one the previous summer. The Board voted unanimously to reject the North Fork zoning proposal but would allow it to go forward to the County Commissioners with their "no" vote attached. A meeting was scheduled with the Commissioners in October, 1998 at which time they ignored the negative recommendation of the County Planning Board and approved the zoning proposal. Sue and I were at our home in California when we heard the news. We were shocked at the Commissioners' decision and to this day still do not know what motivated them to approve the first zoning in the North Fork. Like most of our fellow North Fork residents, we were thrilled that, at long last, there was some County protection against North Fork land being cut up into tiny pieces.

Almost a soon as the threat of subdivision was alleviated, another worry began; commercial development. There were no limits on the number, type or size of businesses that might be established in the North Fork. If McDonalds wanted to put up a restaurant, no

286

problem and Holiday Inn could move in right next door. Rumors about new saloons and stores and guest ranches were circulating. Out-of-state business people were buying up land with who-knows-what purpose. People were afraid of what might be happening. Members of the three North Fork civic organizations decided something needed to be done to prevent uncontrolled commercialization of this tiny piece of America that had somehow escaped commercialization. The NFLUAC got to work again. The agonizing process that led to the subdivision zoning proposal had taught Committee members and landowners a great deal about how to proceed and the process of developing a commercial zoning proposal went more quickly – if not more smoothly.

Lines were drawn between landowners who wanted to put limits on commercial activity in the North Fork and those who didn't. A third group argued that limits were OK if they didn't prohibit commercial enterprises that they themselves might wish to develop. Public meetings were called, input solicited, ideas argued and tempers got hot. Unable to cope with the pressure, the chairman of the NFLUAC resigned. Fortunately, Jon Cole, a full time North Fork resident agreed to take his place. Jon had a level head and steady hand. He and his Committee members worked tirelessly with the County Planning Department to develop an amendment to North Fork zoning that would regulate commercial activity. The Committee made sure the planning process was transparent through broad and frequent communication with landowners.

The goal of this proposal was, like that of subdivision zoning, to preserve the rare qualities for which the North Fork was traditionally known. The proposal specified the type and number of businesses that were appropriate in the North Fork. It identified three distinct zones, one of which was Polebridge, and concentrated economic activity there, allowing fewer businesses in the other zones. The proposal, along with a survey soliciting opinions about it, was sent to all landowners. Two-thirds of respondents were in support. In the summer of 2002, the community was ready to face the County Planning Board again.

Many of us were not, however, prepared for the person the County Commissioners had appointed as Chairman. Russ Crowder was an outspoken supporter and lobbyist for Montanans for Multiple Use. This organization is driven by a hard-core ideology that opposes environmental legislation and Forest Service rules that regulate access to and activities on public lands. MFMU has been equally opposed to zoning, contending that a person's right to use the land he owns as he sees fit is a God-given right. Through shrill advocacy and strident activism in support of this ideology, Crowder had created for himself minor local celebrity.

How, we wondered, could the County Commissioners appoint a lobbyist for an anti- zoning, anti-environmental organization as Chairman of the County Planning Board? How would it be possible for anyone to get a fair hearing from a planning board packed with developers and chaired by Russ Crowder? It boggled the mind. Low expectations for our meeting with the Planning Board plummeted.

The meeting format was the same; Jon Cole presented our proposal and landowners spoke in favor and in opposition. This time, nearly everyone who spoke was in support, only three or four opposed. Then it was the Planning Board members' turn.

Crowder dismissed the proposal out of hand as though it represented the lunatic ravings of madmen. With the support of a barrage of derogatory exclamations from other board members, he launched into a diatribe that denounced the intent of the proposal, disputed facts supporting it and ridiculed its underpinning logic. At one point he attacked a key element of our support for the zoning proposal, the results of the landowner survey. The survey showed that two out of three North Fork survey respondents supported it. Crowded disagreed with that conclusion; he argued that if you include all those landowners who did not respond to the survey, then fewer than half supported it! Several of us attempted to point out that only respondents – pro or con – are counted in survey results because the opinions of those who did not respond to the survey are unknown. Crowder flatly rejected that argument. In any event, as far as he was concerned, the will of the people didn't matter. He said, "I don't care if 100% of landowners are in favor of this proposal, I will not support it." Crowder upbraided County Planning Department staff who had assisted in the development of the plan and denounced them as "unprofessional." He admonished them to do better in the future – or else!

The meeting became a series of brow beating lectures from Crowder and other board members about "property rights" and the evils of zoning. As the meeting wore on, it devolved into rambling, nonsensical Babel. People in the meeting began looking around at one another, wondering what in the world they were hearing. At one point, I felt as though I'd fallen down Alice's rabbit hole and had wound up in Wonderland where up is down and down is up. I couldn't decide if Russ Crowder was more like the Mad Hatter or the Queen of Hearts.

When Crowder finally ended the fiasco, North Fork neighbors stumbled out of the meeting in a state of shock, wondering what had hit them. Most agreed it was the most biased, unfair, nonsensical meeting they'd ever experienced.

So, back to the drawing board one more time; the NFLUAC and County planners met to revise the proposal. Creating zones within the North Fork and treating them differently was a legitimate stumbling block, one which would not get by the Commissioners. The new proposal would treat all land within the North Fork the same. Another point of contention was the number of saloons that would be allowed. One local landowner argued that allowing just one saloon would create a monopoly. The number of allowable saloons was increased to two. (Time would show that this landowner intended to open a saloon.) Other minor tweaks were made that planners felt would be important in winning the support of County Commissioners. No one held out hope that the County Planning Board would ever approve a North Fork zoning proposal.

As required, the community went back to the Planning Board, presented the revised proposal and was once again turned down. The proposal would go before the County Commissioners with a unanimous "no" vote. This time some North Fork Landowners held out some optimism. They felt the Commissioners might be distancing themselves from the Planning Board because of their consistent and obvious bias against zoning regulations throughout the County. The Planning Board was becoming an embarrassment. In August 2003, Flathead County Commissioners agreed with our proposal and amended North Fork zoning to provide the protection against commercialization that landowners sought.

Considering the historical propensity of Flathead County Commissioners for putting wide-open economic development, tax revenue generation and "property rights" ahead of environmental concerns, most North Fork landowners felt fortunate to have in place, for the first time, some County regulatory protection against excessive subdivision and commercialization. Some, however, recognized that political sands can shift quickly in Flathead County and the government that gives can also take away. But for the time being, the North Fork would remain essentially as it was a century ago. This valley would continue to be an icon of an earlier day, one of the few places in the lower United States where nature, not man leaves the primary imprint on the land.

But not all of this precious valley lies within the United States. Headwaters of the North Fork of the Flathead River originate some thirty miles north of the border with Canada, in British Columbia. There the river is known simply as the Flathead.

The land through which the Canadian Flathead River flows is Crown Land, land owned by the Government of British Columbia. From the U.S. border to Fernie, B.C. fifty miles north, no settlements, private land, permanent dwellings or paved roads exist. A confusing spider web of logging roads throughout this primitive wilderness led to a tenuous connection between Fernie and the North Fork, crossing the border at a US Customs station one hundred yards west of the river and one mile north of our place.

Lands drained by this river north and south of the border form a single, undivided ecosystem, a vast, largely empty, landscape of trees and lakes and mountains where lines on a map don't matter much. Wildlife found in Glacier National Park, the Flathead National Forest and Canadian Crown lands migrate freely north and south through this wild place. Aquatic species found in the river and its tributaries are dependent upon the sparkling clean waters flowing south. They are affected by whatever flows into the river from the very source of these waters high in the Canadian mountains to their outlet into Flathead Lake.

We weren't aware of any of this when we first came to the North Fork. We certainly didn't know that, seven years earlier, planning that would establish an open pit coal mine just nine miles north of our property had begun.

In 1974 the Province of British Columbia issued a Stage I permit to Sage Creek Coal Ltd. for the purpose of exploring the Flathead for coal. High grade low sulfur coking coal used to make steel was found in quantity. By 1985 Sage Creek had secured a Stage II permit from the government which allowed it to move to the development of a detailed plan for creation of the mine and infrastructure needed to support it. The mine site was at the confluence of Howell and Cabin Creeks in the Flathead River drainage, eight miles north of Glacier Park.

Sage Creek's plans called for an open pit coal mine. Two mountain tops would be removed to get at 50 million tons of coal which would be shipped out to Japan over a 21 year period. During the construction phase of the project, activities would include logging, land clearing, earth moving and construction of paved roads and bridges, electric transmission lines, plant site facilities, sediment control structures and a tailings pond.

The mining phase would involve open pit mining, pit, waste and refuse dump development, blasting operations, coal washing and processing, coal loading and hauling out of the valley by several hundred outsized coal-hauling vehicles. The mine would operate 24 hours a day, 7 days a week. Contaminated waters from mining operations would be collected in ditches and routed to any of 4 settling ponds. One of these ponds would discharge into Cabin Creek. Three ponds would discharge directly into the (North Fork)

Flathead River. Runoff from coal processing operations would enter the tailings pond.

The project was first reported in the press in 1974. Within a few months, opposition to the Cabin Creek project developed downstream from the mine - in the Flathead Valley and across Montana. Images of British Columbia towns blackened by coal dust from the Crowsnest and Elk Valley coal fields adjacent to the Flathead Valley came to mind. People were concerned that the North Fork, the Flathead River, Flathead Lake and Glacier National Park would fall victim to inevitable mine discharge and runoff, fouling the pristine waters and destroying marine habitat forever. The public was fearful that wildlife habitat in the Canadian Flathead forests– closely intertwined with those south of the border - would be seriously compromised by mountain top removal and by development and operation of the massive infrastructure Cabin Creek mine would require.

People throughout northwest Montana came out of the woodwork and a groundswell of opposition developed, opposition that would ultimately create or bring together 26 organizations determined to fight the Cabin Creek mine. The issue caught the attention of local, state and even national media and in the process, captured the interest of a young congressman, Max Baucus who saw the danger that mining in the Canadian Flathead posed to the Flathead Valley and Glacier Park. Baucus and a succession of Montana governors – both Democrat and Republican – sought a dialogue with the Province of British Columbia, pushing for an agreement that would protect Montana from the adverse affects of mining north of the border.

The British Columbia government saw things differently. The Province had mined adjacent Crowsnest and Elk Valley coal fields for decades and reaped the economic rewards. Coal was the second largest Provincial export. There was no reason, they insisted, that they should not take advantage of the coal that lay beneath the ground in the Flathead, thereby creating jobs and spurring economic development. Besides, the Canadians considered it their right to do whatever they chose with Crown land and seemed to resent interference by their large neighbor to the south. They insisted that the Cabin Creek plan would contain sufficient safeguards to protect the environment. There would be no harm to Montana, they insisted.

In 1985, a century-old threat to the North Fork environment re-surfaced. Shell Oil Company of Canada began drilling several exploratory oil and gas wells just north of Glacier Park. We could see lights from their rigs at night in the otherwise inky-black valley and hillsides across the border. It was the first time we'd ever seen man-made light at night from our property. Shell announced that they were prepared to spend hundreds of millions of dollars to build pipelines and other infrastructure if the test wells proved successful.

This was not the first time geologists believed the North Fork sat above oil and gas deposits; far from it. In 1892, prospectors located oil seepage in the ground near Kintla Lake in what is today Glacier National Park. They filed the first oil claims in Montana that year. Due to a lack of capital combined with the depression of 1893, their claims were abandoned. But in 1900, interest in oil in the Kintla drainage revived and drilling began in 1901. The first oil well on the shore of Kintla Lake reached a depth of 1400 feet but did not reach a profitable pocket of oil and, after a derrick burned in 1905, efforts there were abandoned. Interest in oil developed north of the border as well, and in 1930 three unsuccessful wells were drilled.

While Shell was drilling in the Flathead north of the border, Cenex, a Canadian energy company applied for a permit to drill a well on the U.S. side, just south of Polebridge. Following several months of contentious hearings, Cenex was given permission to drill at Home Ranch Bottoms, a portion of the 1,600 acres owned by Tom Ladenburg. This was the worst possible news for those worried about creation of a massive oil field north of the border. Cenex began drilling at their closed well site. No outsiders were allowed in and employees were forbidden to talk to anyone. Several groups concerned about pollution of the North Fork River and potential health hazards from sulfur dioxide which might escape from the well filed suit. Plaintiffs asked that a rubber-lined containment pond be required to hold contaminants produced by the well. They also asked that air quality monitoring be conducted and that a helicopter be stationed at the site to evacuate people should deadly gas be detected. The court agreed. The increased cost to Cenex combined with the failure of the well to produce significant quantities of oil convinced the company to abandon oil exploration on the U.S. side of the North Fork. Shell eventually abandoned their efforts in Canada as well when test wells failed to produce sufficient oil and gas.

In 1985, Canada and the United States submitted the Cabin Creek issue to the International Joint Commission, an organization established by the Boundary Waters Treaty of 1909 to address trans-boundary water quality issues. Max Baucus, then a Senator, secured funding for the Flathead River Environmental Impact Study the goal of which was to establish baseline values for water quality in the Flathead River. That led to the establishment of the Flathead Basin Commission, a quasi-State organization that monitors water quality issues in Flathead Lake and River on an on-going basis.

The IJC issued its report in 1990, stating that "migratory fish populations, important to the entire Flathead Lakes/River system, would experience significant long-term population declines because of severe damage to spawning and rearing habitat in the vicinity of the mine." The IJC recommended against the establishment of the Cabin Creek Mine unless adverse impacts could be mitigated – which the proposed plan could not accommodate. One of the most important IJC recommendations was that Canada and the U.S. work together to agree on permissible activities in the Flathead drainage. History would prove that objective to be elusive.

The North Fork River was given protection by Congress under the Wild and Scenic Rivers Act and in 1995, the United Nations designated Glacier/Waterton International Peace Park a World Heritage Site, both efforts meant to convey the unique value of these places and importance of preserving them.

Because of trans-boundary environmental issues combined with a softening in the price of coal, the Cabin Creek mine project was ultimately sidelined. Sage Creek Mining Ltd., however, retained its licenses and rights to resume its interest in the project at some future date. Most people in Montana worried that the Canadian coal mining issue would reappear. The coal was still in the ground.

They were right. In 1997, Fording Coal Ltd., Canada's largest mining company, applied for licenses to explore for coal in the Canadian Flathead. Fording – which operates coal mines in adjacent Crowsnest and Elk Valley coal fields - is a subsidiary of Canadian Pacific Ltd., a giant company that owns the Canadian Pacific Railroad, an ocean shipping company, hotels and oil and gas operations. Fording was awarded licenses in three areas within the Flathead drainage just north of the Cabin Creek site.

Jack Potter, Chief Science Officer of Glacier Park at the time was quoted as saying, "The bombshell is that nobody knew this had been reopened up there. If you thought that coal mining in the North Fork was dead, you'd better think again. The potential for large-scale pollution is real again and it all flows downstream."

Bob Cyr, Fording Coal's chief mine engineer made it clear they intended to succeed where Sage Creek Mining had failed. "Our plans are straightforward. We will try to be good neighbors. But we intend to stay in this business a long time, and that means long-term planning and identifying possible resource sites for the future." Sage Creek, too, indicated renewed interest in the Cabin Creek project.

In 2001, a third Canadian company, Cline Mining Corp. sought to develop another new coal project on the Cabin Creek site, bringing to three the number of mining companies planning – with the encouragement of the British Columbia government – to create massive coal mines in the Flathead drainage, all less than a dozen miles north of Glacier National Park.

Opposition to industrializing the Canadian Flathead grew steadily in Montana. Max Baucus took on the issue of protecting Glacier National Park and the Flathead as a personal crusade. He raised awareness of the dangers from Canadian mining in Washington and made his opposition known in both Vancouver and Ottawa. The scientific community in the United States, alarmed by the accelerating pace of developments in B.C., began to study the impact of mines on water quality and marine species downstream from Crowsnest and Elk Valley operations.

But the Government of British Columbia was not impressed. Supporting and encouraging mining in the Flathead was deemed a logical extension of the long history of mining activities in the southern reaches of the Province and officials showed not the slightest inclination to accommodate what they insisted were the specious worries of American meddlers.

People living in Fernie and other parts of British Columbia, however, began to be concerned that large scale mining operations in the Flathead was not a good thing. They began to worry about threats mining would pose, not only to the pristine Flathead environment, but also to their economy which benefitted from revenues generated by hunting and outdoor recreation. Canadian news media and environmental groups like Canadian Parks and Wildlife Society became engaged. Public interest in and opposition to what was afoot began to spread to Vancouver and even Ottawa. Concerned Canadian citizens and environmental groups in British Columbia joined forces with their Montana counterparts in opposing mining, forming the Flathead Coalition.

Faced with opposition and political pressure both south and north of the border, in 2005 the Provincial government announced a moratorium on coal exploration and mining in the lower third of the Flathead drainage of British Columbia. Celebration by opponents was short lived. Cline Mining soon applied for and was given approval to develop plans for an open pit coal mine on Foisey Creek, a tributary of the Flathead in the northern third of the drainage. Having made a concession to opponents in the lower Flathead, the Government of British Columbia seemed more resistant to opposition, more committed than ever to mining the upper valley. Efforts by Senator Baucus to talk with the B.C. Government in Vancouver were rebuffed and, so far as they were concerned, the matter was closed. Mining on Foisey Creek would go forward.

It was clear to opponents that moving mines further north in the Flathead drainage would not alleviate their concerns. Effluent still flows downstream and large scale mining would still destroy parts of the pristine Flathead forests in B.C. Little was gained by the government's moratorium. It was seen as smoke and mirrors meant to deflect criticism and afford the B.C. government some cover.

One major problem on the U.S. side of the border was lack of definitive data on the quality of water coming down from Canada at the border. If we could not say for sure what was in the water – and equally important, what was not in the water – prior to actual mining in Canada, there would be no way to prove that planned Canadian mines were – or were not – polluting the river. During the summer of 2006, The North Fork Compact, North Fork Preservation Assn. and North Fork Landowner's Assn. joined together for the first time and petitioned Federal, State and Local governments to fund definitive studies of water quality in the North Fork River that could provide indisputable base-line data prior to mining and energy development upstream. The intent was to put B.C. on notice that the United States would know when, what and how much pollution was produced by mining activities upstream should they be allowed to begin. In February 2007, the Flathead Basin Commission secured $300,000 from the Montana legislature for water quality monitoring. In 2008 Senator Baucus secured nearly $900,000 for the same purpose.

After unsuccessful negotiations with the Province of British Columbia, Governor Schweitzer, in early 2007, petitioned the Canadian Federal Government in Ottawa to invoke the Canadian Environmental Assessment Act. Unlike the U.S., the federal government in Canada has no voice in what happens in Crown lands unless an issue with a foreign nation arises. In that case,

Ottawa can require the Provincial government to conduct a federally designed environmental review. Schweitzer's petition was unsuccessful. Ottawa would only invoke a watered-down element of federal law which lacked teeth.

Just when it seemed things couldn't get any worse, they got worse, a lot worse. In July 2007, British Petroleum announced that they had been given approval to explore for coal bed methane in the Canadian Flathead. Their announcement said they planned to invest $100 million in that exploration effort and if exploration proved successful as expected, BP was committed to investing several billion dollars in development of a CBM field.

Coal bed methane is the gas that causes explosions in coal mines. The gas is trapped in coal seams as much as 1,400 feet below ground. Extracting the methane requires pumping massive amounts of water out of the ground, thereby lowering pressure and releasing the gas which, along with the water, is then pumped above ground. The gas is compressed and becomes a liquid which is then pumped by pipeline to buyers outside the area. Residual water is either pumped back into the ground or discharged into streams and rivers. Discharge water generally contains chlorides and sometimes heavy elements like selenium. High alkalinity in the water has led to deforestation and loss of vegetation downstream of many CBM fields.

Drilling deep wells and constructing compressing stations and pipelines requires a large-scale infrastructure of roads, bridges and power lines. Given the required investment in infrastructure, a large number of wells must be drilled to make development of a field economically viable. The Black Warrior Basin CBM field in Arkansas consists of 2,200 wells, for example. The well-known Wind River Basin field in Wyoming is made up of 8,000 wells.

Considering that each well site requires the clearing of 30 acres of forest, combined with the creation of required infrastructure – let alone affects of water discharge – some Canadian environmental engineers estimated that a CBM field in the Canadian Flathead would result in a "dead zone" twenty miles deep by two hundred miles wide. Couple this with the fact that British Petroleum had arguably the worst safety record in the oil and gas industry and you have a problem.

Opponents of BP Canada's Mist Mountain CBM project, as it was called, sprang into high gear. Canadian environmental groups like Wildsight and a new British Columbia grass roots organization called Citizens Concerned About Coal Bed Methane joined the Flathead Coalition to fight BP Canada and the Provincial government. National press coverage was given to the threat to Waterton-Glacier International Peace Park in both the U.S. and Canada. Senator Max Baucus travelled to Vancouver to look over the situation and express his opposition to the Mist Mountain project. He was met at the airport by a crowd carrying "Baucus Go Home" signs. In Fernie, he was greeted by a friendlier group of concerned Canadian citizens who lived closer to the proposed Mist Mountain project.

The B.C. Government, as usual, insisted that the project would do no harm to Montana and would not go forward if the required environmental analysis indicated otherwise. British Petroleum Canada would conduct the environmental analysis.

Few opponents to Mist Mountain – north and south of the border – were reassured. If BP was allowed to go forward with a CBM field, it would create an environmental disaster in what scientists considered one of the least-disturbed ecosystems in North America. Senator Baucus summoned the Canadian Ambassador To the United States to his office to discuss the matter and his insistence that it not go forward. Condoleeza Rice, then Secretary of State, met with her counterpart in Ottawa to the same purpose. Opposition grew heated in Fernie, B.C. and early in 2008 the city council passed a resolution against construction of the Mist Mountain CBM field.

In February 2008, Max Baucus travelled to Kalispell and announced that BP Canada had agreed to cancel its Mist Mountain project. BP Canada quickly issued a press release saying that Baucus had exaggerated their agreement but, in fact, the

Government of British Columbia had rejected BP's proposal to put a CBM field in the Flathead. Vancouver had caved to the enormous bi-lateral pressure against it. But the Cline Mining Co. project to develop its open pit coal mine on Foisey Creek was a "go." On top of that, the B.C. government granted leases for gold exploration and mining just north of Glacier Park.

It was clear that 30 years of fighting British Columbia over the environment, one project at a time, was not productive. A definitive agreement between Canada and the United States on the proper use of lands within the Flathead drainage was required as the IJC had said twenty years before. The problem of how to achieve that agreement remained.

Governor Schweitzer resumed negotiations with the Premier of British Columbia, Gordon Campbell. Wisely, they kept these negotiations out of the press. Barak Obama, in his presidential election campaign swing through Montana, stated that he opposed mining in the Flathead. American Rivers, a national environmental organization and the Outdoor Council of British Columbia both voted the North Fork of the Flathead River as the most endangered river in the United States. Early in 2009, Dave Hadden, president of Headwaters Montana, sent a letter to the World Heritage Committee of UNESCO requesting a place on their July meeting agenda in Seville, Spain to discuss Canadian mining in the Flathead. To his surprise, his letter resulted in an invitation to Seville. Hadden presented the case against mining and requested that Glacier/Waterton be declared a World Heritage Site In Danger, a singularly rare designation. None existed in North America. Hadden's request resulted in UNESCO sending a delegation of two top-level environmental scientists to the Flathead in September 2009. Their mission was to visit both the U.S. and Canada to assess the situation and write a recommendation regarding Endangered Site status to the UN commission. Based on the scientists' comments after their investigation, there was little doubt about the conclusion they had reached. Their report, issued in December 2010, stated that coal mining in the Flathead valley would be inimical to Glacier/Waterton International Peace Park. Without a change in Canadian policy, there was little doubt the

World Heritage Committee would declare it a Site In Danger at their next meeting.

Feeling pressure from their constituents, the State of Montana, a new President of the United States and UNESCO, the Province of British Columbia reached an agreement with Montana on the activities that would be allowed within the Flathead. A Memorandum of Understanding was signed by Governor Brian Schweitzer and Premier Gordon Campbell in Vancouver in February 2010. Mining and oil and gas exploration and development would not be allowed in the Flathead/North Fork Valley on either side of the border. Traditional activities including timber harvesting, hunting and recreation would be allowed.

Thanks in large part to patient, persistent negotiations by Governor Schweitzer and Premier Campbell, thirty-six years of wrangling over the fate of the Canadian Flathead/North Fork were at an end. Legislation was subsequently enacted by the British Columbia Parliament to protect the Flathead in perpetuity while oil and gas leases in Flathead National Forest were retired as agreed. At long last, Glacier/Waterton Park, the Canadian Flathead and U.S. North Fork are no longer threatened by mining and drilling. The land will remain quiet, the waters pure, as they had been in eons past.

William F. Butler, an officer in the British Army, had an important role in creation of the Royal Canadian Mounted Police. Butler was an intelligent observer and a man who loved wild country. Writing about Canadian wilderness in 1872, he said, "One saw here the world as it had taken shape and form from the hands of the Creator." He might have been talking about the North Fork. May it remain as it was when it left the hand of the Creator.

CHAPTER 8

FIRE!

The summer of 2003 was a sober reminder that not everything is in man's control and that nature can play a far more dramatic role in shaping the world we live in. Around noon on the 18th of July, thunderstorms began rolling over the Whitefish Range, sweeping across the North Fork Valley. These storms produced no rain. In fact, spring and early summer had been dry, with just 66% of average precipitation April through June. July had seen no rain at all. Following a five year drought, the forest was tinder-dry. Stepping outside our house, the grasses and understory crunched when we walked on it. County and Forest Service fire restrictions were at Stage III, the maximum; no outside fires, no running chain saws or other small engines by day, no smoking, no driving or parking vehicles in high grass. While the storms sweeping through produced no rain, they did produce lots of lighting.

Every crack of thunder caused us to worry. In the years following our arrival on the North Fork, Sue and I had sat on our front porch nights, nervously watching red splotches of fire burning Starvation Ridge in Glacier Park across the river from our place. We worried over smaller lightning-caused fires behind us on Mount Hefty. We'd lived through the 1986 fire behind Tom's house and seen the blackened trunks of trees around Polebridge following the 1988 Red Bench fire that burned 35,000 acres in Flathead National Forest and Glacier Park. Only heroic efforts by John Frederick, Karen Feather and other residents saved the North Fork Hostel and Polebridge Mercantile. The Moose Fire of 2001 was a big one; it burned 69,000 acres. That fire swept down from the Whitefish Range, jumped the North Fork Road and River and raced up Huckleberry Mountain in Glacier Park. Lightning over a dried-out sea of trees was definitely cause for worry.

Late in the afternoon, the two-way VHF radio that linked us to neighbors crackled with the alarming news that a Forest Service spotter plane had reported smoke in the Whitefish Range near

Hornet Lookout about eight miles south of our place. My heart rate increased and I felt a pit in my stomach. Sue and I ran outside to look into the southern sky, in the direction of the fire, but of course, with the thick forest crowding our house, we could see nothing. We went back inside and stayed glued to the radio, listening for news. Chatter on the Forest Service channel indicated that fire fighting resources were being assembled. The calm tones of Forest Service personnel had an edge to them.

The following morning we learned that winds in the Whitefish Range had kicked up, fanning the flames and rapidly spreading the fire. Traffic on the Forest Service radio channel was now continuous. Terrain in Wedge Canyon where the fire had started was steep and difficult to get to. Fire retardant fixed wing bombers and helicopters were on scene, dropping on the fire and more were being requested. Bus loads of fire crew were reported to be on the way. Everything we heard indicated this was going to be a big deal.

Sue and I put our daughter Heather and her small daughters Briana and Kelly who were visiting from back East, in our truck and headed south to Trail Creek. We needed to talk with Larry Wilson, Lynne Ogle and Duke Hoiland, knowledgeable men who had long lived on the North Fork and were experienced fire fighters. We wanted to know how much danger the Wedge Canyon Fire, as it was called, posed. No on could say but everyone worried. The men were getting their volunteer fire gear ready. One thing was clear; the winds were spreading the fire rapidly, burning east toward the North Fork Road and north toward Trail Creek. The many people living along Trail Creek and south of there on the North Fork Road were directly in the path of the fire. Above the open meadow south of the Hoiland's house, we caught our first glimpse of the white plume, rising high into the sky three miles distant.

Heather and the girls were anxious to make the most of their two week vacation. We'd promised to take Briana and Kelly and their mom on a white water raft trip down the Middle Fork of the Flathead with a commercial raft outfit near West Glacier. Since we'd been assured there was no immediate danger to our place from the fire, we set out the morning of July 23rd for adventure on the Middle Fork. On the way down the North Fork Road, we passed dozens of vehicles carrying fire crews and equipment north toward Wedge Canyon. As we passed by the fire which was high in the Whitefish Range, we could see how it had grown. The smoke was no longer a single well-defined column; it had become an amorphous dirty-grey mass that darkened large portions of the western sky.

Glacier Guides, the raft company, is located a few miles west of West Glacier, below Apgar Mountain. The morning sky there was bright blue, not a cloud in it. The sun warned that the day would be hot. About eleven o'clock, we set out in Glacier Guide's rickety bus for Moccasin Creek, ten miles to the east, where our rafts would be put in for the thrilling white water ride down the Middle Fork. I hoped it would get all our minds off Wedge Canyon.

As the young guide pushed our raft out of the creek into the fast-flowing Middle Fork, he warned that we would probably have our work cut out for us. The wind was forecast to be strong out of the west, right in our faces. Even with white water pushing our raft down the river, we would have to paddle like crazy to keep it moving, he warned. He was right. A half hour into the float the wind began to whistle through the canyon we were in, slowing and then stopping forward progress of our raft. Everyone in the raft was ordered to paddle. We were all soon sweating under the hot sun but despite everyone's best efforts, the water continued to rush rapidly past our barely moving raft. This was not fun, though no one said so. When we reached the narrowest part of the canyon where the water runs fastest and is the most turbulent, the raft picked up speed, rode up over three foot high waves and down, and bounced off a rock or two. Everyone squealed with delight as frigid water splashed over our hot bodies. This was fun!

Near the end of the big white water, the river turned left and as it did, we all gasped. We could scarcely believe our eyes. In the distance, a giant white mushroom cloud was rising thousands of feet above Apgar Mountain. The cloud immediately brought Hiroshima to mind. I realized it was a second wildfire, one of massive proportions. How could that happen so quickly, I wondered? We'd been very close to Apgar Mountain three hours earlier and there wasn't a wisp of smoke anywhere, just bright sunshine and sparkling blue sky. As everyone in the raft gaped at the nuclear-shaped cloud, the wind raging up the river from the west hit the raft again and it actually began moving backward against the strong Middle Fork current. We all bent our backs to our paddles, anxious to get the raft moving so we could get off the river and back up home. We could only imagine what this wind was doing to the Canyon Creek Fire.

Heading home on the North Fork Road, we encountered fire crew being deployed near Camas Creek. It was hard to believe; now two fires driven through bone dry forests by hurricane winds were raging through the North Fork; Wedge Canyon Fire on the north end and now one on the south end - to be known as the Robert Fire.

We drove north in a convoy of Forest Service vehicles on their way to the Wedge Canyon fire. We passed Polebridge, climbed Vance Hill and, at the top, gasped once more. In the far distance directly ahead, we saw what looked like a massive black rain cloud rising thousands of feet above the valley. It wasn't a rainstorm, it was smoke from Wedge Canyon. It was frightening to see how massive the fire had become in just hours. My heart leapt into my throat. From our vantage point, the fire appeared to be centered on our property! Were we being burned out? It certainly looked like it. Anxiety jangled my nerves and gnawed at my stomach as we crawled north among dozens of fire vehicles.

When we finally neared Trail Creek, we could see to our great relief that the fire was still in the Wedge Canyon area. Our place was safe for the time being. Still, the size of the fire and the rapidity with which it was spreading was frightening. The fire, we figured, wasn't more than six miles from Reynolds Ranch. Sue, Heather and I decided that she and her small daughters should return back East as soon as possible.

In the following days and weeks, one question was constantly on everyone's mind; what's happening with the fire? The Forest Service incident commander who had overall responsibility for fighting the Wedge Canyon Fire established daily briefings to give residents the latest information. Briefings were set up for 9AM at Larry Wilson's house near Trail Creek. Neighbors we'd never met came every morning, expanding our circle of North Fork friends. A special camaraderie developed at those meetings. We were all in the same boat, worried sick about the fire that threatened us and our properties. Satellite images, maps that showed daily changes in the size and location of the fire, reports on fire fighting resources and strategy and importantly, weather forecasts were presented every morning. Most days red flag warnings were up; expect hot, dry, windy conditions.

Wedge Canyon and Robert fires weren't the only ones racing through Montana forests. A big lightning-caused fire was reported in Glacier Park near Heaven's Peak, the Trapper Fire. It closed Going to the Sun Road. The Middle Fork Complex fire sprung up three miles east of West Glacier followed by the Rampage Complex Fire twelve miles east of that. Northwest Montana, it seemed, was on fire!

Sheriff's deputies showed up at North Fork residences with mandatory evacuation notices. It was too dangerous to stay, they warned. We, like nearly all our neighbors, chose to sign a waiver and stay. We couldn't imagine leaving and not knowing day-to-day, hour to hour what was happening. Besides, Sue and I were busy with chain saws and brush cutters, clearing low-hanging branches and high grass around our house, cabins and outbuildings. We would do all we could to save our home.

The fire continued to race down the mountains toward Trail Creek and the North Fork Road. We began to see red flames light up the smoke at night before we went to bed. Even though we knew the fire was several miles off, it was difficult to get to get to sleep. The fire, we were told, could leap-frog ahead rapidly if very high winds arose, blowing red-hot embers as much as a mile ahead of the fire, starting new ones. The fire could conceivably reach our place overnight, not a comforting thought as we went to bed.

That summer we were staying at the cabin we'd built for my Uncle Bob because work was being done on Tom's house – our house. A few years before Tom died I was looking at his house. "Tom, this house needs a proper foundation." I said. Without heavy equipment or even power tools, Tom had built his house on large boulders mortared together. It never had a proper foundation. "Oh, it'll last as long as I need it," he replied. As usual, he was right: it did last as long as he needed it but not as long as we would need it.

Before the Robert and Wedge Canyon Fires had closed the North Fork Road to commercial vehicles and outsiders, we employed Steve Kinniburgh's construction crew to raise up the house, excavate a deep crawl space under it and put in a solid concrete foundation. When the Wedge Canyon Fire started, the house was jacked up, sitting three feet above the ground waiting for the concrete to cure. Kinniburgh's crew had planned to return and set the house down on the foundation the day after the County Sheriff closed the road, so there it sat, high and dry. We realized this was a major problem. If burning embers were to hit the house or fall under it, this historic structure would be gone in a flash.

We alerted the incident commander who came to our place to size up the situation. "Call your contractor," he said, "and get him back here immediately. This house has to be set down right away. I'll send word to the Sheriff to let them come up the road. Tell them to be at the gate tomorrow at 6 AM." Using our satellite phone, we called Steve and told him he needed to have his crew and equipment at the Sheriff's blockade on the North Fork Road early the next morning. He said his crew was deployed on another job but would try his best. Late the next morning an 18 wheeler transporting an excavator and other heavy equipment ground noisily up our road. By evening, our house was back down, sitting solidly on its new foundation. We will be eternally grateful to the dedication and hard work of Steve Kinniburgh and his crew of Russian workers.

One day Sue and I went to Glacier Park International Airport in Kalispell to check on some maintenance that had been done to our airplane, a twin engine Beech Baron 58P. An incredibly rare four engine airplane sat on the tarmac near our plane. It was a Navy PB4Y-1 patrol bomber, the single-tail version of the twin-tail B-24 the army flew in World War II. This, I knew, was the only aircraft of its kind still in existence. I could scarcely believe that it was being used as a fire retardant bomber. How could anyone risk a one-of-a-kind 60 year old airplane? While on the ground, fifty gallon oil drums sat beneath each engine to catch oil leaking from the ancient 18 cylinder radial engines. After the aircraft was filled with red diatomaceous earth, a tall, blond young man sauntered out, climbed up into the airplane, started one engine after another and taxied out. It was an awesome sight and I had to watch the takeoff. The PB4-Y1 lumbered down the 5,000 foot runway, slowly gaining speed. The temperature that day was close to 100 degrees which would reduce the power of the old engines. At the very end of the runway, the old girl separated herself from the earth and rose slowly, ever so slowly, barely clearing trees a quarter mile south of the runway. With its heavy load, it struggled for altitude and began circling the field to gain enough to clear the Whitefish Range to the north on its way to Wedge Canyon. I watched it until it disappeared, admiring the skill and courage of the young pilot.

A couple weeks later, Sue and I returned to take a flight in our plane. I saw the young pilot in the lounge. He was waiting for the PB4Y-1 to be fuelled and loaded for another run. I introduced myself and said, "I watched you take off a week ago and wasn't sure you'd make it. It looked like your climb rate wasn't more than 200 feet per minute."

The friendly young man grinned. "Two hundred feet – that's on a good day," he replied.

By early August, fire crew began visiting our place to look over the situation and make plans to defend our house, cabins and out-buildings. At times, as many as five fire fighting vehicles were parked around our place, including several fire engines. Morning briefings were not encouraging. One red flag day followed another with temperatures remaining in the 90's, humidity in single digits and southwest winds raking the mountains at 25 to 35 mph every afternoon. The fire was bearing down on Trail Creek. If it jumped the road, it would race up Ketchikan Creek and down to our property. The Forest Service fire crews decided it was time to wrap three of our historic structures in fire-retardant foil.

Sue and I discussed what to take with us should we be forced to leave. We gathered up picture books, records, clothes, guns and the like and put them in our truck. One afternoon a few days later, smoke began to filter through the trees at our place and reports on the Forest Service radio channel indicated both the North Fork and Trail Creek Roads were threatened. It was time to go. If these roads were overrun by fire, we'd be trapped. We could not flee north to Canada because the border was closed and the gate locked. We gathered up Raja, our beloved Siamese lilac point cat, and got into our truck. As we drove down our lane, I wondered if we'd ever see our place again the way it was.

Three miles down the road at Holton's corner, I put on the brakes. The road was blocked by a dozen or more fire trucks and maybe a hundred fire fighters. I rolled down my window as a fire fighter approached. "You're not going anywhere," he said, "and neither are we. The fire jumped the road north of Trail Creek. The road is closed." We got out and talked with men and women blackened by soot and dirt. They'd come from California and Alaska and New Jersey and Texas to fight our fire. They described what was happening but did not know any more than we did about whether the fire would reach our place.

There was nothing we could do but return home and pray. We were trapped in a sea of parched trees with a massive wildfire raging uncontrolled not more than three miles away. It was unsettling to say the least. The attentiveness and concern of fire crews that patrolled the road and stopped in frequently was reassuring. We knew they would do all in their power to keep us and our buildings safe. Still, they like we, were trapped.

The road remained closed the next day but the following afternoon the fire had swept farther east, beyond the North Fork Road and we were told we could leave but to be careful; fire was burning on both sides of the road in some places. Indeed it was; when we got a few hundred yards beyond Trail Creek Road, tree trunks shorn of their branches smoldered and flickered with flame to either side of our truck. We drove quickly but carefully through the fire, anxious to escape a scene that brought to mind Dante's Inferno. As we proceeded south, we could see that land owned by friends had been burned over and we wondered if they and their homes had escaped the flames. It was a bewildering, frightening landscape that scarcely resembled the land we'd known and loved so well.

The fire hadn't reached as far as Sondreson Hall and from there south, the forest was as it had always been. Soon after we reached the patch of pavement south of Polebridge, we were startled once more. A meadow by the side of the road was filled with vehicles, tents and equipment. Giant satellite dishes pokes skyward like a field of mushrooms. Thick cables snaked from an 18 wheel semi truck to a large white tent we figured was the fire command center. Huge generators on the back of flat-beds roared. A dozen other 18 wheelers, some bearing food service logos, were circled like wagons expecting an Indian attack. At least two dozen yellow busses crowded the meadow in front of row upon row of blue porta-potties. Tents large enough to accommodate a hundred firefighters – mess tents, we guessed - were erected here and there amid a colorful sea of small individual backpack tents. The whole thing looked like the camp of an invading army. And indeed it was; an army of fire fighters. At one point, more than six thousand men and women were deployed in the North Fork to fight the Robert and Wedge Canyon Fires.

South of Camas Road near Huckleberry Mountain we came upon fire fighters battling the Robert Fire. It was burning on both sides of the road. The temperature was in the 90's. The crews were dirty. They looked tired. The wind blew and the fire burned.

Sue and I spent two days in Flathead Valley but on the third day, we could stand the uncertainty no longer; we needed to return to Reynolds Ranch to find out what was happening. Fire crews were at our place when we got there but the fire was still several miles distant. We resumed our schedule of attending morning briefings, talking with neighbors and watching the smoky sky. One morning we awoke to overcast skies. We'd seen this before – clouds mixed with smoke but no rain. That the morning, Forest Service officers were warning that the fire was closing in on Trail Creek and the two dozen residences along that road. They sounded pessimistic that the fire could be stopped in the red flag conditions that were forecast to continue. As they spoke, a light rain began to fall! Everyone looked up, expressions of amazement on their faces. Where did this come from, we wondered? None of us could believe it, least of all the Forest Service weather man. This turned out to be a totally unexpected break the fire crews desperately needed. Higher humidity slowed the fire, giving them time to run 27,000 feet of fire hose up Trail Creek, set pumps in the water and install hundreds of sprinklers. Their objective was to continuously wet the trees along Trail Creek Road and increase humidity, thereby giving fire crews a better chance of preventing the fire from jumping the road. Nobody thought the fire could be stopped short of the Canadian border once it breached the road and began roaring up thickly timbered Ketchikan Creek.

Rain soon stopped, clouds dissolved, humidity dropped, temperatures soared and winds picked up again. The fire raced down the south side of Trail Creek Canyon and approached within a few hundred yards of the creek. It appeared that, given the conditions, it would certainly burn the homes along Trail Creek, breach the road and start up Ketchikan Creek. In fact the fire did jump the creek in the steep uninhabited Trail Creek Canyon to the west and near the North Fork Road but it did not reach the houses along Trail Creek or the heavy timber in the Ketchikan basin. Miraculously, the fire suddenly stopped short. Once again, Trail Creek and those of us living north of there were saved.

Everyone wondered what had happened. The next morning Forest Service briefers were at a loss as well. But after a few days, fire experts explained that the wind had shifted. Instead of blowing out of the southwest as it had for weeks, it swung around and came out of the north. They conjectured that when it did, the wind accelerated as it hit the face of a mountain known as Cleft Rock, causing a low pressure area around the fire. That stopped the fire's northward movement and blew it back on itself. Lacking fuel, the fire died down – at least along Trail Creek. Where did that north wind come from, we wondered? It surely saved many homes and maybe many lives. I took to calling it our kamikaze – our Divine Wind.

When the fire danger along the North Fork and Trail Creek Roads had passed, we visited our neighbors to see how they'd fared. Duke and Naomi Hoiland's marvelous log home and outbuildings just 50 yards from Trail Creek nearly burned when the fire raced down the mountain and jumped the creek there, turning east at the last moment. Duke's well-planned defense along with the efforts of Forest Service fire fighters saved them. Larry Wilson's, Lynn Ogle's and Bill Meeker's places nearly burned when the fire raced over the North Fork Road and down to Kintla Ranch. Only their brave efforts saved their homes.

Annmarie Harrod's home on the south side of Trail Creek stood amidst a dense stand of six-inch lodgepole pine, perfect fuel for a wildfire. It swept through her property but, thanks to the amazing efforts of firefighters, it did not burn her home. It did, however, overtake her late husband's immaculate 1953 Chevy pickup. The tires were burnt off and the entire vehicle was reduced to a blackened hulk. I was amazed to see that the windows were not broken. The glass had melted instead. Molten glass from the windshield had flowed down over the instrument panel like so much thick molasses. A fire fighter on scene told us that glass melts at 2,000 degrees Fahrenheit. How in the world did they save Annemarie's home, we wondered? While we were there, a fire fighter spotted smoke coming from the top of her roof. The intense heat had, in fact, caused the top purling to catch fire. The fire crew got busy again and put it out. To everyone's dismay, other North Fork residents were not so fortunate. Seven homes and 29 outbuildings burned to the ground.

We, like many residents, were astonished at how fire had changed the landscape. Seas of lush green trees had been turned into oceans of blackened masts. Understory vegetation was replaced with blackened earth. Views not seen before were opened up. Colors and shapes and perspectives were changed. We were saddened to realize that the portions of the North Fork that burned were, so far as we were concerned, changed forever. Burned forests would not recover fully in our lifetime. But that is nature's way; birth, life, death, renewal. The areas burned over would sprout new life in the spring. Burned trees would provide habitat for birds not seen on the North Fork for decades. Open areas would provide new forage for deer and elk and moose and bear. In time, Lodgepole pine seedlings would sprout and rise up, followed decades later by aspen, fir, spruce, larch and other species. The land would heal itself and become what it had been.

In the end, 2003 proved to be an historic year in terms of wildfire. The Robert Fire burned 60,000 acres, Wedge Canyon 55,000 acres, Trapper Creek 20,000 acres, Rampage and Middle Fork Complexes 25.000 and 12,000 acres respectively. Sixteen wildfires burned 135,000 acres in Glacier National Park, more than the great fire of 1910. The fire season provided proof that man cannot control nature. I believe that once a wildfire grows to 100 acres, the best fire fighters can do in dry, windy conditions is steer it away from inhabited areas and protect some structures. Only nature has the power to put it out. The early onset of snow in mid-September was needed to extinguish the fires burning in the North Fork, Glacier Park and elsewhere in northwest Montana.

The danger posed by wildfire tends to unite a community. So too does the distance that separates people in sparsely populated areas; it tends to draw them together. North Fork neighbors generally stand ready to lend a hand, are quick to offer an invitation, happy to give encouragement even when they don't agree on things. After all, they may need a hand themselves one day and town is far away.

One thing that people have had trouble coming together on, however, is the North Fork Road. Controversy over what should – and should not – be done with the road has inflamed more passions and lasted longer than any other issue. Cecily McNeill says that people were arguing over the road before she arrived in 1949. It continues to this day.

In the late 18th Century and early 20th, settlers used a rut through the forest on the east side of the North Fork River in what is now Glacier Park to gain access to Polebridge and the North Fork. In the 1930's the County built a road in essentially today's location, running from Columbia Falls to Coal Creek where mining operations were being conducted. Over time, a track running north of there was extended to the Canadian border. The Forest Service gradually improved it to assist loggers and in the 1970's the County took over, constructing the present roadway from Coal Creek to the border. Good pavement was put down from Columbia Falls north to Canyon Creek but there the pavement ends. The road remains unpaved from that point to a six mile patch of poorly engineered pavement that was quietly and quickly put down along Tom Ladenburg's property. (Some folks say Ladenburg, then-owner of 1,600 acres, used his considerable clout with County Commissioners to get the pavement.) For some reason, the pothole-riddled pavement stops just short of Polebridge. The road remains unpaved from there to the border. One can truthfully say that the North Fork pavement patchwork is illogical, an artifact, perhaps, of poor planning and lack of money by Flathead County combined with local politics within the North Fork community.

North Fork landowners divide themselves into two camps regarding the North Fork Road; those who want the road paved and those who don't. It seems there's no one who doesn't have an opinion.

Some paving advocates say they want to pave only the section from Canyon Creek to the paved road leading into Glacier Park at Camas Creek. That would provide an uninterrupted ribbon of asphalt from Columbia Falls to Apgar and Going to the Sun Road.

Other proponents want the road paved to Polebridge and still others would like to see it paved all the way to the Canadian border. Dust, they argue, is the big problem. Though labeled a gravel road, there is precious little gravel on the North Fork Road. The road bed is just plain dirt. When dirt dries out and vehicles travel over it, clouds of dust are inevitably raised, dropping visibility, filling vehicles with powdery grit and fouling the air. Proponents argue, not illogically, that paving would eliminate dust, improve visibility and safety and reduce health risk. And by the way, it would make getting to town faster and easier.

Opponents of paving generally oppose any paving at all. They argue that paving the southern Canyon Creek segment would lead to a domino effect, resulting a few years later in demands to pave the road to Polebridge and beyond, possibly all the way to the border. Opponents believe that paving would cause a multiplicity of ills leading eventually to the ruin of environmental and cultural values unique to the North Fork. Paving poses a threat to water quality and wildlife, especially grizzly bears, they believe. Higher speeds afforded by paving would make the twisty, windy, often wet and snowy mountain road more dangerous, not less, they argue. Easier, faster access to what is now a relatively hard to reach remote area would spur subdivision and residential development. The "footprint" of each new house and family would intrude upon the essentially empty wildlife habitat necessary for many North Fork species. More residents would create demand for more products and services which, in turn, would lead to commercialization and demand for electricity, telephones and County services. This, along with increased traffic, pollution and noise would eventually result in ex-urban sprawl and change the culture of the sparsely settled valley. The rough dirt road is essential to preserve the North Fork and its way of life, they argue.

In the mid-1980's, pressure was brought to bear on Flathead County Commissioners to pave the Canyon Creek segment. The County requested and received approval for Federal funds. However, the National Environmental Policy Act requires an Environmental Impact Study for all projects using Federal funds and affecting public lands. In 1988, the U.S. Fish and Wildlife

Service that conducted the EIS issued a report stating that road paving would jeopardize the continuing existence of the grizzly bear, an animal protected under the Endangered Species Act. That effectively put a halt to the project and, in subsequent decades, has been a major impediment to other paving initiatives.

People in both camps are passionate in their beliefs and no subject leads more quickly to elevated blood pressures and raised voices. Bob Grimaldi has been a forceful, articulate proponent of paving. John Frederick, founder and president of the North Fork Preservation Assn. has been a persistent, effective opponent. Oddly, they both live in Polebridge, directly across the street from one another.

The heat of controversy waxes and wanes from season to season. When we arrive for the summer, we're always wondering if road paving will be a hot issue this year. In the middle years of the first decade of this century, Bob Grimaldi, Ray Brown and others got fed up with County Commissioners turning a deaf ear to their complaints about the road and with the North Fork Landowners' Assn. for its reluctance to push County Commissioners to pave it. They formed the North Fork Road Coalition for Health and Safety (NFRCFH&S), a group of landowners who wanted to push for road improvement, ideally paving. Meetings were held behind closed doors, ambitious plans to secure paving were rumored, members were recruited and fundraisers were organized. All this, of course, got the attention of paving opponents. It spread fear and motivated them to begin mobilizing their defenses.

The rising controversy focused on monthly meetings of the North Fork Landowners' Assn. held in Sondreson Hall. Established in the late 1940's, the NFLA was importantly the nexus of social activities within the North Fork. Over the years, that changed as a more or less united community used the people and resources of the NFLA to fight for County zoning protection. In the early years of the new century, the NFLA had essentially dropped its central social function and became, instead, a meeting place for residents to argue over issues affecting the North Fork, most importantly the road. NFLA politics heated up; some landowners felt that the organization had been hijacked by a small clique of elitists. Those in charge sometimes acted as though they lacked respect for rank and file NFLA members. More than a few North Fork residents stopped attending meetings to avoid two hours of contentious argumentation punctuated by occasional personal attacks.

To the fury of paving proponents, the NFLA was not about to take a position on road paving because the president and board of directors knew it would loose half of its members if it did, either way. The division within the community was that sharp.

Dry weather at the time made road dust and paving an issue not only in the North Fork, but also in the much more populous Flathead Valley. Various groups lobbied the County to pave various roads. The problem was that Flathead County has over 700 miles of unpaved roads, many of them busy residential and commercial routes people have to use every day to get to and from town and conduct their business. Paving costs several million dollars per mile and the County had no money. One or more Commissioner might have liked to pave some roads if they had the money, but the North Fork Road – which paving opponents pointed out leads nowhere – would be at the bottom of the list. The 1988 US Fish & Wildlife "jeopardy opinion" combined with opposition from Flathead National Forest and Glacier Park virtually guaranteed the North Fork Road would not soon see paving.

Still, the County tried to mitigate dust on the North Fork and other unpaved roads as best it could. It experimented with various techniques, one of which was a colossal failure. The County borrowed a large machine from Billings that was supposed to dig down into the road bed and grind large rocks into small ones. They tried it north of Polebridge. Unfortunately, the North Fork Road is built on dirt, not rock. The machine malfunctioned and wound up pulverizing dirt and rocks into a fine powder the consistency of flour, leaving it twelve inches deep and nearly impossible to drive through. The big machine was returned to Billings.

Eventually the County put down a layer of gravel and magnesium chloride, a compound that holds water and binds dirt together, on a number of roads in Flathead Valley and most of the North Fork Road south of Polebridge. That, along with wetter summers, significantly reduced road dust and blunted the shrill demands of paving advocates. It also silenced paving opponents who could not argue against road improvement that left it unpaved.

That's the good news. The bad news is that to remain effective in holding down road dust, gravel and magnesium chloride need to be re-applied every few years. Gravel and magnesium chloride cost money - about $3,000 per mile. And Federal funds – which helped pay for the applications – are, like the road in summer, drying up. The controversy over paving the North Fork Road will arise again as it always has. The beat goes on.

CHAPTER 9

GOD'S COUNTRY

Belief in God – any god – requires that one accept the existence of something greater than one's self. Faith requires such acceptance to be more than an intellectual nod to self-serving humility. It requires denial of the ego's persistent demands on us. In the competitive climate of our high-energy society, those demands are powerful, constant, even necessary. Not so on the silent forest floor or windy mountain top. There, close to the earth, exposed to the natural world, we are sheltered from the constant demands and thousand distractions of modern life and afforded the luxury of contemplation. The big sky and land beneath it tells us how small we are.

Gazing across our lawn and seeing an unborn fawn move within the belly of a doe, the Livingston Range as the backdrop, I am hard pressed to believe there is no power, no existence, no intellect greater than my own. I confess I am less and therein lies the foundation of my faith.

Such was not always the case. When Sue and I were married, I was proud of my atheism, quick to use my knowledge of history and the physical sciences to "prove" to ignorant, naïve believers that God was a myth. But not long after, I experienced something that trumped argument and wiped out my smug arrogance. I believed.

In the intervening half century, spirituality has played an important role in Sue's and my lives. One of the first women candidates to become an Episcopal priest, Sue studied for her Master of Divinity degree at the Episcopal seminary in Berkeley, California in the early 1980's and founded a street ministry. We both became lay ministers in the Episcopal Church and as we moved around the country, established or participated in a number of programs to help people. We attended church regularly and often took part in the conduct of liturgies. But not during the summer. The North

Fork had no church services. The closest Sunday service was in the Apgar campground amphitheater, 45 miles away.

But that wasn't always the situation. In fact, Christian church services were very much a part of the history of the North Fork and the community hall. For three decades, from the late 1940's to the mid- 1970's, Sunday church services were held during the summer in Sondreson Hall. A minister from Columbia Falls drove up each Sunday morning to conduct the services. There was even a Sunday school. A collection was taken up during the service and given to the minister to pay his travel expenses. Christian symbols were – and are – permanent fixtures in the Hall. A 30 inch cross is mounted on the front of the podium that speakers and NFLA officials have always used and a smaller one hangs on the wall. But for one reason or another, church services ceased and, for nearly four decades, Sondreson Hall stood empty on Sunday mornings.

One summer Sue and I began asking people what they thought of re-starting church services on Sunday. Nearly everyone we talked with thought it was a good idea, though many said they themselves would not attend. We concluded there was a need for church services in the community and, during the winter, we made plans to conduct them ourselves, having been trained and licensed by the Episcopal Church to do so. Since we figured there were few Episcopalians in the North Fork (there are only 3 million in the US), we planned to make them non-denominational Christian services which we hoped would appeal as broadly as possible.

In the spring of 2008, we called Larry Wilson from our home on the East Coast and discussed our ideas. Larry has been a leader in the community since first coming there in the late 1940's and has held every office in the NFLA – several times. He thought starting up church service again was a good idea. Like us, Larry assumed the Sunday services would be held in Sondreson Hall, venue for all North Fork community activities. He said he'd mention it to the NFLA president. Larry called back a few days later and told us we'd have to speak to the president about using the Hall for church services. We figured that by speaking to Larry instead of the president, we'd raised her sensitivity about protocol and prerogatives. We'd make amends when we got back to the North Fork.

When we arrived, we told the NFLA president what we'd discussed with Larry and said we assumed we could use the Hall. She said we'd have to come to her house to lay out specifically what we had in mind. We arranged a meeting. After we arrived at her home, she ushered us to a wooden bench in a hallway and sat us down. We explained that our plan was to hold non-denominational Sunday church services that would be open to everyone. They would last about an hour and be followed by coffee and fellowship. She clearly was not conversant with Christian liturgy and wanted to know exactly what these services would consist of. We explained. She said she would discuss our request to use Sondreson Hall with the NFLA Board of Directors. Based on her attitude and demeanor, we were worried. Was it conceivable, we wondered, that the Hall could be used for every possible community activity but not church services? That seemed preposterous.

The Sunday for which we'd planned the first church service came and went. Shortly thereafter, the president drove up our driveway and announced that we would be able to use Sondreson Hall for church services. We were excited. Then she said we'd have to rent the Hall at $75 for the two hours we planned to use it and would have to arrange for its use on a week-to-week basis. We would not be able to rent it for all summer Sundays at one time, she said, because someone else might be renting it on any given Sunday. To our knowledge, the Hall had stood empty every Sunday morning for decades. That requirement meant we could not advertise Sunday services because we would not know, week to week, if we would be able to rent the Hall. Anyone who wished to attend church services on Sunday could not plan to do so because they could not know if we would be able to hold them. And why, we wondered, should the NFLA require us to "rent" Sondreson Hall when community-wide meetings, potlucks and Thanksgiving dinner were held there for free? And isn't $75 a bit much for two hours of rental? We were shocked. Her demands essentially made our entire proposal impossible. We asked her and the Board to reconsider our request in light of the issues we raised.

A letter arrived in the mail the following week; the Board had been polled, she said, and our request to use Sondreson Hall for church services on a seasonal basis without a rental fee was denied. Her demands stood.

Sue and I felt that the Board members must not understand that our intention was to provide a service to the North Fork community, open to all, exactly like all the other events held without charge in the Hall. We sent each Board member an email detailing what we planned and why church services should be treated as every other community-wide event when it came to the use of the Hall. The following week another note arrived; our request was denied. Obviously the Board did understand our proposal and rejected it anyway. We were astounded and felt their decision was discriminatory and unfair.

The NFLA annual meeting was coming up in August when many members would be in attendance. I wrote to the president and asked for time on the agenda to discuss NFLA policy on the use of Sondreson Hall. We believed the Board's policy was not only discriminatory but inconsistent with traditional use of the Hall. Sue and I planned to make the membership aware of our request to use the Hall for Sunday church services and the Board of Directors' unique demands and restrictions. We wanted to ask the membership to establish a committee to review Hall rental policy. We figured the community at large would see the need for a review of a policy that allowed free use of the Hall for every community-wide event except church services.

About fifty North Fork landowners assembled at 8 PM. Toward the end of the meeting, the president stated that I had asked for time on the agenda. I was prepared to make my case. But to my surprise, the president made her case first! She framed the issue in her terms. She said that we wanted to rent the Hall for church services and, like every member who wants to hold a private event, the Board informed us that we would have to pay the standard

322

rental fee of $75 per day. She handed out charts and graphs showing how much it cost to operate the Hall for a year. She stated that she and the Board were not going to make an exception for the Sullivan's church services. If they did, she said, they would have to make an exception for everyone who wanted to rent the Hall.

I could scarcely believe what had happened. The NFLA president violated standard meeting protocol by putting me on the agenda, then pre-empting my presentation, framing the issue in her terms and declaring her opposition before giving me a chance to say a word. It seemed to me to be a clear abuse of the power of her office. I knew the deck was stacked heavily against me when I stepped to the podium, but I would do my best to lay out the issue as Sue and I saw it. I explained that we hoped to provide a service for the community. I said the president mis-spoke; we did not wish to rent the Hall for a private event. We wished to use the Hall to conduct an event that would be open to the entire community exactly like a dozen other events that are allowed use of the Hall without charge. I explained that by requiring us to rent the Hall on a week-to-week basis, it would be impossible to plan a season of community church services.

In the discussion that followed, the President stated that "NFLA sponsored" events enjoyed use of the Hall without charge. "Non-NFLA sponsored events" did not. Church services were not "NFLA sponsored" events, she said. Larry Wilson made a motion that was seconded. His motion was to make Sunday church services "NFLA sponsored" events. That would solve the problem. At that point, one member – a man known for proselytizing his atheism – stood up and shouted, "I will not allow my NFLA dues to subsidize church services!" (Annual dues are $10.) His wife worried that folding chairs might be stolen. Larry's motion was defeated.

At that point, the president told me to relinquish the podium; I was given time on the agenda to discuss one issue, she said, and the motion was defeated. I reminded her that the motion was made by Larry Wilson, not me. My issue was different and I had no intention of yielding the floor until I had finished. I made a motion that the NFLA establish a committee to determine what the policy regarding use of Sondreson Hall should be, with their report made for review by the membership the following summer. My motion was seconded. The President stated her opposition to such a study and the motion failed. That was that. I thanked the membership for their time and said I accepted the will of the majority. There would be no church services on the North Fork.

A couple months later, I learned that, at the following NFLA meeting, the Board established a committee to review Hall rental policy - exactly as I had proposed. The next spring Sue and I were informed that NFLA members would be allowed to rent the Hall for two hours for a fee of $10 if the member rented it eight or more times per year. Though this policy continued to be discriminatory, it allowed the resumption of Sunday church services. We sent a check for $130, rental fee for 13 Sunday services. When we told our priest the good news, he said, "It happened in God's time."

A new slate of NFLA officers was elected in August of 2010 and Hall rental policy was changed again; any member wishing to hold any event open to the community-at-large would be allowed free use of the Hall.

The first North Fork church service in four decades was held at Sondreson Hall at 10:30 AM on Sunday, July 5, 2009. Though we'd spread the news via word of mouth, Sue and I had no idea if anyone would show up. Just before 10:30, three vehicles pulled into the parking lot. Eight North Forkers – including Sue and myself – came together to worship God. The following Sunday the congregation grew to 12 and by August, average attendance was close to 20. People came from both the upper and lower North Fork, from the Canadian border to Polebridge 25 miles south, bringing together some people who had never met one another before. One Sunday in 2011, more than forty people showed up. Clearly, we had been right; a need for Sunday church services does exist in the North Fork.

It all happened in God's time. Since re-starting church services, we've shared with friends and neighbors our gratitude for the magnificent place God has given us and thanked God for the opportunity to experience what so few people ever have. Along the way we've made new friends and deepened friendships with others. We've been given the opportunity to comfort some in their sorrow, celebrate joy with others and help one or two find their faith.

Sue and I have lived many places over the years and we've made dozens of friends with whom we stay in contact. But the friends to whom we feel closest are folks in the North Fork. Some we've known for more than 30 years. We've stood shoulder to shoulder, fighting the County to gain subdivision and commercial zoning protection, debating road paving issues and lobbying to stop Canadian coal mines. When wildfire threatened, we banded together, providing each other whatever protection or comfort we could.

There exists continuity among North Fork people rare in mobile, high-energy America today. Some people, like Tom Reynolds, Larry Wilson, Cecily McNeil, Naomi Hoiland and Karen Maas McDonough, to name a few, have lived in the North Fork – off and on – for sixty years and more. Their kids and their kids kids have come to the North Fork, met together, played together and formed life-long friendships. There is a strength of character, an element of caring for one another, a resourcefulness and kindness not often found in 21st Century urban America. We feel a kinship, a spiritual bond with our North Fork friends, even though we usually don't see one another eight and nine months a year. I've often said that the best part of the North Fork isn't the natural beauty or peacefulness or wildlife; it's the people.

In July 2011, some of those people came to my rescue. Heather, Briana and Kelly had just arrived from the East Coast a few days earlier for their summer vacation. I'd notice some red spots on my left shin and figured they were bug bites. I radioed Karen McDonough and asked her what she put on bug bites. A few days later I planned to cut a tree that had fallen onto one of the access roads on our property but, when I got up in the morning, decided to wait. I wasn't feeling 100%. After breakfast I went out to wash our truck. About three quarters of the way through, I suddenly felt dizzy and fell to the ground. Sue and Heather picked me up, carried me inside and put me on our bed. By that time, I felt as though I was freezing and began to shake. I asked Sue to pile blankets on top of me, but that didn't help. I felt as cold as I did in the stone hut atop Gunsight Pass when Patrick and I suffered hypothermia. My shaking became uncontrollable.

Sue and Heather told me I needed to go to the hospital but I refused. Sue radioed for help. Lynn Ogle – a retired county deputy sheriff with EMT training and Larry Wilson – an acting deputy sheriff trained in search and rescue - were monitoring the radio, thank God. When they heard what had happened, Lynn barked in his most formidable drill-sergeant command voice, "Get him to the hospital NOW! Head down the road and we'll meet you at Trail Creek. Do you want us to call for the medevac helicopter?" Sue and Heather asked me. I shook my head, no helicopter. Heather told Larry to order the chopper. I said, "Tell Larry to kiss my butt." I was obviously out of my head!

Sue and Heather carried me to our truck and, with our granddaughters, headed south toward Trail Creek. When we got there, Lynn told us that the helicopter he'd requested had been diverted to Glacier Park to assist in recovery of a climber who had fallen. An ambulance was headed up the road toward Polebridge. Larry looked at me and said, "You're going to make it. You're not going to die." I didn't know if he was just trying to be reassuring or if he really believed I'd live. I wasn't at all sure myself. Since I live with several heart problems, we all thought I was having a heart attack.

Lynn and Larry were in radio contact with Mark Heaphy who lives ten miles south, just north of Polebridge. Mark has a telephone and was able to call the County for the helicopter, then the ambulance. The trio alerted emergency facilities and law enforcement in Kalispell and kept in contact as we drove down the road. It was a team effort.

Just north of Polebridge a Border Patrol car, lights flashing, intercepted us and escorted us on our way. Shortly thereafter, the ambulance met us. After getting me inside, the emergency medical technicians stuck IV's in each arm and wired me up for a continuous ECG. They put Sue in the front seat of the ambulance with the driver and we headed for the hospital, still sixty miles distant. At Polebridge, a dozen and more of our friends had gathered near the Polebridge Mercantile – the only store in town - to wish me well and say a prayer or two. I didn't see them but Sue and the girls did. It buoyed their spirits.

My mind began to clear and I started to feel a little better but began to feel a sharp pain in my left shin. The pain grew steadily and when the ambulance bounced over bumps in the North Fork Road, it became severe. The medical technician told me that he was continually monitoring the ECG and if it started to "go south," he'd call for the helicopter again. But fortunately, the irregular beat of my heart showed little change.

Two and a half hours after leaving Reynolds' Ranch, we pulled up to the emergency room at Kalispell Regional Medical Center. I was whisked into an exam room and immediately examined by a man who introduced himself as Dr. Dismal – or at least that's what his name sounded like to me. I said, "Oh, Dr. Dismal! This is a great way to start out!" We both laughed. At least I hadn't lost my sense of humor. I told Dr. Desmal that I thought my problem was connected with my heart condition. He shook his head. "No," he said, "it's this leg." He pointed to my left shin which by that time was seriously red and swollen. "You have an infection in this leg. Your temperature is 104 degrees. If you hadn't gotten IV's in the ambulance, you probably wouldn't have made it. Your temperature caused severe dehydration."

My North Fork friends had saved my life. When I was well enough to return home, Larry said, "We always wondered if our plans to deal with a medical emergency way up here would work. You gave us the opportunity for a trial run. It works!" Two weeks later, a neighbor fell and dislocated his shoulder. Larry and the gang's plan worked again.

The subcutaneous antibiotic-resistant bacterial infection in my leg was tough to treat but, after seven weeks of experimentation with a variety of drugs, I was back on my feet, grateful for my North Fork friends who saved my life and looked after Sue and me during my recovery.

CHAPTER 10

FULL CIRCLE

Two years before my medical emergency, the summer of 2009, Heather, Briana and Kelly came in late July for their annual summer visit. They brought Sarah McMahon, our granddaughters' best friend with them. Like Kelly, Sarah was 14, a schoolmate we all knew well. An "A" student, Sarah was vivacious, polite and full of fun – a great kid. However, she was strictly a city kid. She'd always lived in the Washington-Baltimore-Annapolis megalopolis and had never been west of the Mississippi. I wasn't sure how readily she would adjust to the absence of hair dryers, internet, shopping malls and inside bathrooms.

Maybe my first clue should have been Sarah's request to buy a cowboy hat immediately after getting off the plane. We went to Western Outdoor in Kalispell where she selected a straw hat that appeared stylishly beat-up. We stopped in Apgar to give Sarah her first glimpse of the ragged mountains at the head of McDonald and took a group picture with the lake and mountains in the background. Then we headed up the road to Reynolds' Ranch.

We'd learned that the expression on the face of visitors when they first arrive at our place in "the deep woods" reveals a lot about what's going on inside of them. We've had visitors from back East who looked amazed or hesitant or down-right scared. When Sarah got there, her eyes sparkled; I sensed in her a combination of wonder and excitement.

Briana and Kelly who had been to Reynolds' Ranch every year of their lives, were anxious to show her everything. After unpacking in the middle cabin where the girls would stay with Heather, they walked up the hill to our place. When they got there, Sarah and the girls were laughing like a pack of hyenas, having the time of their lives. After checking out our house, Sarah and the girls went off down the road, poking here and there, exploring. If Sarah gave a thought to the possibility of encountering a bear, she never showed it.

The next day we drove everyone to the U.S./Canadian border where the girls mugged for the camera next to an obelisk put there by the 1857 U.S. survey crew. One of my favorite pictures is of Sarah straddling the border, one foot in Canada, the other in the United States, arms spread high above her cowboy hat in jubilation. Then we headed for the river a hundred yards away. Before we knew it, the girls were wading in the shallows, giggling and laughing as they negotiated the slippery stones on the bottom. It wasn't long before the stones won out and they were all submerged in frigid water, squealing with delight.

One night Heather called the girls out of the cabin to see the stars. Sarah, in her jammies, stared up at the sky, mouth open in wonder at the long white smudge of uncountable stars spread out above her head; the Milky Way. Like most people who live in today's light-polluted beehive cities, she'd never seen it.

Heather drove Kelly and Sarah from their cabin up to our house one day in our Jeep Wrangler. Sarah decided to sit on Kelly's lap in the front seat. When Kelly opened the door to get out, the girls were laughing so hard, Sarah fell out of the Jeep onto the ground, spurring new peals of laughter. They reminded me of hilarious little pine squirrels that scamper about our yard, chattering noisily as they chase one another up and down tree trunks

The girls liked to have Heather drive them to Polebridge. The Merc's incredibly tasty baked goods and gaggle of interesting characters "just hanging out" -especially the boys -were powerful magnets. Bouncing down the road in the Jeep, the girls sang "Eye of The Tiger" at the top of their voices – over and over and over. Neither they –nor we - will ever hear that song without thinking of those boisterous trips to Polebridge. It was all good.

When Heather first arrives each summer, our practice is to discuss which hikes we'd all like to take. The popular Highline Trail that runs along the Garden Wall is usually on the list. When we described the trail and its destination – Granite Park Chalet – Sarah wanted to go. I worried that she didn't have hiking boots, but she assured me she'd be just fine hiking the 12 mile trail in her tennies.

I watched Sarah's eyes when we stepped out onto the narrow ledge below Logan Pass. I saw her expression as we observed a sow grizzly and her three yearling cubs dig camas root in a meadow below Haystack Butte. I sensed her mood when we ate our lunch atop box-car sized boulders in the shadow of the Garden Wall. When Heather pointed out delicate alpine flowers and mossy ledges beneath sparkling waterfalls, the delight in her eyes was familiar. The awe and wonder and joy I saw in Sarah as she hiked the Highline Trail brought back memories nearly five decades in the making. The emotions that filled Sue and me the morning we stepped out of our tent and beheld Rising Wolf Mountain and Two Medicine Lake for the first time reflected in Sarah's eyes. This young person from another time, another place, another generation, felt the spirit of the land, as we had. The spirit of the land lives on so long as the thirst for freedom and adventure lives in our hearts.

Wallace Stegner, Pulitzer Prize winning author who was born and raised in the West, has written, "remaining wilderness is the geography of hope." I believe he understates the case. Remaining Wilderness is the geography of hope, freedom, joy and peace.

The End

Made in the USA
Lexington, KY
08 December 2019

58304529R00184